An Introduction to
Transactional
Analysis

An Introduction to
Transactional Analysis

PHIL LAPWORTH and CHARLOTTE SILLS

Los Angeles | London | New Delhi
Singapore | Washington DC

© Phil Lapworth and Charlotte Sills, 1993, 2011
Transactional Analysis Counselling published by Winslow Press in 1993.
Reprinted 2006
This fully revised edition published 2011

SAGE Publications Ltd
1 Oliver's Yard
55 City Road
London EC1Y 1SP

SAGE Publications Inc.
2455 Teller Road
Thousand Oaks, California 91320

SAGE Publications India Pvt Ltd
B 1/I 1 Mohan Cooperative Industrial Area
Mathura Road
New Delhi 110 044

SAGE Publications Asia-Pacific Pte Ltd
33 Pekin Street #02-01
Far East Square
Singapore 048763

Library of Congress Control Number available

British Library Cataloguing in Publication data

A catalogue record for this book is available from the British Library

ISBN 978-0-85702-907-2
ISBN 978-0-85702-908-9 (pbk)

Typeset by C&M Digitals (P) Ltd, Chennai, India
Printed and bound in Great Britain by Ashford Colour Press Ltd.
Printed on paper from sustainable resources

Contents

About the Authors

Phil Lapworth is a psychotherapist and supervisor in private practice near Bath. He has been an external examiner, consultant and supervisor for several integrative counselling and psychotherapy courses and was Director of Clinical Services at the Metanoia Institute before moving to Bath.

His interest in psychology and psychotherapy began while a teacher in Special Education, particularly through his work at the Maudsley Psychiatric Hospital School in London. His subsequent deputy headship at a school for troubled children and adolescents provided him with the opportunity in 1981 to undertake counselling training at South West London College which encompassed several approaches to counselling.

From these eclectic beginnings Phil qualified as a transactional analyst, trained in gestalt therapy and, later, integrative therapy, establishing a psychotherapy and supervision practice working with adults. With Charlotte Sills and Sue Fish, he published books on transactional analysis and gestalt approaches and, as sole author, several chapters in therapy publications.

Through his clinical experience, personal therapy and further MSc studies Phil's perspective widened in the nineties, and gave rise to another book with Charlotte and Sue on integration. A second edition of *Integration in Counselling and Psychotherapy: Developing a Personal Approach* by Phil and Charlotte was published by Sage in 2010 and, due to their popularity, their earlier introductory books on transactional analysis and gestalt (rewritten and updated to include coaching and other applications) will also be published in 2011.

Phil has also written a book of short stories, *Tales from the Therapy Room: Shrink-Wrapped*, published by SAGE in 2011. Though fictional, these tales reflect Phil's continuing interest in, and encouragement of, an integrative, personal approach to psychotherapy.

To contact Phil: phil@murhill.com

Charlotte Sills has been a teacher and supervisor of counsellors, therapists and coaches for almost twenty-five years. Her original introduction to working in the 'helping relationship' was in the field of bereavement, when she worked as a counsellor and subsequently the organizer of a local authority service for bereaved people. It was there that she began to learn about the healing power of the relationship – a fundamental value that still underpins her work using transactional analysis in a variety of settings.

After these beginnings, Charlotte trained in psychotherapy in various approaches and in particular in transactional analysis. For many years the head of the Transactional Analysis Department at Metanoia Institute, she still works as a senior tutor there in TA and integrative approaches to psychotherapy and is a Visiting Professor at Middlesex University. She is also in private practice as a therapist, coach and supervisor in West London. Since 2000 she has worked at Ashridge College, UK, where she is the co-director of the Coaching for Consultants course as well as a tutor on Ashridge's Masters programme in Relational Executive Coaching. She has a further major interest in groupwork and works as a group facilitator and team coach using TA and other approaches.

Charlotte has published widely in the field of therapy and coaching, both alone and in collaboration with colleagues. Books include: *Transactional Analysis: A Relational Perspective* with Helena Hargaden (Routledge, 2002) and *Integration in Counselling and Psychotherapy* also with Phil Lapworth (Sage, 2010). In 2007, Charlotte was co-recipient of the Eric Berne Memorial Award.

To contact Charlotte: contact@charlottesills.co.uk

A further book in this series – *An Introduction to Gestalt*, co-authored with Billy Desmond – will be available from January 2012.

Praise for the Book

'This is an extraordinarily clear and accessible introduction to transactional analysis, whilst at the same time a comprehensive and profound guide to its application. The authors have adapted their original text with examples taken from across the helping professions, making it eminently usable for executive coaches as well as counsellors.'
Erik de Haan, Director of Ashridge Centre for Coaching

'I really welcome this book as a fresh perspective on transactional analysis for today. The authors' relational approach and realistic examples will be invaluable to coaches, educators, consultants, psychotherapists and counsellors, with case studies and stories that show how TA can be applied pragmatically and creatively. In language that is direct, humane, lively and practical they explain current theory in straightforward ways, engage us in self-discovery and invite us into new ways of working with clients.'
Trudi Newton, Teaching and Supervising Transactional Analyst and Chair of Training and Certification, International TA Association

'In his development of transactional analysis now more than 50 years ago, Eric Berne challenged his psychoanalytic colleagues by arguing that analyzing what actually happens between people is as important for self-understanding and change as analyzing what happens within their minds. With their revised introduction to TA, Lapworth and Sills bring a wise and lively accounting of contemporary TA, situating it firmly within a relational perspective. Berne's thinking foreshadowed our current relational thinking. This thorough introduction puts relational thinking at the front and center of transactional analysis, while retaining its usefulness in understanding the experience of individuals.'
William Cornell, psychotherapist, coeditor of Transactional Analysis Journal, 2010 winner of the Eric Berne Memorial Award

'A very well written book with many practical examples and good exercises. I can really feel that it is written by highly experienced practitioners. A very good introduction to TA and it roots.'
Berit Daugaard-Freese, Independent consultant, Denmark; Associate, Ashridge Business School

'Practitioners from a variety of situations and contexts, as well as the layperson, will find this book a rich, valuable and practical resource. The authors use an accessible and easy-to-follow format and explain complex concepts in a way that makes them readily understandable. It is an engaging and practical demonstration of transactional analysis theory and practice.'
Heather Fowlie, Head of the Transactional Analysis Department at Metanoia Institute, London

Preface

Relational skills are now becoming more and more recognized as an essential part of effective helping. Nowhere is this more true than in social services, psychological therapy, education, organizations and the health care professions. This book on transactional analysis (TA) should be of immediate practical benefit to anyone in the 'people business'.

The book has emerged from our earlier work *Transactional Analysis Counselling* (Winslow Press/Speechmark, 1993) in response to the requests of many colleagues, teachers and students of TA who have asked us to revisit and expand our ideas according to developments in the field both of TA theory and its applications. In particular, this involves a focus on a relational approach to using TA in a wide variety of 'helping conversations', from counselling and coaching to mentoring, managing and guiding. Of course, each of these roles will require different skills and some specialist knowledge. However, what they have in common is the intentional use of a relationship to help clients understand something about how human beings work – to understand themselves, their relationships and their patterns of being in the world, as well as how they can develop and be the best that they are able to be. This is what our book is about.

The Book

In Chapter 1 we will give an overview of TA in order to place it in a general context. In the chapters that follow we will introduce the major TA concepts for you to explore and experiment with for yourself and in your work with others. In each chapter we will give a definition or description of the concept, some everyday examples to clarify the concept, suggestions as to how it may be usefully applied, a case study that runs through the book, and some exercises for you to practise for yourself and with your clients. In Chapters 10 and 11 we offer some ideas on the process of engaging, assessing and working with clients along with some longer examples. At the end of the book there is a list of TA organizations for those of you who are interested in furthering your knowledge and skills in using TA in your relationships with clients, colleagues or employees.

Many of the illustrative examples and case studies in this book are derived from actual practice – for example of counselling or coaching. In the interest of confidentiality, the real identities of these clients have been changed and in most cases are composites. Where real examples are used, the permission of the individual has been obtained.

A word about language – as the book aims to address those who are involved in a range of different activities, we have chosen the word 'practitioner' as the catch-all term which we hope can represent anyone from the psychotherapist to the organization consultant.

Phil Lapworth and Charlotte Sills

Acknowledgements

First and foremost we would like to acknowledge the contribution of our late friend and colleague Sue Fish to the original version of this book. Reworking and updating the text has constantly brought her lovingly to mind, especially in the exercises where her suggestion of getting a massage seems to occur not infrequently! Charlotte would also like to appreciate Phil for his generous work as lead author on the original version of this book.

Our grateful thanks to Leo Lapworth for his computer-graphic wizardry in providing all the figures for this book; to Andrew Day for being our 'coaching consultant'; Berit Daugaard-Freese for her valuable feedback on the first edition as we prepared the revision and Alice Oven and the team at SAGE for all their support as usual.

We would like to extend our appreciation and respect to our clients, trainees and supervisees who have taught us more about counselling, psychotherapy and coaching than any book can possibly teach and to whom this book is dedicated.

1

An Introduction to Transactional Analysis

What is Transactional Analysis?

Transactional analysis (TA) is a theory of personality and relationships based on the study of specific ego states, a theory of social interaction or interpersonal communication and a system of group and/or individual psychotherapy used as a tool for personal growth and personal change. It involves four methods of analysis – structural, transactional, games and script – and has taken its name from the second of these, though it clearly comprises all four.

TA is a way of inquiring into what goes on between people and inside people in order to help them make changes. The transactional aspect is exactly what it says: a two-way communication, an exchange, a transaction. Although this word can sound unattractively businesslike, the concept actually captures a wealth of understanding and meaning about the way human beings relate. A transaction may be of spoken words, expressed feelings, physical behaviours, shared thoughts, stated opinions or beliefs and so on. A transaction may be a raised eyebrow that is responded to with a smile. It may be a comforting hug when another is crying, or it may be a silence at the other end of the telephone following some unexpected news.

We may look at and analyse what goes on between people in terms of the words that they are using or the gestures they are making or the beliefs they are expressing and learn something of each of these people. But how does this apply 'inside' people? How can one person transact? Here is an incident as described by a client:

> I was really scared when the lift stopped between floors. I said to myself, 'Don't panic whatever you do!' But this didn't help much. In fact, I started to panic more. So I said, 'I'm really scared,' and I told myself this was all right. I felt a lot better knowing this and got myself thinking about how to deal with the situation. I told myself I could feel scared and still think of what to do. Of course, it was simple, I just pressed the alarm button. A man on the intercom reassured me I'd be out soon. The lift started to move while he was still talking. 'Well done,' I said to myself. 'A year ago you'd have been a gibbering wreck.'

This person is simply doing what we all do: he is talking to himself. Notice that sometimes he refers to himself as 'I' and sometimes as 'you'. In this way, though he is still one person, he can hold an internal dialogue between different parts of himself. He is transacting internally.

TA provides a model which defines these parts of oneself as different ego states. Whether it is thoughts, feelings or behaviours that are being exchanged externally or internally – usually it is all three, whether we are aware of this or not – they will be coming from one of three types of ego state: the Parent, the Adult or the Child ego state. Early in this book, we will introduce the concept of ego states and will return to the concept many times, as these ego states are the building-blocks of TA theory.

This three-part model is both simple and profound. Unfortunately, like many good ideas which have immediate appeal, the model is open to misuse. It can be seen in a rather simplistic way or used manipulatively for selfish and exploitative ends. Eric Berne, the originator of the model, was astute enough to recognize this possibility and in his catalogue of psychological 'games people play' included one called 'Transactional Analysis', which is when people use TA to belittle themselves or others. The simplicity and immediate usefulness of the TA model lies not only in the colloquial language adopted to describe the various and often complicated concepts, but also in the ease of understanding and identification people tend to show in response to TA theory. It is not uncommon to hear people using ego state language adeptly and creatively within minutes of its introduction. The profundity of the TA model lies in the depth and breadth of its psychological understanding and exploration. The list of contents of this book, including ego states, transactions, functional and behavioural options, life script, and assessment and the process of change, indicates the range to which this three-part model may be applied. We hope this introductory book will show some of the depth and breadth of understanding that TA can bring to many aspects of life, living, relating and communicating.

Since its introduction and development by Eric Berne and others who will be mentioned in this book, many people from varied professional backgrounds have been attracted to TA and found in it something useful and exciting. Clearly, they still do. What is it about TA that has attracted psychotherapists, counsellors, psychologists, doctors, coaches, social workers, nurses, teachers, children and others over the years? Here are some of the reasons we think TA is so popular:

- The basics of TA theory are expressed in simple, colloquial and easily understood language with words like 'games', 'scripts' and 'strokes' (a term that has now been included in several English dictionaries as well as being commonly found in songs and TV programmes).
- Though there is now common reference to the 'inner child' both in popular and in mainstream psychology, counselling and psychotherapy literature, the term 'Child' and the concept of part of oneself remaining phenomenologically alive as a child throughout one's adult life has been a central tenet in TA – a concept that is appealing and experientially validated and validating for many people.
- TA concepts are often shared with clients, so there is a talking *with* rather than talking *at* clients. In this way the content and process of psychotherapy or coaching are demystified and developed into a shared endeavour.

- TA lays stress on personal responsibility for one's experience and in so doing puts the client in a central, proactive and therefore potentially powerful role in his or her situation. In this respect, TA is referred to as a decisional model. If we are personally responsible for our own experience, we must be responsible for the choices and decisions that we make about how we behave, how we feel, how we think and what we believe, even though many of these decisions may not be made in awareness, but at a pre- or non-conscious, somatic and emotional level. Even as children we made such decisions in response to the environments of home, school and society. Clearly, some of these decisions were misinformed, misperceived, skewed by immaturity, but nonetheless the best we could manage in those early circumstances. Hope lies in the fact that as we become aware of the meaning we have made of ourselves and the world, and the patterns we are enacting, new and reparative decisions can be made in the present to replace the now dysfunctional and maladaptive decisions of the past.

The appeal of TA to some may also be due to its embracing and integrating the three main streams of psychology within its theoretical model: the psychoanalytic, the behavioural and the humanistic/existential. As mentioned earlier, Berne's formative training was in psychoanalysis. TA theory owes much to the psychoanalytic thinking and experience with which Berne was familiar – to Freud, Klein, Fairbairn, Federn and Erikson, to name but a few – and to the concepts belonging to traditional psychoanalysis, ego psychology, social psychology and object relations, particularly intrapsychic phenomenological structures. For example, Parent, Adult and Child ego states are not the Superego, Ego and Id of psychoanalysis, but there is no denying that they are derivatives. It is also clear that the Freudian concept of the repetition compulsion was developed by Berne into one of the central notions of TA: that of the life script and the repetitive games and rackets that support it.

An example of the inclusion of behavioural concepts is the emphasis given in TA to the effect of positive and negative reinforcement (operant conditioning) or 'stroking' as an important element of script formation. Our hunger for strokes influences how we adapt to the perceived wishes of others in terms of the feelings we have or show, the thoughts we have, the beliefs we hold and the behaviours we exhibit. This adaptation will be based particularly upon our experience of our parents when we were little and how they responded to our hunger for strokes. The humanistic/ existential component has already been touched upon. TA emphasizes personal responsibility, growth, self-awareness and choice; even when circumstances are not chosen, people can still choose their attitude towards these circumstances in a positive and creative way. Central to the humanistic philosophy also is the intrinsic value of human beings, and this too is a core belief in TA: the concept of 'OKness'. In the twenty-first century, a fourth stream of psychological thought is recognized – the transpersonal. Transpersonal approaches (such as mindfulness, Buddhist therapy, psychosynthesis and the like) see the interconnectedness of all creatures to each other and indeed to the universe itself. This fourth strand did not traditionally have a place in TA, which on the contrary has had rather a pragmatic approach. Therefore there are no direct links between it and the original TA concepts. However, recent developments and applications of TA have been influenced by its attitude of acceptance towards the inexplicable or the liminal and it contributes to a turn towards a relational perspective in TA, which has grown in popularity in the new century.

Relational Transactional Analysis

Relational TA sees the process of *relating* – to self, to others, to an organization, within the organization or community – as the key channel of self-expression and as the key vehicle for change.

Why this Emphasis on Relationship?

In recent years, a focus on relationship and relating has become a major trend in the world of psychology, philosophy, organizational and management theory, and consulting. Many influences combine to bring this about. Developments in post-modern philosophy and complexity theory highlight the interconnectedness of discourse and the importance of pattern in organizations and communities, which are seen not as entities but as processes of communicative interaction – as Stolorow and Atwood put it, 'a continual flow of reciprocal mutual influence' (1992 p. 18).

In the field of psychology, neuroscientific research and infant observation demonstrate the vital importance of early relationship to the development of the human brain and sense of self. What is more, a substantial body of research into successful outcome of therapy and counselling – and more recently coaching – identifies relationship factors as one of the best predictors of effectiveness. Last but not least, psychological theories as well as life experiences tell us that patterns of relating repeat themselves and are often the source of difficulties. Consequently, our clients will need us to help them in this area.

To summarize: relational TA sees relationships of all kinds as central to the work and identifies the relationship between practitioner and client as the chief vehicle for change. It is based on the fact that there are two 'subjectivities' in the meeting – each engaged in shaping and being shaped by the other. Relational practice therefore involves:

- First and foremost the provision of a relationship based in mutual respect and empathy, as well as shared agreement about direction and goals.
- Acknowledgement of the 'bi-directionality', the mutuality of influence, which co-creates a relationship in which there are a multiplicity of possible responses or 'selves' and in which patterns emerge and can be changed.
- Working in collaborative dialogue in the relationship as these selves emerge and meet. In other words, an inquiry into the process of relating will reveal important information about the client's (and the practitioner's) ways of meeting the world.
- Use of the practitioner's subjective experience as a valid source of information and, potentially, as part of the inquiry.
- Change, not just for the client but for the practitioner who will – indeed must – change in the process of the work. We will talk more about this later in the book.

TA is an ideal approach with which to work relationally. Many of its theories focus on understanding the co-created nature of relationships. Within the relationship, it integrates psychoanalysis's careful understanding of unconscious patterns with the authentic here-and-now focus of cognitive and humanistic methods; it recognizes multiple ego states (or 'self states' as they are sometimes called) and it is grounded in a humanistic philosophy that values human experience and trusts people to be responsible to themselves and their community. In recent years that humanistic philosophy has been underlined and emphasized in relational TA to recognize the importance to healing of an authentic, empathic meeting between two people.

Transactional Analysis Philosophy

Much of what has been written above touches upon the philosophical underpinnings of TA. The first of the three central philosophical beliefs is the notion that people are born 'OK'; in other words, free from original sin and with an innate 'drive' to grow and be healthy. The second is that people with emotional difficulties are nevertheless full human beings who can think and take responsibility for themselves. The third is that all emotional or behavioural problems, given adequate knowledge and resources, are changeable. These beliefs mean that all people have a fundamental worth and as such should be valued and respected. This does not mean that we accept and approve of a person's behaviour, if for example it is cruel and damaging, but that beneath the behaviour we try to see the person and value that person's humanity. This involves working with the person from a position described by Carl Rogers, the grandfather of humanistic therapy (1951), as 'unconditional positive regard'. We need to hold ourselves in the same regard if we are to approach another person with human equality. Thus the position of I'M OK – YOU'RE OK, a well known shibboleth of TA, existentially acknowledges your and my being in the world – separate yet connected – along with the value statement that humans are 'OK'. This tenet is paramount in TA. As practitioners (and people), if we are coming from a position of I'M OK – YOU'RE NOT OK or I'M NOT OK – YOU ARE OK or I'M NOT OK – YOU'RE NOT OK, we are coming from a position of inequality (or, in the last instance, equal hopelessness) which cannot be conducive to growth and change.

Implicit within the I'M OK – YOU'RE OK philosophical position is the belief that our core selves are lovable and creative and that our intentions are normally positive and constructive, even when our behaviour is undesirable, misguided or destructive. We think the following anonymous quotation with which we end this chapter expresses well this essential philosophical attitude towards ourselves and others:

> Every single human being,
> when the entire situation is taken into account,
> has always, at every moment of the past,
> done the very best that he or she could do,
> and so deserves neither blame nor reproach
> from anyone, including self.
> This, in particular, is true of you.

A Brief History

Eric Berne (1910–70), the originator of transactional analysis, was a Canadian-born psychiatrist who began his psychoanalytic training in 1941 at the New York Psychoanalytic Institute. His analyst was Paul Federn, a student of Freud's. Before he came to write about TA, his writing was more psychoanalytic in nature, as in *The Mind in Action* (1949).

In 1943, Berne's studies were interrupted by service in the army. It was here that he began practising group psychotherapy and developing his intuitive and observational skills which were later to appear as observations and definitions of ego states. Between 1949 and 1962, he developed these ideas and presented them in several journals: these articles were later to be compiled as *Intuition and Ego States* (1977). It was in 1958 that his ideas were first published in the *American Journal of Psychotherapy* under the title 'Transactional analysis: a new and effective method of group therapy'. He went on to publish eight books and numerous articles on the subject of TA. His final book *What Do You Say After You Say Hello?*, rated by some as his most erudite and comprehensive work, was published posthumously in 1972. It certainly combines the creativity, originality, wit and wisdom of the author into a book of enormous appeal.

After his work in the army, Berne pursued his psychoanalytic training at the San Francisco Psychoanalytic Institute and went into analysis with Erik Erikson but, perhaps because of his unorthodox and innovative – even, on occasion, confrontational – ideas and manner, he never gained recognition as a member of the psychoanalytic establishment. Clearly, Berne was attracted to psychoanalysis – much of his work testifies to the respect and esteem he held for psychoanalytic thought – yet he found the psychoanalysis of his day too rigid, too cumbersome, too complicated, too precious; above all, too slow. In response, he devoted his energy to combining individual and social psychiatry into a unified system he was to call Transactional Analysis. The theories he developed, therefore, include the rigour of psychoanalytic attention to unconscious processes, transferential dynamics and relational repetitions. They also integrate the pragmatic results-orientated attitude of the behavioural school and its cognitive behavioural approaches that were emerging during this time. These are contained within a humanistic philosophy that trusts in the healthy process of the human organism and empowerment through self and social responsibility.

Around the time of his first TA publication in 1958, Berne began to hold seminars to discuss and develop transactional analytic ideas. They were called the San Francisco Social Psychiatry Seminars. Six people attended the first meeting. By the end of the first year, attendance and TA theory had grown so much that there was both an introductory course – known as 'the 101', which continues to this day as the official introductory course – and an advanced seminar known as a '202'. By 1962, the first quarterly *Transactional Analysis Bulletin* (*TAB*), later to become the *Transactional Analysis Journal* (*TAJ*), was published and in the following year the first annual summer conference was held. In the mid-1960s, the San Francisco Seminar was renamed the International Transactional Analysis Association (ITAA). The word 'International' was to honour the membership of one Canadian! Throughout this time and until his death in 1970, Berne continued to develop TA theory.

The ITAA swiftly developed a worldwide membership. It was complemented in 1976 by the European Association for Transactional Analysis (EATA) and in 1982 by the Western Pacific Association for TA (WPATA). Both ITAA and EATA have their own respective and mutually recognizing examining bodies and are dedicated to the enhancement of TA theory and practice in psychotherapy, counselling, organizational and educational development through the maintenance of standards of training and accreditation as well as journals and conferences.

Today more than 90 countries have regional or national organizations, each associated with one or other of the larger organizations. In the UK the major organizations are the Institute of Transactional Analysis (ITA) and the Institute of Developmental Transactional Analysis (IDTA). The UK was also the founding site of the International Association of Relational Transactional Analysis (IARTA), which now has members worldwide.

2
Making Contracts

The practice of transactional analysis (TA) involves the use of contracts. A contract is an agreement between two or more people. Its purpose is to clarify matters so that there is no confusion about what everyone expects of themselves and other people. TA practitioners make contracts with their clients about how they will work together, what is to be expected and what goals the person wants to achieve through the process of the work.

Eric Berne first developed his ideas at a time when psychotherapy and counselling usually followed the 'medical model', whereby therapists, like doctors, were considered to be the experts with all the learning and skill. They employed this expertise to 'cure' the patient who was regarded as having the problem and as being in the position of weakness or 'illness'. Berne felt very strongly that this was a position that could not effect lasting change. It disempowered the patients, making them reliant on the helper. He also thought it was disrespectful as it implied an inequality between human beings, categorizing them as the well and the sick. Therefore, he used a language that was understandable to his clients and he encouraged them to read his books and to study the theory. He believed that most people can take responsibility for themselves and, therefore, have the ability and the right to decide what they want in their lives. Consequently, he would ask his clients what they saw as the problem, what they wanted to change in their lives and what they wanted from him. He would explain to them how he worked and then together they would decide if and how he could be helpful to them in achieving what they wanted for themselves. From this position a client would make a contract, an agreement, not only about the time and duration of sessions, fees to be paid and so on (the *business* or *administrative contract*), but also about the specific change the client wanted to make (what Berne, 1966, called the *treatment contract*, often called the *development contract*).

In what follows, we want to stress that such contracts are made in the service of the people involved, that they are made to enable, not to bind or restrict. The aim is not that later one person can take another to a court of law and prove how bad that person is for not having met the contract or for wanting to change it. The only exception to this flexibility is where there is some breach of the ethical or professional practice guidelines relating to the professional body to which each practitioner

Level 1: The contract with the world – society, the planet, the law

Level 2: The contract with the organization and its parts – *The Administrative Contract*

Level 3: The development contract – *The Learning Contract*
The Contracting Matrix

Level 4: The sessional contract

Level 5: Moment by moment contracts

Note: *Beware the 'psychological contract' – that which we cannot control*
Contracts are reviewed regularly and updated as appropriate

Figure 2.1   The five levels of contract (Sills 2006)

should belong. The essence of contracts is that they are made in order for both parties to feel safe and clear about what they are going to do together, to define the nature of the work and the skills and tasks that each person will require.

Figure 2.1 lists the five levels of contract described by Sills (2006).

The framework starts with the largest contextual container and then works down the levels to the micro-moment. Our colleague Brigid Proctor likens this to a set of Russian dolls. Each one nestles safely inside the container of the previous one, each separate but contributing to a whole. The dolls capture the idea that the contract, at best, acts as a safe container for the creative work. It is also one of the key elements in differentiating the various types of helping relationship that this book addresses. Whether you are a counsellor or therapist, coach, teacher or manager, your role and task will be defined, contained and clarified by the contract.

Level 1: The Contract with the World – Society, the Planet, the Law

This first level of contract is a type of personal contract or commitment that each of us makes with the world we live in and the context we work in. Different practitioners may be committed to different values but essentially each of us has some principles and values we will not transgress. They may be to do with harming human beings or degrading the planet. They may be to do with keeping within the law or respecting diversity. Many practitioners believe that it is necessary to make clear to the client the professional organizations to which they belong, and the ethical codes to which they adhere.

Exercise

Ask yourself these questions:

1 What is important to me and what values do I live by?
2 What work would I need to refuse or give up in order to remain true to myself?
3 What would I be willing to lose my job over?

Level 2: The Contract with the Organization and its Parts

Figure 2.2 depicts the *three-cornered contract* of Fanita English (1975). The model starts with a triangle.

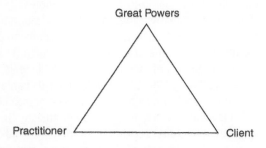

Figure 2.2   The three-cornered contract (after English 1975)

The 'Great Powers' are the organization, or the HR department, the school, the mental health agency or whoever is purchasing the practitioner's skills and has the power to dictate how the work will go. The other two points on the triangle are practitioner and client. Where the practitioner is in private practice, the person of the client is also the 'Great Powers' (in that they are employing you) and it still may be helpful to consider that there are three positions.

The important implication is that there are certain things that must be transparently agreed, on all three vectors of the triangle, in order for any engagement to be safe and effective.

You can expand the diagram to have many points and vectors to represent multiple stakeholders and lines of authority (see Tudor 2006). For the purposes of this chapter, however, we will stay with the simple three-cornered contract. What are the elements that must be agreed on all sides?

- *Clarify the role:* This first element involves a recognition of the skills and knowledge that is required in the particular role being offered. For example, in addition to understanding and using the ideas described in this book, a coach or manager will need some understanding of business or organizational dynamics, a teacher will need to know the field of education and learning theories, a psychotherapist will need to understand psychopathology and the workings of the unconscious mind and so on. Understanding the nature of your role, even where there are overlaps, for example between counsellor and coach, contributes to clarity in the work. Equally, the role of the client – what you expect of him as your client – is also important to define. You are likely to describe how you see the work and ask his agreement and commitment to it. It may be especially important to give a fairly detailed explanation of the approach when proposing to work cross-culturally. The role of the practitioner can vary enormously between different cultures – from advice-giving leader in one culture, to spiritual guide in another, to awareness facilitator in a third.
- *Clarify the administrative contract:* Sometimes also referred to as the *business* contract, this type of contract deals with all the practical arrangements such as time, place, duration, fees, confidentiality and its limits (for example, for a counsellor or therapist, would risk of harm mean a limit to confidentiality? For a coach, what will be the required report-back to the HR Director when coaching is part of an assessment centre or change process?), how the work can be reviewed and evaluated and so on. These are all apparently straightforward but it is surprising how often the practitioner, with their eyes firmly fixed on the development work to come, can be unclear about them or overlook their importance. This importance is fundamental. Not only is clarity about administrative agreements essential to clarifying the nature of the helping relationship, but the creation of this structure significantly contributes to the provision of the area of 'bounded instability' in which true creativity can emerge (Critchley 1997; Stacey 1993/2007) within the safe container of the contract.
- *Clarify the reason for the work:* It may be at the request of the client herself who, for example, seeks counselling as a way to address her anxiety. Or it may be a referral from a doctor or friend. It might be a sort of mentoring imposed on an adolescent as a result of concern about his behaviour. If it is coaching, it might be part of a wider consulting intervention or as an adjunct, for example, to a leadership development

programme. Alternatively, coaching may be part of the professional development that is routinely offered as 'talent management' to managers at a particular level. The context – including whether the engagement is chosen or imposed, considered as a punishment or a life enhancement – will play an important part in the nature of the administrative contract (and indeed in the *development* or *learning contract* – see below).

- *Discuss the possibility of changes to the contract and how they will be negotiated:* Any one of the three parties to the contract may at some time want to change the agreed contract. This may be unforeseen or it may be planned according to the needs of the client or the practitioner. Where possible, changes in frequency, duration or fees can be predicted at the initial stage of the work so that they are part of both people's expectations. Many practitioners draw up a written contract that outlines the business contract.
- *Outline the learning and development contract:* Once the business contract is made, practitioner and client (and sometimes the great powers) will also make an agreement about what they will be doing together. This initial learning or development contract – a mutual commitment to a particular focus – is sometimes referred to in therapy as the treatment contract.

The Initial Contact/The Initial Contract

When clients first come to see a practitioner, many will almost certainly be feeling anxious. This is especially true in the case of a counselling or psychotherapy client. They will probably be experiencing some sort of unhappiness in their lives which has caused them to seek help and they are coming with a mixture of fear and hope. It may be distressing for them to talk about what is painful. They may not know what is going to happen. They may worry that the practitioner will think them silly or bad or they may see themselves as having failed in some way in needing to come for counselling. Equally, they are really hoping that a practitioner will help: maybe counselling can work magic and turn their lives around. In any case, they will need two things: one is to feel that the practitioner is sufficiently caring and trustworthy for them to risk spending their time, and perhaps money, coming to talk about very private things; the other is a clear idea of what is going to happen. Later in the book we will look at 'structure hunger' and how anxious people can become if they do not have enough order in their lives. This includes clear expectations. If you think back to the last time you went somewhere new, where the people and surroundings were unfamiliar to you, you can probably remember what your initial concerns were. For example, who were the other people? Where were the relevant rooms? Where were the washrooms? What time would lunch be? What were the rules? It is the same for your clients.

In order for practitioners to be experienced as caring, trustworthy and interested, they have to give their clients space to talk and be listened to. The most important thing is that, from the first moment of the relationship, clients feel encouraged to trust that the consulting room is a place where they can bring all their concerns in an atmosphere of support and safety. For that atmosphere to feel supportive and safe, the practitioner will need to be experienced by the client as providing protection and potency, and to achieve this there must be a clear structure – a contract.

Level 3: The Development Contract

From the start, some clients like, or are able, to be very specific about what they want to change in their lives. For example, 'I want to make a good relationship with a woman – up to now my partners seem to get bored with me', or 'I've been depressed all year since I was made redundant and I want to start enjoying my life', or 'I want to discover how I keep getting into arguments with my colleagues and find better ways of communicating with them.' With people like this there are some useful formats for clarifying treatment contracts, which we will discuss later.

Many clients, however, do not have a clear idea about what they want from the work. They are conscious of their distress, anxiety or depression but may not be aware of the reasons for feeling this way or what they can do about it. They may have some vague feeling of unease or they may be aware that there is something missing in their lives. With these clients, it would be wrong to insist upon getting what is sometimes referred to as a *hard contract*. At the very least, it is a waste of time. At worst, it could be abusive, as the client might receive the impression that they have to know everything about themselves before they start or that they are being asked to restrict what they talk about.

In his book *Till We Have Faces*, C.S. Lewis (1978) wrote, 'How can we meet the gods face to face until we have faces?' Broadly, he meant that we cannot attain a higher understanding of anything until we know who we are. He was talking about spiritual growth, but the same truth obtains in this sort of work. We cannot know exactly what it is that we might want to change about ourselves until we know and accept ourselves the way we are at the moment. For these clients, the initial contract may consist of loosely naming the problem and making a commitment to focus on understanding and exploring until such a time as the goal can be clarified. Even then, this may be a gradual process, with the contract being updated sensitively as time goes on.

Example

At the start of counselling, Andrew said, 'I've been feeling low for months. I don't know why. I'm successful at work – I just feel low.' The initial contract was to explore this. After several weeks of counselling, Andrew said, 'I realize now that I'm living my life as if to please my mother. I need to start living it for me.' The practitioner agreed, and for the next few weeks they worked together to fully understand the implications and significance of this. It was not long before Andrew discovered that 'Living my life for me is harder than I thought. I don't really even know what I want to do.' The contract then became for him to learn to listen to his own feelings and needs and to figure out what he could do to get them met. Yet later, after Andrew had spent a painful and exciting time truly getting to know himself, including some of the feelings he had shut out of his awareness over the years, he began to be more in touch with what was missing in his life. He had found his own 'face' and was ready to make decisions for his future. He was now able to identify behavioural changes that he wanted to make in his life in terms of how he spent his time and how he related to people. This was the focus of his work which ended when he achieved intimate, enjoyable and interdependent relationships in which he could express his feelings, ask for his needs to be met, have fun and reciprocate from an I'M OK – YOU'RE OK position.

A useful tool for clarifying the contract at this stage is the contracting matrix shown in Figure 2.3.

The vertical axis of the matrix is the polarity of hard (observable, measurable outcome) and soft (subjective, experiential outcome) contracts; the horizontal axis is 'known' and 'unknown' – the extent to which the client is aware of what his issue is and what he wants from working with the practitioner. This matrix gives rise to four types of contract, which vary according to how clear the goal is and how behaviourally

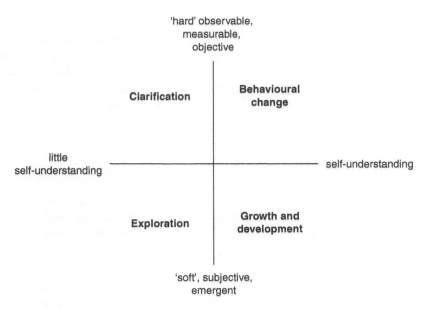

Figure 2.3 The contracting matrix

definable it is. It also leaves space for whatever emerges from the encounter between practitioner and client. It encompasses contracts for skills acquisition or performance improvement through to an emergent process of self-discovery (cf. Holloway and Holloway's 1973 *social change contract* and *autonomy contract*). As such it is very useful for differentiating, for example, between a therapy engagement and a coaching or mentoring one. Figure 2.4 gives examples of the four types of contract. Inevitably, as the work proceeds and the client's awareness increases, the contract evolves and moves fluidly between the four aspects.

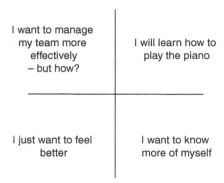

Figure 2.4   Four types of contract

Level 4: The Sessional Contract

Some practitioners find it effective to have a structured start to the session, perhaps reviewing actions that the client had agreed to carry out since the last session. Alternatively some practitioners wait to see where the client is and what is in the forefront of his mind, perhaps beginning with 'So what is important today?' or simply waiting for the client to speak and set the focal theme.

Level 5: Moment by Moment Contracts

These are the here-and-now *instant contracts*, offered in order to clarify something or find a way forward in a session. They might involve the client saying what she wants and the practitioner agreeing; or the practitioner making a suggestion which the client accepts, as in:

P.   'Do you want to say more about that?'
Cl.   'Yes, I have been worrying about … etc.'
P.   'I have a suggestion for an experiment, do you want to hear it?'
P.   'Do you want some information about that?'

Example

Beth is spending her time in the session talking about her daughter rather than herself. The practitioner may wonder if this is useful to the client and may say to Beth, 'You seem to want to tell me the story of your daughter today, is that right?' To which Beth answers, 'Yes, really. I don't know why but I need to tell you about her.' This is a contract. It has clarified the situation for the practitioner. It has also highlighted for the client that she has charge of the session in the sense of choosing what she talks about. She is, therefore, more likely to be aware of when she wants to change the focus. If later, she discovers that talking about her daughter was not useful after all, she has the option of exploring this with the practitioner in order to understand how or why she did this and how to do it differently next time. However, it may be that in talking about her daughter something very important emerged for her which might have been lost if the practitioner had been in the habit of starting the session by immediately requiring her to name something that she wanted to do that day that would have an observable outcome for her.

Breaches of Contract

A breach of contract on either side is likely to be a serious matter and probably symbolic of significant issues that must be addressed. There may initially be pragmatic issues to be resolved. However, for a relational practitioner, breaches can be welcomed as valuable and rich sources of out-of-awareness information for both client and practitioner about what is going on between them or for the client and his situation. For example, 'forgetting' the time of a session and arriving late may, on the one hand, be an indication of the level of stress in the client's outside life but, equally, may be an expression of some disturbance in their relationship with the practitioner (as in our case example in Chapter 11).

It is important to remember what is sometimes called the *psychological contract*. This means the unspoken and, indeed, out-of-awareness (or unconscious) emotional exchange between practitioner and client that is not accessible to cognitive contract making. This psychological level of contract can be a positive one; a mutual enjoyment and appreciation of each other, based on personal preferences or even positive transferences. Or it can be a negative process, whereby both parties are trapped in a limiting or harmful dynamic enacting fixed patterns and co-creating destructive outcomes.

Example

Jonathan, a successful and charismatic CEO, claimed he wanted to be challenged but, by his voice tone and facial expression, sent the implicit message that he was

(Continued)

(Continued)

too vulnerable and would be unforgiving of confrontation. His coach picked up the unspoken agenda and complied with it. She was half aware of doing so, guiltily thinking that she didn't want to lose the work. Only in coaching supervision did she realize that her bullying father was being evoked in the countertransference.

We cannot control this level of psychological contract. We can only be alert to its emergence in enactments in the relationship and be ready to welcome the learning it will bring.

To sum up so far, there are many benefits to contract making when this is sensitively undertaken:

1 Contracts stress the equality and respect inherent in a working relationship in which the client has the right to say what they want from the work situation.
2 They encourage self-responsibility, in that clients not only have the right to say what is wanted but also are asked to fully 'own' that want, to be aware that they have some control of their own lives, that they have options and that only they can change their lives.
3 They provide clarity of focus and, in naming a goal, give both client and practitioner something to aim for. Another meaning of the word 'contract' is 'to make smaller'. In this sense, the clarity of goal can mean economy of time and energy for client and practitioner. The time spent in clarifying a contract constitutes an important part of the total work to be done. Furthermore, the contract acts as a 'mind set' such that the client not only moves towards the goal consciously but also holds it as an internal frame of reference.
4 They help to avoid misunderstandings: for instance, they challenge the belief that the practitioner has some magic potion that is kept in a secret drawer and handed out to any client who has the password. Specifically, they go some way to avoiding what in TA are called 'games'. These will be discussed later in the book. Games are partly the result of lack of clarity and hidden agendas – hidden to all parties – which would seriously impede or prevent effective work.
5 Contracts provide a useful yardstick for measuring the effectiveness of the work. This is essential if we are to work ethically with our clients. If contracts are not being achieved, either they are the wrong contracts – in which case, the focus of the work needs to shift – or the client and the practitioner are not suited – in which case, the work will need to be brought to an end and the client referred elsewhere.
6 The achievement of a contract instils hope and optimism in a client, along with a sense of power. This can be a fine foundation for future changes.
7 They provide a container in which many meanings can emerge and be explored.

The possible disadvantages of contracts, especially of hard contracts, are:

1 Clients may experience themselves as not being listened to or seen in all their dark and hidden parts but only in the specific area they have named.

2 Contracts can sometimes feel like homework assignments to some clients. For instance, Cleo, who has spent her life being 'good', getting things right, always achieving 'A' grades and so on, may feel as if this is another test and that the practitioner will be marking her on her performance.
3 Clients who 'don't know' what they want can feel inadequate, 'bad', despondent or hopeless when asked to name their goal. Some may comply with the expectation and invent something to please the practitioner, while others may be rebellious in response.
4 If a goal can be named, it comes by definition from the known frame of reference. This creates a danger of excluding spontaneous or other issues that may arise in the relationship.

These disadvantages can be avoided if the practitioner sees contract making not as static but as a flexible, growing process in which the practitioner and client together are aware of the journey they are making and are responsive to the changing needs and goals of that journey. The Contracting Matrix can support the practitioner in this.

Application

Several transactional analysts offer models of contract making. Holloway and Holloway (1973) suggest:

What do you want to change? How will you and I know you have made those changes? By their second question, they encourage translating even the softest contract into behavioural terms. The exploration should be as detailed as possible as the client imagines a possible future, engaging all senses.

Some examples of contracts for behavioural change could include the following:

- A mother who is overwhelmed and angry during the school holidays makes a contract to do something enjoyable with her children every day.
- A lonely man makes a contract to make three new friends.
- An anxious and housebound person makes a contract to travel, gradually increasing distances outside the house week by week.

Though these contracts emphasize an observable behavioural change, they are likely to involve the client in exploring why they are, respectively, miserable and angry, lonely or anxious, and what they are doing or not doing to keep it that way.

There are other formats for making contracts that have been suggested by TA practitioners. We include two of them here.

Muriel James (1977) provides a list of contracting questions which have been expanded by our colleagues, Petruska Clarkson and Shona Ward:

1 What do you want that would enhance your life?
2 What do you need to change to achieve this?
3 What would you be willing to do to effect this change?

4   How would other people know when the change has been made?
5   How might you sabotage yourself?
6   How will you prevent sabotage?
7   How will you reward yourself on completion?
8   How are you going to spend your time when you have changed?
9   Where and how will you get your strokes, now that you have changed?

Allen and Allen (1984), offer some simple questions to focus the client:

1   What will you be doing when you are well that you are not doing now? (It is inter-
    esting to note that they use the word 'well', which suggests a medical model of
    illness and health. However, we think they intend 'well' to mean having a sense of
    'well-being' within yourself.)
2   What are you doing now that you will not be doing when you are well?
3   How will we both know when you are well?

The answers that two clients gave to this last set of questions demonstrate the
flexible way in which they can be used. Ann answered without hesitation. She had
thought a lot about what she wanted from her life. To the first question she replied,
'I will have friends whom I will see regularly. I will sing in a choir and I will be
training as a counsellor.' To the second question she responded with, 'I'm having
panic attacks when I go out and I certainly won't be having those any more.' There
was no need for the third question, as it had been answered implicitly in the first
two. But Sally was different. She needed a long time to explore (*exploratory contract*)
the implications of the questions and she spread them over several sessions in her
exploration. She needed to understand what it was that lay beneath her general
feeling of malaise in order to start to let herself know what she wanted to change
in her life. Eventually, she knew that what she would be doing when she was well
was expressing her feelings, asking for what she wanted and managing creatively
those situations in which she could not have what she wanted. What she decided
she would not be doing was telling herself that she was not important and that
others should come first. She said we would both know when she was well when
she looked, acted and sounded more energetic and had taken up a new hobby –
she was not yet sure what. (The 'new hobby', incidentally, turned out to be several,
including a regular aerobics class and squash. She also started a new relationship.)

A Final Word about Contracts

In order to make contracts as useful and effective as possible, they need to be stated
in clear, precise language understood by both practitioner and client. A contract to
'perambulate diurnally in a recreational outdoor amenity while inhaling and exhaling
diaphragmatically' is less likely to be achieved than a contract to 'take a daily walk in
the park and breathe deeply'.

   The practitioner should also be alert for contracts which contain hidden loopholes.
Often these take the form of qualifier words such as 'more', 'less' and 'better'. These
obscure the real meaning. For example, what does it mean to 'make more and better

contact with others'? How much is more? What constitutes better contact? Who are these others and how many are there? These unquantified aspects need to be avoided by careful questioning on the part of the practitioner to elicit more precise and specific goals. Similarly, there are phrases like 'try to', which implies a lot of effort and no success, or 'be able to', which contains possibility but no action. Either the client is going to do something or they are not. This needs to be clear within the contract.

Note that TA practitioners do not encourage their clients to make what are called *Parent contracts* – those which please our parents (or others we may see in a parental role). A TA practitioner is interested in helping people to truly discover themselves and what they want, not parenting models from their childhood. This encapsulates the difference between a promise and a contract. Though the content may be similar, the process of making a contract is different in that a contract is a commitment primarily to oneself (witnessed and supported by the practitioner), whereas a promise comprises a commitment to or for another. Most of all, avoid contracts which involve 'getting rid of' some part of the self. For example, 'I'll stop being vulnerable' or 'I'll cut out my angry feelings'. These contain a belief that there is something wrong with the client as they are and invite the practitioner to collude with this belief.

Our Contract with You, the Reader

Though we are not meeting face to face, we can in a sense make a contract with you now about this book. We undertake to present some of the major concepts in TA and show how they can be used by a practitioner. For each theoretical concept, we will include a section on its application and a section of exercises to be used by readers for themselves and for their clients. We do not undertake to cover every aspect of TA theory but we will widely reference other TA writers for those readers who would like to learn more. Where, for clarity, we use our own terms instead of the more commonly used TA terms we will indicate this with reference to the original terminology.

Your side of the contract, as the reader, is that you have acquired this book, from a shop, library, the publisher, friend or colleague. This means that, at some point, payment has been made for our services and those of the publisher. This is the extent of your side of the contract. You have not contracted to read it. You may even have bought the book because it's just the right thickness to prop up that wobbly table in the kitchen. However, if you do decide to read it, we hope you will find it interesting and helpful to you. We would be happy to hear your comments on it (see the 'about the authors' pages for our e-mail addresses).

Exercises

Self

1 Make a list of five things you want to do today. Choose one. Do it. This may sound simple but you have just made a contract with yourself and kept it. How do you

feel? Do you have a sense of satisfaction in having made a plan for yourself and fulfilled it? What do you think and feel about the experience?

2   This time, make a list of five things you want to do or ought to do but have been putting off. Choose one. Why have you been putting it off? Do you still want to do it? What could you do to make it easier? Are you willing to do it? If so, how will you reward yourself for having done it? Now do it. How do you feel? You can do the same with the other things on the list if you want to.

3   Choose one of the contracting methods we have introduced in this chapter and answer the questions for yourself. You may choose to do this with your own practitioner.

4   Experiment with a friend or colleague (someone with whom you feel free to be open) in having two separate conversations. In one, start by saying what you want to talk about and what you want to get out of having the talk. In the other, just talk about whatever is on your mind at the time without making a plan and ask your partner to listen empathically to what you are saying. Notice the difference in the two experiences and assess for yourself the advantages and disadvantages of each.

Working with Clients

1   While you are listening to and talking to your client, stay aware of your own experience and notice when you need clarification of what the client wants. Gently, find out what your client wants either by asking directly, as in 'What would you like from me about this?' or 'How would you like to be different?' or by checking assumptions, as in 'Do you want to do something about that?' or 'It sounds as if you need to let off steam about that right now, is that right?'

2   Invite your clients to picture themselves as they want to be, paying attention to how they will be different from the way they are now. How will they feel, think, walk, sit, talk, eat, dress and so on? (You could ask them if there is any detail of the picture that they could start doing right now?!)

3   Use one of the contracting methods or one of your own and invite your clients to be specific about what changes they are going to make in their lives.

CASE STUDY: A COACH'S STORY

Anita was pleased when she got a call from Ladli, the HR Director of a multinational furniture manufacturer. Ladli explained that Gunther, the manager of their European operations, had asked for coaching through a stressful reorganization that had happened as a result of a recent merger. Though German, Gunther was based at their Head Office in the UK, not far from where Anita lived and worked. Anita's name had been given to her by a colleague. Would she like to meet the potential client? Anita said she would, and talked briefly with Ladli about what involvement HR would want to have. None, was the reassuring answer. Ladli was happy to authorize an initial six sessions over the coming nine months and suggested that perhaps a three-way meeting at the end of the series would be useful. They agreed a fee and a system of invoicing and Anita promised to contact Gunther. Following the call she wrote a brief e-mail to Ladli, confirming their conversation, and then got in touch with Gunther to arrange a meeting. He answered immediately and seemed pleased to set up a short session to 'look each other over'.

At their meeting the following week, Anita arrived promptly at Gunther's office where he met her immediately in reception and took her to the cafeteria for a chat. They got on well. Gunther, a tall, kindly man in his mid-forties, talked about some of the issues facing him but said that he thought there were others that he didn't know about. It seemed that Gunther had been very relieved that HR had agreed to the coaching, and Anita suspected that he was more anxious than he appeared. They settled on the six sessions that Ladli had suggested, starting with a contract to explore his situation. Anita assured him that their sessions would be confidential and suggested that once the coaching started in earnest, they meet somewhere where they could be private.

3

Ego States: a theory of personality

As mentioned in the introduction to this book, ego states are the building-blocks of TA theory.

Definition and Description

In his last book, *What Do You Say After You Say Hello?*, Berne defined ego states as 'coherent systems of thought and feeling manifested by corresponding patterns of behaviour' (1972 p. 11). Simplified further, structurally, an ego state is a state of being or experience which involves our thinking, feeling and behaving. You may already be asking yourself if there are any states of experience which do not involve thinking, feeling and behaving. The answer is no. At any moment in time an experience will, in some way, involve all three. As you are reading these words you will be having a feeling response to what you are reading, thinking about the meaning of the words and your response to them, and simultaneously exhibiting a behaviour called reading, involving looking, seeing, body posture, manner of holding the book, facial expression and so on. Inevitably, then, at any given moment we can be said to be in an ego state.

Now that you have read a further sentence or two you are in another ego state with the thinking, feeling and behaviour belonging to the new moment. Looking back in time, you can now see that by this definition your life has been made up of millions upon millions of ego states, one after the other. But how can this possibly be of any use to us in our quest for some understanding of ourselves and other people? To answer this question, we need to look yet more closely at ego states. On closer inspection, we observe that some of these ego states are not new. They are not fresh, 'of the moment' states of experience but repetitions of past ego states. In other words, they involve thinking, feeling and behaving in the same way we once did in our near, mid or distant past.

A further question arises: does this matter? It matters only insofar as how much the re-experiencing of a past ego state interferes with our current functioning in life. For example, you may be reading this book right now, yet at the same time reliving a negative experience you had when struggling to understand a book on, say, calculus when you were nine years old. Your thinking is confused and has a nine-year-old's capacity, you feel sad and despondent and your behaviour is agitated (you put the book down, you pick it up, you clean your fingernails with the cover and so on). We hope this is not the case, as clearly this will be interfering with your enjoyment and learning.

Conversely, you may be reading this book and reliving a positive experience of learning a new subject as a student. You are thinking clearly, you feel excited by the ideas being presented, you read with concentration and do not even notice your fingernails. We definitely hope this is more the case. The latter experience, of course, may not be an old ego state at all. It could be a purely current experience, in which case, all well and good. The point of the examples, however, is to show that, even if we are reliving an old ego state, it is not necessarily dysfunctional for us. What we are looking at, then, in our own lives as well as those of our clients, are those ego states which are interfering negatively with the way we are functioning or want to function in the present.

Already we can see that there are distinctions we can make between ego states. First, we can say that some ego states are current – our set of feeling, thinking and behaving is in relation to the here-and-now reality – while others are historic – our thinking, feeling and behaving belong to the past. Second, we can make another distinction by applying some assessment and judgment as to whether an ego state is functional or dysfunctional, whether it enhances or interferes with our experience.

The Adult Ego State

The term used to describe an ego state that is in direct relation to here-and-now, consensual reality is an 'Adult' ego state. We talk of being 'in' an Adult ego state or 'in Adult' where there is no historic interference. We are thinking, feeling and behaving in the moment. The words that might be used to describe a person in an Adult ego state could include 'responsive', 'alive', 'vibrant', 'in good contact', 'spontaneous' and 'autonomous'. This is not synonymous with being happy or persistently 'full of the joys of spring'. We are talking about reality here, and reality involves being appropriate to whatever is the situation. For example, in response to the death of a friend, people might feel sad and despairing, they question their own existence and the point of life, they cry and get angry. All of these are Adult ego state responses to the here-and-now reality of bereavement.

Experientially, we see the Adult ego state as an 'empty' ego state that is filled in each co-created moment as we respond to a new situation from the wealth of our experience and potential and the situation responds to us. Moment by moment the reality changes, as does our response to that reality. Once past, each Adult ego state becomes one of the many historic ego states from which it was distinguished only by its current nature, its here-and-now relation to the situation.

Clearly, in an Adult ego state we are not totally 'new'. What is new is our unique experience and response to a particular situation as it shapes and is shaped by us. However, we can draw upon our past experiences (historic ego states) constructively and creatively. Indeed, if we are to grow and change, it is vital that we do just that. Our whole learning process is dependent upon our ability to use the past in this way and benefit from our experience. This capacity for drawing upon other ego states or integrating them is suggested in the fuller labelling of the Adult as the *Integrating Adult* ego state (Tudor 2003). The historic becomes integrated into the here–and–now.

Further Distinctions

Unfortunately, we do not always use our past experiences constructively or creatively, nor do we necessarily use them consciously. As stated earlier, sometimes the past impinges upon the present without being consciously integrated and interferes with our current functioning. We cathect or 'go into' historic ego states sometimes partially, sometimes totally.

The concept of 'going into' historic ego states implies that these ego states are stored within us. Recent developments in understanding about neural networks and the development of the brain tempt us to hypothesize about links between areas of the brain and ego states (see for example Allen 2000, 2009; Mazzetti 2010). Yet exactly where and how we store such experiences remains largely a neurobiological mystery. Berne posited the concept of 'psychic organs' but these remain merely as conceptual constructs. Suffice it to say that there are reservoirs of past experience and that they can be re–experienced. Such re–experiencing involves more than thoughts about our past experience. It is not an act of remembering. It is a timeless 'reliving' of a past experience in the present involving all three of our criteria of an ego state, namely, thoughts, feelings and behaviours in a coherent system. Let us take a look at these reservoirs of past experience, known in TA structurally as the Child ego state and the Parent ego state.

The Child Ego State

In order to emphasize its historic nature, the Child ego state is more fully referred to as the 'Archaic Child' ego state. This label, though the singular form is commonly used, describes the multitude of historic ego states which constitute the person's own past experiences. Gregoire (2004) talks about 'generalizations' of experiences that make up ego states. They are called Child ego states to emphasize that these ego states often have their origins in childhood. Much of the work that we do in psychological therapy is likely to focus on childhood experience. We conceptualize all past experience as being stored in the Child or Parent ego states, including the moment just past. Thus Adult ego states form in the present but, once past, are stored within one of the two types of ego state reservoirs – either as easily integrated, fluid responses to the world or as more rigid ego states that have become stylized in an unchanging response to similar situations, What makes a pattern become a fixed way of being is likely to be the level of stress or emotion that is aroused in the original experience. Alternatively, frequently repeated experiences create a habitual and fixed ego state.

When a person thinks, feels and behaves in ways that are a repetition of past, often childhood experiences, we say they are in a Child ego state.

Example

John, on arriving home from work, realizes he has forgotten to pick up the groceries. As his wife moves to greet him, John's first thought is that she will be angry with him, he feels very scared and hurriedly leaves the room. Outside of his awareness, he has responded to a current situation in the way he responded when, as a six-year-old, he forgot to run an errand for his mother. In the past situation his mother was often, in fact, violently angry and he fled the room in fear of her wrath. Thus the past experience has been generalized, stored as a pattern of relating to others, and is relived in the present triggered by the similarity of the circumstances. In the Child ego state John thinks, feels and behaves in ways inappropriate to the current reality. Had he remained in an Adult ego state, he could have greeted his wife, told her he had forgotten the groceries, apologized, offered to return for the groceries and so on, even if his wife did get angry.

A second example illustrates how a fixed pattern can arise in adulthood.

Example

Gunvati starts a new job in an advertising agency where creative ideas are highly prized and the culture is relaxed and spontaneous. She won the job because of her first class degree and superb references. Before going to university, she had a job as a PA, where she was terrorized by the critical and perfectionist attitude of her boss and she learned to check everything before she spoke. Being 'at work' seems to trigger old work patterns. In the new situation, she comes across as unimaginative and rigid. This is a Child ego state that she is using inappropriately in the present.

The Parent Ego State

The second store or reservoir of historic experience is called the 'Parent ego' state. This singular label again describes a multitude of past ego states. These are distinct from Child ego states in that they are not our own direct experiences but rather the ego states of our parents or parent-figures which we have taken in (introjected) as our own. This ego state reservoir is consequently often more fully referred to as the 'Introjected Parent'.

Again, though the emphasis is upon introjection that occurred in childhood, we conceptualize the Parent ego state as also accommodating introjections of anyone who was significant or had power over us when we were growing up, as well as later important figures in our adult lives, which may include friends, colleagues, bosses, counsellors, coaches, teachers and others. When a person thinks, feels and behaves in ways that are unconsciously borrowed from parents or parent-figures, we say they are in a Parent ego state.

Many actual parents, though determined *never* to treat their offspring in the way their own parents treated them, nonetheless 'find themselves' (often to their dismay) admonishing their children with the same words and phrases, intonation, gestures and feelings to which they were exposed by their own parents. In other words, they 'go into' a Parent ego state. But responding to others in this way is not the prerogative of actual parents. Each of us, at times, transacts from a Parent ego state. Observers and teachers of even small children will often observe how children 'become' their parents at times.

Let us go back to John who, in the previous example of the Child ego state, forgot the groceries. As much as he has access to a Child ego state wherein he is scared and runs away from his angry mother, equally he has access to a Parent ego state which contains the introjection of his angry and chastising mother. (It is most likely that the experience of this internal Parent ego state, and the projection of this Parent ego state onto his wife, reactivated the fear in his Child ego state.)

Having access to this Parent ego state, it would not be surprising if, had the situation been reversed and his wife had forgotten the groceries, John thought, felt and behaved towards her from his Parent ego state in the violently angry manner in which his mother had once dealt with him, by responding, for example, with, 'You stupid fool, how could you forget such a simple thing!' This is why we often come to the uncomfortable realization that our fear of the way others may think about us, feel about us and behave towards us arises precisely because it is the way we could easily think, feel and behave towards them (and are internally treating ourselves).

The PAC Model

You now have the basic Parent–Adult–Child structural model (known in shorthand as the 'PAC model') of ego states. When referring to these ego states, the initial letter is always capitalized to differentiate the ego states Parent, Adult and Child, from actual parents, adults and children. The basic PAC structural model of ego states is shown in Figure 3.1.

The Identification of Ego States

In his book *Transactional Analysis in Psychotherapy*, Berne (1961) suggests four ways of identifying from which type of ego state a person is transacting. These are detailed below.

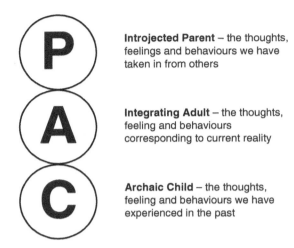

Introjected Parent – the thoughts, feelings and behaviours we have taken in from others

Integrating Adult – the thoughts, feeling and behaviours corresponding to current reality

Archaic Child – the thoughts, feeling and behaviours we have experienced in the past

Figure 3.1 The PAC structural model of ego states

Identification by Behavioural Diagnosis

By observing the demeanour, gestures, body posture, voice tone, vocabulary and facial expression of a person we may find some clue as to which ego state that person is in. For example, a man waving a fist while issuing words of command with an angry facial expression may be in a Parent ego state, reproducing the thoughts, feelings and behaviour of his father. Equally, it could be a person in an Adult ego state rehearsing his part in Shakespeare's *Henry V*.

As another example, a woman observed to curl up in the corner of the sofa crying piteously may be seen to be in a Child ego state. Equally, she may be behaving as her mother did when under stress, in which case, though her mother may have been in a Child ego state at the time (or behaving as her mother did), this woman would be said to be in a Parent ego state, having introjected her mother's thinking, feeling and behaviour. Clearly, a behavioural diagnosis, though perhaps giving some clues, is not enough to be certain.

Identification by Social Diagnosis

Social diagnosis is the most relational of the ego state diagnoses. It concerns the reactions of others to the person being diagnosed. In our first example above it may be that, in response to the fist-waving man, others feel vulnerable and scared, think they are about to be dominated and, therefore, avoid confrontation with him. If such is the case, it is possible that our man is in a Parent ego state eliciting a complementary Child ego state response in others. If, however, this is a Shakespearean actor rehearsing his role, the social response of others is likely to be Adult and indicate the complementary Adult ego state of our actor.

In our second example, if others respond to the crying, curled-up woman from Parent ego states ranging from over-protective urges to nurture her to equally strong urges to shake her and tell her to 'Grow up!', it is likely that she is in a Child ego state. But what if, as suggested earlier, she is in a Parent ego state, behaving as her mother once did under stress? The others might still respond from Parent ego states as if to a child because this is the Child in her Parent ego state (mother's Child) although, technically, this is her Parent ego state. Clearly, even with the behavioural diagnosis, a social diagnosis is not enough.

Identification by Historical Diagnosis

This simply means checking the origins of the observed behaviour, feelings and thinking with the person in question. For example, we could ask the fist-waving man to be aware of how he is behaving, thinking and feeling and ask him if this is how others in his past behaved. If he says his father used to behave in this way, use the same gestures, express the same thoughts and feelings, it is a pretty good indication that he is in a Parent ego state – unless, of course, he tells us that he is consciously copying his father's behaviour for his role of Henry V, in which case he is in Adult.

In the example of the crying woman whose behaviour, along with our social response, has led us tentatively to identify a Child ego state, we may ask if she remembers being like this as a child. She may even remember how old she was at the time and fully corroborate the identification of a Child ego state. Conversely, she may remember her mother being like this and identify a Parent ego state. Or she may even be entertaining her grandchild with an enacted story, in which case she could identify being in Adult. By now, being corroborated by the person in question, the diagnosis may be getting much clearer.

Identification by Phenomenological Diagnosis

Here the identification is encapsulated within the subjective experience of the person re-experiencing the past. The person experientially relives the original event. The fist-waving man in our example may verify being in a Parent ego state as he currently 'feels' himself to be his father waving an angry fist and giving commands, just as his father had done 30 years ago when our subject was a child. Our hypothesis that the woman is in a Child ego state may be verified as she continues to sob deeply and, feeling sad and abandoned, cries out, 'Mummy, don't leave me!' just as she had done as a child when her mother left her alone in the house at a very early age.

We hope we have here emphasized enough the importance of including all four means of diagnosis when identifying ego states. It is fine to have hunches when working with your clients, especially those relating to your own feeling response to the person; this is a helpful starting-point. It is even better to check them sensitively before acting on them. If you do not, at best you may be unhelpful, at worst you may be insulting or even harmful.

Application

How is the identification of ego states useful? In our introduction we wrote that TA is a way of looking at what goes on between people and inside people in order to help them make changes. The identification of structural ego states is an important step in this direction. If we learn to identify our own ego state responses, we provide ourselves with important information and widen our choice of response options.

Example

Susan, a successful and competent businesswoman, faced hundreds of people in conference rooms all over the country but avoided social situations. This was because, when entering a room where others were informally gathered, she would feel acutely embarrassed and would want to run from the room. She turned down invitations to parties, dinners and drinks with the neighbours and was becoming more and more socially isolated. This was the problem she brought to her employee assistance counselling. The counsellor asked her to talk about the differences between the two situations. She made the following distinctions:

- lecture hall as opposed to people's front rooms
- formal as opposed to informal
- presenting ideas as opposed to presenting myself
- seats in rows as opposed to casual seating
- feeling confident as opposed to feeling nervous and embarrassed.

The counsellor shared with Susan the concept of ego states and his hunch that when lecturing she was in an Adult ego state and in the social situation in a Child ego state. She agreed that in the social situation she did feel extremely little. The counsellor suggested that she close her eyes and imagine herself as a child and to 'take herself' into a situation where she was in someone's front room, at an informal gathering where people are casually sitting around and where she was presenting herself in some way. Almost immediately Susan said she felt scared and embarrassed. She experienced wanting to run away. She thought, 'They think I'm silly. They're laughing at me.' The counsellor encouraged her to stay with these thoughts, feelings and behaviours even though they were uncomfortable. He asked her where she was and she told the counsellor, 'I'm at my aunt's house. I'm six years old. I'm very excited to be here at a grown-up party. I'm dressed as a fairy ... (Susan here is looking very frightened, wringing her hands in her lap and trembling slightly) Yes, of course!' At this point, Susan 'came back' to the present. She did not need to stay in her six-year-old Child ego state any longer. She reported that she had run into the room where the grown-ups were casually seated. Wanting to present herself as a 'real fairy', she'd leapt into the air as an entrance. Unfortunately, she fell awkwardly, snapped her wand and tore the paper wings which fell about her as she lay on the floor. All she could hear was the laughter of the grown-ups as she ran from the room in great distress, feeling acutely embarrassed.

Susan could see that, outside of her awareness, she had been repeating the feelings, thoughts and behaviours of this archaic event each time she had presented herself at an informal gathering. She had generalized a specific event and, outside of her awareness, repeated this pattern in similar situations of informal gatherings. Making the conscious connection, in other words identifying the Child ego state, helped Susan recognize that she had options in such situations. With this recognition and some work on her original embarrassment, she began to attend social gatherings and would stay in her Adult ego state. If she felt nervous or embarrassed, she would remind herself that she was not six years old, she was not about to leap awkwardly into the room and that others were not going to laugh at her; they would be seeing the attractive, confident and competent woman that she was.

In this example, Susan's Child ego state had been interfering with her Adult functioning. By identifying that ego state, Susan could choose to respond to current reality in an appropriate way.

Exercises

Self

Now you are familiar with the three types of ego states of the structural model, you can practise being aware of whether you are in Parent, Adult or Child ego states. Being aware at the time you move into a particular ego state (even better, predicting which one and when you might move into it) will enhance your options in any particular situation. However, it may take some time to reach this level of self-awareness. To begin with, observe which ego state you have been in after the event. Think back over the many different situations in which you were engaged. Isolate certain events and for each situation ask yourself the following questions:

1   Did I think, feel and behave in ways that my parents used to (or other grown-ups used to) when I was little?
2   Did I think, feel and behave in ways that were appropriate and a direct here-and-now response to what was going on?
3   Did I think, feel and behave as I did at some time in my recent, mid or distant past?

Work through several events until you come up with an example for all three ego states and write them down as follows:

PARENT: I felt ....
          I thought ....
          I behaved by ....

ADULT: I felt ....
                   I thought ....
                   I behaved by ....

CHILD: I felt ....
                   I thought ....
                   I behaved by ....

In the case of the Child ego state, see if you can identify the origins: what was happening for you in your life; how old were you; who else was involved?

In the case of the Parent ego state, see if you can identify the person whose feelings, thoughts and behaviours you re-enacted today. Why do you think you were influenced by this person? Why do you think in this particular situation you went into a Parent ego state?

Given that you could have been in any of the three ego states in the situations in which you have chosen to self-observe, let us experiment with alternatives:

1 Imagine what would have happened if, in your example of a Child ego state, you had been in a Parent ego state.
2 Imagine what would have happened if, in your example of a Parent ego state, you had been in an Adult ego state.
3 Imagine what would have happened if, in your example of an Adult ego state, you had been in a Child ego state.

Note: The exercises above may also be useful to give to your clients if you are thinking of introducing TA into your practice. Though the following exercises are to help your clients to become aware of their own ego states, clearly, in the counselling, coaching or teaching situation, *your* ego states will play an important role. Much of the time you are likely to work effectively with your clients from your Adult ego state, while being willing to draw upon historic ego states in order to resonate with and understand your clients at a deep level. However, there may be times when you move unknowingly into a Parent ego state, subtly controlling your client in the way your father subtly controlled you, for example, or into a Child ego state, perhaps responding to your client with the thoughts, feelings and behaviours of the eight-year-old you once were. What will be important at such times is your ability to move back into a reflective Adult ego state in order to acknowledge what has happened, to be curious about it and to be willing to explore and understand these dynamics with your client, if it seems appropriate, or in your supervision, for the enhancement of their therapy. We will address such co-created occurrences later in this book, particularly when discussing *games* and *rackets*.

The aim is for your transactions to be filtered through Adult. This will mean constant self-supervision, supervision by others and personal work for yourself in order to integrate unresolved past experiences and parental influences. Becoming an integrated Adult is clearly an ongoing process, and by 'ongoing' we mean lifelong.

Working with Clients

Choose a client with whom you will go through the exercises in this book. One of the best ways to learn to use TA concepts and skills effectively is by making audio or visual recordings of the sessions for self-supervision or supervision by others. Do inform your client that you will be recording the sessions and clarify the extended confidentiality contract involved.

Using your Intuition

When working with your client (and when listening to or watching a recorded session) use your intuition to assess which ego state your client is in at any particular moment. Watch and listen for behavioural clues as your client moves in and out of ego states. Remember that each client's ego states will be unique to that individual. Observation will need to take place over several sessions before you begin to notice certain patterns. Remember, the pattern should include thoughts, feelings and behaviour.

Behavioural Clues

Use your intuition to make tentative hypotheses as to the type of ego state to which these patterns belong. Make a note of these under Parent, Adult and Child headings (leaving space for further notes and further ego state diagnosis). Remember that these behaviours will belong to one of the three types of ego state particular to the individual client – one person's Child behaviour may be another person's Parent behaviour, and so on. For example:

- **PARENT:** This particular client folds arms across chest, clenches fists, jaw rigid; voice sharper, staccato, higher pitched; uses words like 'should', 'have to', 'never'; short of breath, angry and frustrated; speaks contemptuously of self and others. (Like father?)
- **ADULT:** This same client sits with feet well-grounded, relaxed; makes good eye contact; breathes fairly deeply and regularly; thinks clearly and talks of self and others in a lively and interested manner; expresses feelings clearly and directly.
- **CHILD:** This same client sits with shoulders dropped, head bowed; speaks softly (often inaudibly); avoids eye contact; agitates fingers, expresses anxiety, thinks others (including me) are angry with her; fears she has done something wrong; looks about five years old.

Social Clues

The social clues are your experience in response to these behavioural clues. What are your feelings, thoughts and behaviours at these times? Check them against the intuitive identification of your client's ego states so far. Do you experience yourself in Child when your client is in Parent? In Parent when your client is in Child? In Adult when your client is in Adult? Check the consistency of your responses and add these under each of the headings.

Historical Clues

By asking appropriate questions, you can check further on your ego state identification so far. When you think your client is in a Child ego state, the following types of questions may be useful:

> Do you remember feeling/thinking/behaving like this in your childhood?
> How old do you feel right now?
> What was happening in your life then?
> What are the similarities between your past experience and your current one?

When you think your client might be in a Parent ego state, the following types of questions may be useful:

> Who in your past used to say what you're now saying?
> Who in your past behaved like this towards you?
> Are you expressing your feelings or are you expressing familiar feelings expressed by someone from your childhood?
> Who was this? What was the situation?

Familiarity on your and your client's part with the historic ego states will help identify the Adult ego state by a process of elimination. You can directly ask your client if they experience themselves in Parent or Child right now, or if they feel in the present.

Phenomenological Clues

In Parent or Child ego states your client may be aware of re-experiencing the past. If you think your client is in a Child ego state it may be useful to ask directly what is happening right now, what is the client's experience, what the client is feeling and thinking, what is the time and place of the client's experience, who else is there and so on. Similarly, with the Parent ego state, ask your client to express their experience right now: who is it that is grimacing in such a way, who is it that is saying these dismissive words, who is it that feels so despondent at such times? And so on. For the Adult ego state again, asking your client to express what they are experiencing at the moment will help to confirm your identification of an Adult ego state according to the response.

CASE STUDY: A COACH'S STORY

Anita and Gunther met for their first official coaching session. They had decided that two hours would give them time to explore the situation and clarify some of the immediate issues. At their initial meeting, Anita had let him know that she used TA in her coaching, but he wasn't familiar with the approach so she had in mind to share some of the concepts with him. In the event, she didn't. For the first hour he talked almost non-stop, describing the build-up to the merger – actually, it seemed more of a take-over of his own firm by a slightly bigger one – and the hard work he had put into clarifying the processes and procedures for his new team. The head-count of employees had needed to be 'rationalized' as he called it, but this had been managed through voluntary redundancies and some sideways moves. He said that he had told the team that he would make no major job moves or leadership interventions without their support and agreement, so one or two decisions were still unresolved because the team were acting rather passively and appeared unengaged.

Anita felt slightly anxious. The merger was taking place in troubled economic times and she thought that perhaps a stronger leadership stance might be appropriate. She was also somewhat disconcerted to find that she felt a little bored with Gunther's account (*Social diagnosis, hypothesizing a Parent ego state in Gunther, with an absent Child*). His English, like his dress, was punctilious and even. He showed no feelings – not even as he described how hard he was finding it to understand his team's passivity (*Behavioural diagnosis – perhaps more indication of a Parent ego state*). He went into detail about the new processes and she found herself glancing at her watch. However, he appeared to find telling the story a relief, so she did not challenge his presentation. At the end of an hour however, she said, 'I am curious about the meticulous care and precision with which you are treating your team, and yet you have said nothing about how they – or you – feel about what's going on. I find myself wondering about where you learned your way of leading the team.' Gunther looked surprised for a moment; then he smiled and his kindly eyes twinkled unexpectedly, 'Your description of me reminds me of what it was like being with my father, after my mother died. He was always absolutely careful and correct when he took care of us boys, but nobody expressed any feelings' (*Historical diagnosis – more confirmation of a Parent ego state*). Anita was surprised how easily Gunther was able to connect his current manner with his father. He explained that his father had grown up during and after the war (World War II) and the psychological legacy from that experience had made him decide to put kindness and correctness above everything – it was a family value. Gunther realized that the situation with the new team, the changes and the job losses, had evoked some anxiety about people getting hurt in the merger and he recognized

(Continued)

(Continued)

that he had adopted his father's somewhat cautious approach to his staff. He also remembered how much he and his brother had yearned for his father to play with them and hug them. He said he was very different with his own children. Anita asked him whether there was anything his 'child self' could teach his 'manager self' about leading the team through the merger. Gunther realized that, in his desire to be fair and calm, he had entirely neglected to connect with his people as people.

After they had discussed how this insight might be useful, Anita shared the PAC model with her client. He was amazed to find that there was a model that explained exactly what he had been describing. Anita also invited him to think that organizations had Parent, Adult and Child ego states too. Berne (1963) called this Etiquette, Technics and Character. In this analogy, the Parent might contain the personality of the founders and leaders including the vision, the rules and the norms about 'how we behave around here', the Adult, the roles, responsibilities and resources of the here and now, and the Child, the way people have traditionally expressed feelings, managed anxiety and adapted to the culture. Anita invited Gunther to think about the confusion that might happen when two cultures met.

4

The Analysis of Transactions: understanding communication

A transaction is a two-way communication. It can either be internal (intrapsychic) or external (interpersonal). In this chapter we will deal with interpersonal transactions: I speak to you and you speak to me; Stanley waves to Bill, Bill waves back; Lara smiles at Neil, Neil frowns at Lara. A communication is made from one person to another and a communication is returned. In the terms of behavioural psychology, a *stimulus* is given to which a *response* is made.

When analysing transactions (which is sometimes called 'transactional analysis proper'), we can use the PAC structural model of ego states introduced earlier to help understand what is going on between two or more people. When two people meet, they each have three types of ego states and we can analyse the various ways in which these two sets of three ego states constellate.

Complementary Transactions

For example, what is going on when Stanley waves to Bill and Bill waves back? Obviously, we would need to talk to Stanley and Bill about this and identify each person's ego state from the various diagnostic clues. If we did, we might discover that Stanley sees Bill, who is an old friend, is pleased to see him and waves in greeting. Likewise, in response, Bill is pleased to see Stanley and waves back in greeting. We would probably diagnose such a transaction as an Adult to Adult stimulus (S) with an Adult to Adult response (R). This is known as a *complementary* transaction: the ego state to which the transaction is directed is the one which responds back to the original ego state. This transaction is shown in Figure 4.1.

Alternatively, we may discover that Bill is Stanley's boss and reminds him of his authoritarian father. Thus when Stanley waves to him it is a placatory wave from a Child ego state addressed to Bill's Parent ego state. In response, we may discover that Bill unconsciously comes from a Parent ego state, waving as his mother used to wave to the neighbours of whom she felt contemptuous and whom she considered beneath her. This is also a complementary transaction, this time between Child and

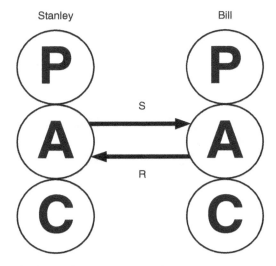

Figure 4.1 An Adult–Adult complementary transaction

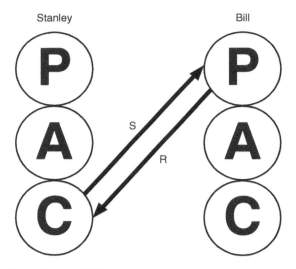

Figure 4.2 Child–Parent/Parent–Child complementary transaction

Parent ego states. Stanley's Child ego state addresses Bill's Parent ego state. Bill's Parent ego state responds to Stanley's Child ego state. This transaction is shown in Figure 4.2.

This is Berne's first rule of communication: *as long as transactions are complementary, communication can proceed indefinitely*. Complementary transactions are not necessarily negative or positive. This can only be ascertained from the context. For instance, a long and boring discussion could be complementary all the way through. In the first example, the Adult–Adult transaction of Stanley and Bill could have continued with:

STANLEY:	Hi, I'm really pleased to see you.
BILL:	Same here, do you have time for a coffee?
STANLEY:	Yes, of course. How's your new job?
BILL:	Well, difficult but I'm getting the hang of it.
STANLEY:	I admire you for changing jobs like you did.

And so on.

Equally, Stanley and Bill could have continued with:

STANLEY:	I'm glad I've bumped into you, I'm so angry with you!
BILL:	Why?
STANLEY:	You said you'd fix my car today and I need it to get to Oxford.
BILL:	Oh no, I thought you didn't need it till the weekend.
STANLEY:	No, I told you! Now, how *am* I to get to Oxford?
BILL:	Look, stop shouting. It won't help. I'll think of something ...

And so on.

This is still a sequence of Adult to Adult complementary transactions, despite the fact that they are arguing. In the second example, the Child–Parent/Parent–Child complementary transactions of Stanley and Bill might have continued with:

STANLEY:	Hello, Mr Thomson.
BILL:	Hello, Stanley. Are you keeping busy?
STANLEY:	Oh, I was just going over to the workshop now, honestly.
BILL:	Step on it then, it'll soon be lunch-time.
STANLEY:	OK, Mr Thomson. I'll run on ahead.
BILL:	Don't run! Don't you know about 'more haste less speed', as my mother used to say?
STANLEY:	Sorry, Mr Thomson.

And so on.

Crossed Transactions

Let us move on to Neil and Lara. Lara smiles at Neil. Neil frowns in return. This could be a complementary transaction similar to the last example of Parent–Child/Child–Parent transactions between Bill and Stanley. In other words, Lara is giving a placatory smile to an authority figure who, in response, provides a disapproving frown from his Parent ego state. Again, in order to be more certain, we would need to use the four diagnostic criteria for identifying ego states (as described in the previous chapter). We may discover that something completely different is going on. It may be that, when Lara smiles at Neil in a friendly way, it is because she thinks he looks interesting and she would like to get to know him. This would be described as an Adult–Adult stimulus. However, when Lara smiles at Neil he sees not Lara's smile but his mother's: the one she adopted when she wanted him to look after her when

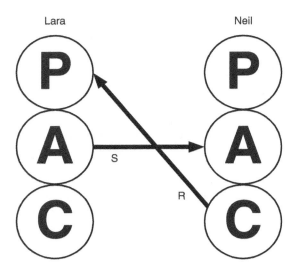

Figure 4.3 A crossed transaction

he was a child. He therefore frowns in response, just as he did as a child in expectation of being manipulated by his mother. This would be described as a Child–Parent response. Lara is probably completely puzzled by Neil's childlike behaviour. If you look at Figure 4.3 you will see why this is called a *crossed transaction*.

Sometimes the vectors do not actually cross, for example where an Adult to Child transaction is responded to by an Adult to Parent transaction, but as, by and large, they do, they are still referred to as crossed transactions because the sender expects a certain type of response but their expectation is crossed. This is the second rule of communication: *if the vectors of a transaction are crossed (which means the responding ego state is different from the one addressed or the addressed ego state responds back to a different ego state than the initiating one), communication is broken off and something different will happen.* As with complementary transactions, crossed transactions may be positive or negative according to the context.

In our example, when Neil crosses the transaction, he interrupts the possibility of smooth-flowing, complementary transactions and Lara is left puzzled. Communication probably stops at this point. If not, it is likely that Lara will now respond (notice that one person's response is another person's stimulus and vice versa) from an ego state other than Adult. She may go into a Child ego state and feel hurt, thinking, 'Nobody likes me!' and leave the room in tears, just as she had as a child in the face of rejection. Or she may move into a Parent ego state and get angry with Neil, shouting at him, 'How dare you look at me like that, you creep!' just as her mother used to shout at her father.

Ulterior Transactions

So far we have dealt with transactions at what is called the 'social level', overt messages between two people. But there are often (some would say, always) covert communications beneath the social level transactions. These are called *ulterior* transactions. Let us move to a new couple, Jean-Pierre and Pamela. Jean-Pierre meets Pamela outside the cinema (where, let us imagine, we are also waiting in the queue). We hear the following simple exchange:

JEAN-PIERRE: What time is it?
PAMELA: It's half-past seven.

On the social level, we would probably represent this as an Adult–Adult complementary transaction: information was asked for and information was given in return. But if we look closer (an action replay), we notice that as Jean-Pierre asks what time it is, he raises his eyebrows and furrows his brow, his hands are clasped together in a supplicatory manner and he avoids any eye contact with Pamela by looking at the ground. We might justifiably suspect that Jean-Pierre is not in an Adult ego state. We would need to mobilize our four diagnostic modes to identify a Parent or a Child ego state. We might then discover that this is how Peter behaved as a child towards his parents (a Child ego state) and that the communication beneath his simple 'What time is it?' is 'I know I'm late but please don't be cross with me.'

If we look more closely at Pamela as she is telling Jean-Pierre the time, we notice that her mouth is tight and her jaw clenched, she avoids eye contact by looking over his head at the sky, her arms folded across her chest, her foot tapping. We may discover, if we questioned her, that this is how Pamela's mother behaved towards her husband whenever he was late. The communication beneath the simple 'It's half-past seven' is 'Yes, you are very late and I'm extremely cross with you!' The complete set of social level and ulterior transactions can be represented as in Figure 4.4. (Ulterior

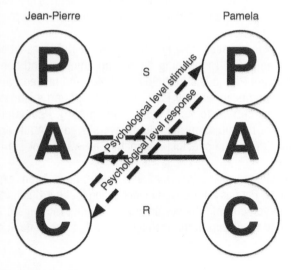

Figure 4.4 The ulterior transaction

transactions in TA are always drawn as a broken line.) Neither Jean-Pierre nor Pamela enjoy the film, but clearly it was not the verbal content of the transaction that led to this outcome. This brings us to the third rule of communication: *the outcome of a transaction is determined by the ulterior, psychological level communication rather than the social level communication.*

Application

Using the structural model of ego states to analyse transactions, we can clarify and better understand what is going on in the process of communication. We can see how historic ego states may be interfering with our relationships and causing dysfunction within those relationships. By being aware of our transactional patterns, we open up options, realize our choices and move towards greater autonomy.

Example

In a counselling group, Paul, in the process of learning to take care of himself, is wanting to find ways of structuring his time in the evenings in more enjoyable ways than hitherto. He is in an Adult ego state asking for information. Other members of the group provide him with some suggestions and to each of these he responds with thoughtful consideration. This procedure continues smoothly with Adult–Adult complementary transactions (Figure 4.5a). Pat, however, says, 'You should be grateful to have time to yourself in the evenings!' at which point there is silence (Figure 4.5b). Paul eventually says, 'I'm sorry, I think I've taken too much time on this' (Figure 4.5c). The facilitator suggests looking at what has just happened in the group by drawing a diagram of the transactions and the group works out the sequence referred to above.

Pat now quite clearly sees how she had crossed the transaction by coming from her Parent ego state (containing the feeling, thinking and behaviour of her mother, who allowed Pat no leisure time as a child) and invited Paul into a Child ego state (easily complied with by Paul, whose childhood experience is almost identical, hence his current focus of work in the group). Paul later realizes that he had a choice in the situation: he could have stayed in Adult and either persisted in asking Pat for the specific information he wanted or simply continued round the group.

When the facilitator asks Pat what she might have been experiencing in her Child ego state, Pat has no problem in identifying that her Child was saying, 'I'm envious – I want some fun in the evenings too!' Having recognized this, she then spends her time in the group more usefully in an Adult ego state, looking at ways of having fun.

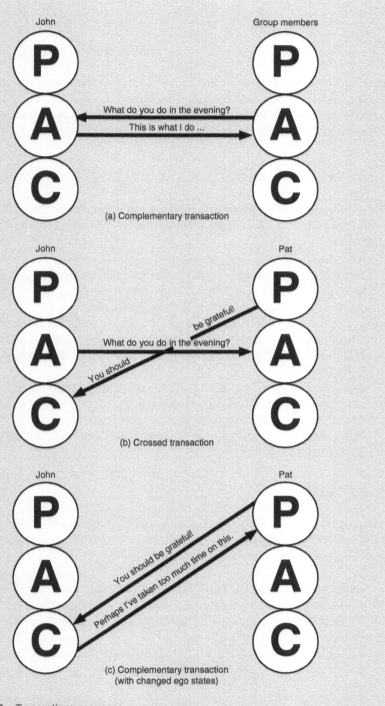

Figure 4.5   Transactions sequence

Exercises

Self

Think back over the past week and choose several conversations you have had with different people in different situations, including those with your clients in your practice setting. Write them down (as accurately as you can remember them) and analyse them transactionally, using the following guidelines:

Complementary Transactions

If the conversation has a flavour of continuity and interconnection from beginning to end (this may be boring or interesting, familiar or novel), analyse the transactions as follows:

1 In each of these complementary transactions, hypothesize which ego state you were in and which ego state you think the other person was in and mark them Adult–Adult, Parent–Child or Child–Parent and so on.
2 If you were in a Parent ego state and the other in a Child ego state, think about whose borrowed feelings, thoughts and behaviours these were and why you might have used them at this time. Was this useful? What might have been a better option?
3 If you were in a Child ego state, think about where you originally experienced these feelings, thoughts and behaviours and why you might be using them at this time. Again, was this useful? What might have been a better option?
4 In the Adult–Adult complementary transactions, what was qualitatively different about them compared to the others?

Crossed Transactions

If the conversations do not seem continuous or interconnected, identify the point at which something different happened. In other words, identify where the crossed transaction occurred. Now follow these steps:

1 Go back a few transactions and identify the ego states up to this point.
2 Now identify the ego states involved in the crossed transaction.
3 If you crossed the transaction at this point, why do you think this was and why did you move into this particular ego state?
4 If the other person crossed the transaction, why do you think this was and why do you think you accepted the invitation to go into the particular ego state that you did?
5 In these instances of crossed transactions, what would have happened if the conversations had remained complementary? Would this have been more constructive/ appropriate/useful?

Ulterior Transactions

Choose one of your conversations that includes a crossed transaction. Go through each social level transaction and see if you can find an ulterior message. Rewrite the conversation using the ulterior transactions only.

Working with Clients

Clients will often bring communication problems to their sessions and provide verbatim accounts of problematic conversations, rows, arguments and frustrations they have experienced. When this next happens, ask your client – who by now is familiar with the ego state model – to do some 'transactional analysis proper' with you by working through the conversation transaction by transaction, using the transactional model of two sets of stacked circles. In this way, using the guidelines you have used for yourself in the above exercises, identify the complementary, crossed and ulterior transactions to show where the 'stuck points' may have been occurring and how the situation could have been handled differently.

Similarly, you may do transactional analysis proper on transactions between you and your client. This is often very helpful in unravelling the parallel process of an outside issue being enacted in the consulting room. For example:

CLIENT:	Good morning, Jean.
SOCIAL WORKER:	Good morning.
CLIENT:	Why are you cross with me?
SOCIAL WORKER:	Cross with you?
CLIENT:	Yes, I know you are but I've not come to argue with you. I'm having enough trouble at home with my kid.
SOCIAL WORKER:	Before we move on to her, let's look at what's just happened between us.

Use the example on page 17 of the CEO who asked for challenge in his coaching but who somehow conveyed in the psychological contract that he couldn't bear to be contradicted and confronted. How would you analyse the transactions between Jonathan and his coach? Can you put in the social level transactions and also the ulteriors?

CASE STUDY: A COACH'S STORY

When he and Anita met the following month, Gunther was eager to continue working with ego states. He had spontaneously realized that if everybody had a full set of ego states, then he could track who was in which state during a conversation and begin to understand how each might be influencing the other. He had started to draw up an analysis of his interchange with one of his team, Joe,

(Continued)

(Continued)

the local UK Sales Manager, using arrows between the PAC models. He had asked Joe for some figures about sales, and while Joe had appeared to agree, a week later nothing had happened. He had drawn up two sets of ego states with arrows from the Adult to Adult. But now he was beginning to wonder: might he have been in his over-careful Parent with Joe, like he had been last time he had met with Anita?

Anita was delighted at his interest and told him that he was pre-empting Berne with his own thinking! She explained about the three types of communication and the three rules that went with them. Immediately he started to think about whether there might have been some ulterior transactions going on between him and Joe. They drew the diagram again (see Figure 4.6).

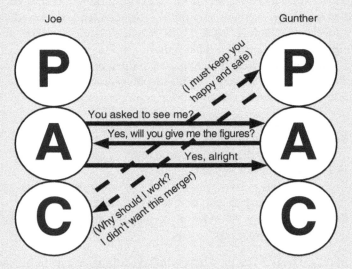

Figure 4.6 Ulterior transactions between Joe and Gunther

It became clear that Gunther's desire not to hurt anybody was a response to Joe's ulterior of resentful resistance to the new structure (of which he saw Gunther as representative). Gunther became very thoughtful. With Anita's empathic support, he began to examine more deeply how he had introjected his father's anxiety about hurting people. He also talked about how guilty he felt when he himself felt angry or hostile to anyone. He realized that the combination of Child and Parent influences (see 'Contaminations' in Chapter 10) meant that he wasn't taking his authority to lead the merger. He began to experiment with Anita in ways of using his power appropriately in an Adult to Adult way.

Towards the end of the session, he drew up two sets of ego states again and thoughtfully started to play with the idea that in merging two organizations, there may be many crossed transactions going on. His team was now composed of eight people – five from his own European division and three, including Joe, who had been part of the small American design firm that had been merged with the multinational. He had attended to the 'Technics' – the procedures, roles and responsibilities – but he hadn't attended to their previous ways of doing things, their founding fathers, their habits and feelings. He decided to have a team day where he would invite everyone to think about the impact of their two clashing cultures. He and Anita discussed questions for the team to consider, like: In your old organization,

- Who were the founders?
- What were the leaders like?
- How did you express yourselves?
- What were your values and passions?
- What were the strengths and what were the weaknesses of the organization?
- How much of all that is happening now in the new structure?

Gunther realized that, as his team did not all work in the same location, it would take a while to set up a team day. In the meantime, he decided to talk to each member individually to see how they were getting on. He realized that they were likely to have some personal Child and Parent ego states that had been activated by the major changes going on.

Anita thoroughly enjoyed their discussion and realized that Gunther seemed far less in his Parent ego state and more able to make spontaneous Adult contact with her. She noticed she was feeling more tenderly towards him.

5

Functional Analysis: behavioural options in relationship

We have mentioned options several times in previous chapters. We have indicated that, by becoming aware of our ego states, particularly the ones which are interfering with our current functioning, we can become more aware of our options in any given situation. The important implication here is that despite the apparently static nature of the structural model of ego states, they are actually dynamic – in other words, they are constantly changing and flowing in the here and now as we co-create each present moment. Awareness means having both responsibility and choice. Once aware that we are responding to a situation from a Child ego state, for example, we are then responsible for exercising choice as to whether we continue in this ego state or look for other options. Awareness implies that we have already accessed an Adult ego state. At the moment we recognize we are in a Child ego state we must already have moved, however partially or momentarily, into an Adult ego state in order to assess what is currently happening. In that moment, from this Adult position, we have the choice of noticing and choosing how we are functioning.

We want to emphasize those words: *how we are functioning*. Here, we are paying attention not to the historical structure of an ego state but *how* it is manifesting in the present – *how* a person is feeling, thinking and behaving and the attitude he is taking to the world. Though the idea of choosing another ego state may be useful, it may also be difficult to shift totally and simultaneously from one set of feelings, thoughts and behaviours to a whole new set. Our awareness may be in an Adult ego state but our feelings may remain in a Child ego state.

In working relationally in the present, it can be very useful to focus on the here-and-now functioning, which may be with a mixture of modes within ego states. Changing the way we are relating to the world in the present – changing our behaviour and the attitudes that reinforce that behaviour – is one of the best ways of also changing our whole state of mind.

Example

Zakir is often in a Child ego state when he goes for a job interview: he is scared, he thinks he will be rejected and he stoops, just as he did when facing his cruel and rejecting teacher as a child. By deciding to adopt a more open body posture, regulating his breathing to relax himself, talking to himself encouragingly and smiling in a friendly way, Zakir discovers that he begins to *feel* more at ease and that he is *thinking* less negatively about the outcome of the interview. Thus, by changing his behaviour and attitude, he has changed his feelings and thoughts and moved out of a dysfunctional Child ego state.

To help look at our functional and transactional options, TA provides a further model that describes a wide range of behaviours. This model is often confused with the structural ego state model. This is because, perhaps unfortunately, the model is usually represented by the same three stacked circles (though some practitioners, for example, Van Beekum (1991), Stewart (2001) and Flowerdew (2006) use stacked squares in order to differentiate the models) using the same Parent, Adult and Child labels and is further confounded by the adoption of the title 'The Functional Model of Ego States'. We consider the term 'ego state' for this second model to be a misnomer, as what the model deals with is behavioural options rather than ego states proper. We therefore suggest 'functional modes' as a preferable and less confusing term.

As the label 'functional ego states' is so much a part of the terminology used in other TA literature, let us explain our two main objections in more detail before presenting the whole model. Let us take one example: one of the terms used in the functional model to describe a certain type of behaviour is the 'Nurturing Parent ego state'. First, according to the definition of an ego state, this implies that we are dealing with a set of feelings, thoughts and behaviours, but, as will be seen, we are often dealing in this model only with behaviour or with behaviour and reinforcing attitude. Second, this label implies that we are dealing with a Parent ego state (ways of nurturing we have introjected from others), yet we know that we can also nurture from an Adult ego state (the nurturing appropriate to the here-and-now reality) and a Child ego state (the ways of nurturing others we used as a child). We suggest using the term 'mode' as a way of avoiding some of the confusion caused by the term 'ego state' when using the functional model. Thus a Parent ego state becomes in our version of the functional model a Parent mode. Though we have kept the terms Parent, Adult and Child for these behaviours, we hope that the use of the term 'mode' in conjunction with them makes it clear that these are purely descriptions of types of behaviours that can be found in each of the three structural ego states (as we will describe later) and that they are not themselves ego states.

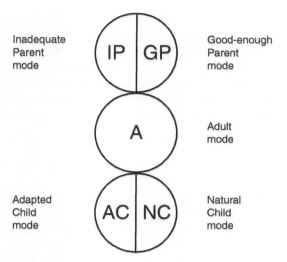

Inadequate
Parent
mode

Good-enough
Parent
mode

Adult
mode

Adapted
Child
mode

Natural
Child
mode

Figure 5.1   The functional model

The Functional Model

This model describes a range of functional modes – by which we mean the gestures, words, voice tones, body postures, facial expressions, attitudes and so on that we discussed in Chapter 3 when dealing with behavioural diagnosis – from which we can choose how to respond in a given situation. They can also be used to describe how a person is behaving whether they have chosen to or not; in other words, they can describe the behaviour in any structural ego state, current or historic. This is useful shorthand when shared with clients but, like most types of shorthand, needs to be used with a full explanation.

Figure 5.1 shows the five basic functional modes.

We have chosen the terms Good-enough Parent (GP) and Inadequate Parent (IP) in preference to the more usual Positive or Negative Nurturing Parent and Positive or Negative Controlling Parent (terms found in the TA literature) as we consider these latter terms exclude other parent-type behaviours and attitudes such as indifference, carelessness, passivity and ignorance.

The Good-enough Parent Mode (GP)

We borrow the term 'good-enough' from the psychoanalyst Winnicot (1958), who introduced the idea of a mother who was not perfectly responsive, constantly attentive and unfailingly accepting, but who manifested enough of these essential relational qualities in order to create a world for her infant which would be accepting, loving and stable enough for him to develop a healthy sense of self in a real world.

In this mode we include those parental behaviours and attitudes that promote the well-being of ourselves and others (an I'M OK – YOU'RE OK position). This mode would also include those behaviours and attitudes that are encouraging, concerned, caring, loving, giving, accepting, comforting, understanding, as well as constructively critical, usefully advising, caringly controlling, appropriately boundary-setting (both protective and permission giving). These are all behaviours associated with a Positive Controlling or Nurturing Parent. Here are some ways we might recognize someone in a GP mode:

- The person leans caringly towards another and keeps good eye contact as they speak.
- The person speaks with a tender tone.
- The person smiles at another's success.
- The person greets another with open arms at seeing their distress.
- The person shouts assertively to prevent some danger to the other.
- The person takes enough holidays for themselves to stay fit and healthy.
- The person sets suitable boundaries and is able to say 'No' appropriately.

The Inadequate Parent Mode (IP)

In this mode we include those parental behaviours and attitudes that disempower the other person or another part of ourselves. Very often this is an unconscious attempt to dispel our inadequacy. This mode would involve those behaviours and attitudes that are destructively critical, belittling, prejudicial, controlling for power, dismissive, indifferent, ignorant, careless, cruel, persecutory, judgmental, authoritarian and moralistic. These are features of the mode that elsewhere in the TA literature, you may see associated with the Negative Controlling (sometimes called Critical) Parent. IP mode also includes patronizing, smothering, condescending, infantilizing, over-protecting, colluding – some behaviours associated with the Negative Nurturing Parent. Here are some ways we might recognize someone in an IP mode:

- The person menacingly towers over another.
- The person, with hands on hips, talks *at* rather than *to* the other.
- The person, unrequested, supports the arm of an elderly but physically able person.
- The person points a finger accusingly while shouting.
- The person shows lack of interest in another's distress by making no eye contact and yawning.
- The person 'fusses' over another as they prepare for some event.
- The person uses judgmental words like 'ridiculous', 'stupid', 'disgusting' and so on to describe their own or others' behaviour.
- The person gives advice to another about something they themselves know nothing about.

The Adult Mode (A)

In this mode we include those behaviours and attitudes that are objective, informative, interested, evaluative, precise, observant, practical, clarifying, rational, goal-setting, analytic, creatively resourceful and constructively questioning. Here are some ways we might recognize someone in an A mode:

- The person clarifies the situation by careful inquiry.
- The person talks in an even voice and is precise in choice of vocabulary.
- The person hypothesizes and processes information.
- The person sits upright with an open body posture.
- The person is alert and thoughtful about a problem they are facing.

The Natural Child Mode (NC)

In the Natural Child mode a person has access to expression of any of the variations of the basic feelings: fear, sorrow, separation distress, love, excitement, joy and anger. In this mode we also include those behaviours and attitudes that are associated with our human needs for relationship, survival and growth as well as for stimulation and rest (see Chapter 6), so behaviour which is spontaneous, energetic, creative, exuberant, free, open, emotionally responsive and curious. There is an uninhibited quality to the actions and attitudes of someone in a Natural Child mode. For the most part this is a positive and creative mode in which to be. There are, however, occasions when such Natural Child responses may be inappropriate. For example, enjoying an exhilarating game of rough-and-tumble with a friend on a spacious beach would be fine. Playing the same game close to the edge of a cliff would be folly. Here are some ways we might recognize someone in an NC mode:

- The person hugs another in the excitement of succeeding in some task.
- The person runs and leaps into the air while out for a walk.
- The person rolls on the floor, doubled up with laughter at a joke.
- The person says, 'I really love you' or 'I really love myself'.
- The person looks startled at a loud noise.
- The person expresses anger in response to an insult.
- The person, in their excitement, takes an unnecessary risk.
- The person goes to sleep when they are tired.

The Adapted Child Mode (AC)

In this last mode we include those behaviours and attitudes that are, as the mode suggests, in adaptation to others or other parts of ourselves. This includes the expression of feelings that are substitutes for those of the Natural Child; for example, where the Natural Child would be angry, the Adapted Child may express sadness (see the discussion of rackets, Chapter 9). This mode can include not only behaviours that are *compliant* but also those which are *rebellious*, rebellion of this type being an adaptation to others, albeit in opposition. Thus we include behaviours and attitudes that are defiant, disobedient, rude, displeasing, stubborn, disrespectful and demanding, as well as those which are yielding, obliging, placating, obedient, polite, censored, pleasing and dutiful.

Compliance or rebellion in the AC mode may be appropriate or inappropriate according to the situation; some people speak of the 'Well-adapted' and 'Ill-adapted' Child mode. Compliance with someone's demand for us to stop as we are about to step carelessly out into a busy road is clearly appropriate. Unquestioningly obeying the same demand when we are safely having fun may not be. In the same way, to rebel against tyranny and oppression may be appropriate, while rebellion against the goodwill of others may not be. Here are ways in which we might recognize someone in an AC mode:

- The person physically and verbally 'digs their heels in'.
- The person questions and challenges the authority of another.
- The person shouts defiantly, 'I won't!' in response to a request.
- The person says 'I will' – but doesn't!
- The person arrives drunk to a coaching session.
- The person drives recklessly, endangering themselves and others.
- The person expresses anger where sadness would be more appropriate.

Or:

- The person cowers, with head down, as they ask for something from another.
- The person says, 'please' and 'sorry' repeatedly in a conversation.
- The person complies with another's wishes.
- The person tries to guess what might please the other.
- The person's voice tone is whining and placatory.
- The person does not ask for things for themselves.
- The person expresses fear where anger would be more appropriate.

Or (more positively):

- The person negotiates a compromised agreement with another.
- The person shares their last piece of chocolate with another.
- The person gives up their bus seat at the request of an elderly passenger.

In order to see how these modes may operate in a given situation, let us go back to the friends who are playing a game of rough-and-tumble on the beach and analyse the various modes they may be adopting. The tide is coming in while Sergio and Stella are playing. Both are in Natural Child mode, oblivious to the incoming tide. Suddenly, Sergio notices:

SERGIO:	Hey, Stella, the tide's almost to the rocks. (Adult mode)
STELLA:	How long do you think we can stay on the beach? (Adult mode)
SERGIO:	It's too risky to stay any longer (*holding out a hand to her*) we'd better go. (Good-enough Parent mode)
STELLA:	Oh, we were having so much fun! (*laughs and hugs him*). (Natural Child mode)
SERGIO:	Well, we'll be trapped if we don't go now. (Adult mode)
STELLA:	It's too soon. I'm not going! (*pulling away from him and making a face*). (Adapted Child mode)
SERGIO:	Come on, now! We really must go. (Good-enough Parent mode)
STELLA:	Look at you! You're just like a scared kid! Pull yourself together! (*pointing at him*). (Adapted Child mode moving to Inadequate Parent mode)
SERGIO:	Don't you talk to me like that, my girl! (*with hands on hips*). (Inadequate Parent mode)
STELLA:	I'll talk how I want! (*pouting*). (Adapted Child mode)
SERGIO:	Look, we have about five minutes before we're trapped (*indicating the tide level*). (Adult mode)
STELLA:	Oh, all right! (*taking his hand*). (Adapted Child mode)
SERGIO:	Let's run! (*laughs*). (Natural Child mode)
STELLA:	OK. Race you to the rocks! (*getting a head start*). (Natural Child mode)

Remember, what we have been analysing here is their functional modes, *what it is they are doing and saying,* their process of communication, *not* their structural ego states, which would give us further information as to the *origin and reasons* for their behaviour. We will return to this later when we look at how the two models may be combined.

Application 1: A Microscopic View

In the above example of Sergio and Stella on the beach, we have in effect taken a microscope to what is going on between two people and analysed their transactions according to their functional modes. By doing so, we open up the possibility of choice and options. The functional model provides us with a ready source of alternatives. At any moment in their communication, there was the possibility of one or more alternative modes. Let us take just one set of verbal transactions:

SERGIO:	It's too risky to stay any longer. We'd better go.
STELLA:	Oh, we were having so much fun!

In response to Sergio's Good-enough Parent mode, Stella had a choice of options. Here she answers from a Natural Child mode. She could also have echoed Sergio's Good-enough Parent by responding from her own Good-enough Parent:

'Yes, I don't want us to get trapped.'

She could also have come from an Adapted Child position:

'OK, if you say so.'

Or:

'I won't! You're always so bossy!'

Or an Inadequate Parent mode:

'Don't make such a fuss. It really doesn't matter.'

Or an Adult mode:

'Yes, I think so too. It's coming in quickly.'

The choice of some of these alternatives would have altered (however slightly) what followed. We know already that the outcome of their total communications was a positive and healthy one but if Sergio had stayed in an Adult mode continually, merely providing accurate observations, the outcome may not have been as effective. Likewise if Stella had stayed in a rebellious Adapted Child mode. The fact that they move between different modes quite fluently and achieve a positive outcome is, perhaps, some indication of their psychological health.

But sometimes people are not so fluent. They get stuck in the same functional mode, with results ranging from the tedious and entrenched to the despairing and disastrous. By developing awareness of their functional options and making more conscious choices, people can avoid such outcomes and ensure more fun, joy, satisfaction and creativity.

Drawing the functional diagram as a transactional diagram when working with clients provides a useful tool for looking at behavioural options (for example Figure 5.2). Here the three rules of communication introduced earlier in relation to the structural model may be usefully applied. Using the model transactionally, it is clearer if the Parent and Child modes are split horizontally rather than vertically.

Example

Freda is developing yet another row with her husband Jeff. The stimulus is from Jeff's Good-enough Parent Mode intended for Freda's Natural Child: 'Can I get you a cup of tea?' But Freda responds from her Adapted Child intended for Jeff's Inadequate Parent: 'No, I'm not incapable!' In other words, there is a crossed transaction. Jeff responds with another crossed transaction, this time from his Adapted Child to Freda's Inadequate Parent, 'You're always cross with me!' And the row ensues.

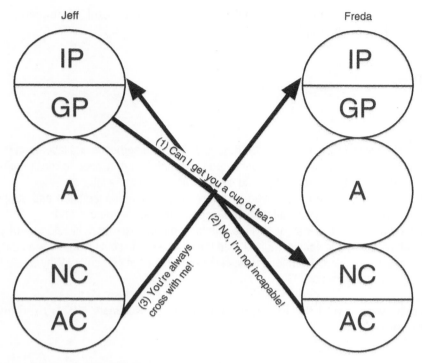

Figure 5.2 A functional transactional diagram

Now, it may be that Jeff was sending an ulterior transaction from his Inadequate Parent to Freda's Adapted Child with the message: 'You are incapable' and that this is what Freda is responding to. It may be that, if we did a structural analysis of Freda's ego states, we might discover she is operating from an Introjected Parent ego state and this is the way her mother always responded to her father when Freda was a child. This may usefully be worked on in the counselling or coaching situation. However, if Freda wants to stop rowing with Jeff right now, she can do so by choosing to respond from different functional modes. So what could she choose?

1 She could keep the transaction complementary by saying: 'Yes, I'd love a cup of tea!' or 'No thanks, not right now' from her Natural Child back to his Good-enough Parent.
2 She could usefully cross the transaction and invite something different to happen by saying: 'I know you mean well, but sometimes I think you do too much for me' from her Adult to his Adult.
3 She could cross the transaction another way and affect the outcome differently by saying: 'Oh no, really, I'll get the tea this time' from her Good-enough Parent to his Natural Child.

When transactions are analysed according to their functional modes and alternatives experimented with, many stuck patterns of behaviour in relationships can be overcome.

For this reason, the functional model is one of the most useful TA models to use when working with couples.

Exercises

Self

1 Write down a recent conversation you have had with someone and label each trans-action according to the functional mode adopted. You may need to recall the body posture, gestures, voice tone and so on to assist in your analysis.

2 Choose one of your transactions at any point in the conversation and supply a response from as many alternative functional modes as you can find.

3 Experiment in this way at various points in the conversation. Would any of your alternatives have considerably altered the course of the conversation? Would these have been preferable options to have chosen? Which in particular? Why would they have been more useful?

You may want to read the article called 'Options' by Karpman (1971) to stimulate your creative ideas.

Working with Clients

1 Introduce your client to the functional model and explore your client's functional modes.

2 As and when your client presents an incident concerning their communication with others (including you), invite them to write down the transactions and analyse them according to the functional modes adopted.

3 Draw a diagram of the transactions that seem to be important turning-points in the conversation. What was going on transactionally? Were the transactions comple-mentary or crossed? What were the possible ulterior transactions?

4 For each of the transactions in the diagram, explore the alternative functional modes that could have been used.

Application 2: An X-ray View

The functional model of behavioural and transactional modes may also be used to look at what goes on inside people, the internal (intrapsychic) transactions we have between various parts of ourselves. You may recall the person we mentioned right at the beginning of this book (page 1) who is stuck in a lift between floors. If you turn back to it, you will most likely now be able to analyse those internal trans-actions in the same way we have analysed transactions between two people using the functional model.

Often these internal conversations are outside our awareness, but by observing ourselves in various situations we can become more attuned to them. We may discover that a lot of our internal transactions are from our own Inadequate Parent mode and are complied with or rebelled against within our Adapted Child mode; or that we are using a Good-enough Parent mode to encourage our Natural Child mode; or that much of our time is spent in observing and objectively clarifying what we are experiencing from a functional Adult perspective.

As with the options we have in our transactions with others, so too we have internal options. The exercises we have used in Application 1 may also be used to explore and change our internal transactions. There is, however, yet another way of using these internal transactions and that is in the service of problem solving and decision making. This technique was devised by Stuntz (1973) and is known as the 'five-chair technique'.

Example

In her coaching session, Sonja informs the coach that she has been offered a promotion to another department in the company which will entail moving to another town. The job requires her to be 'on call' on certain days. Since receiving the news she has been in a state of confusion. The coach suggests she may achieve some clarification of the situation if she brings into awareness her internal transactions and explores her options by using the five-chair technique. They set out five chairs, arranging them like the five on a die to represent the five functional modes as they appear in the functional model diagram (see page 53). The coach suggests Sonja begins by sitting on the Adult chair (in the middle) to outline the problem objectively. A shortened version of this part of the session continues as follows:

SONJA: *(Adult)*: I've been offered a promotion. The pay is much better than my current role but it means I will have to move to another town. I'm really excited by ...

COACH: It sounds like you've moved into a Natural Child mode now. See what you have to say from that chair.

SONJA: *(Natural Child)*: Yes, I am excited by the offer. I think the work will be much more fun and it will be good to meet new people and make new friends. But I don't want to move because I'll see less of my old friends.

COACH: OK, see what you say in Adapted Child mode.

SONJA: *(Adapted Child)*: I don't think I'm good enough really. I think I'll probably be a bit of a failure. Then they won't like me and I won't make any friends and I'll be lonely living in a strange town. (*Pauses*) I think I know where this is coming from.

COACH: OK, move to that chair.

(Continued)

(Continued)

SONJA: *(Inadequate Parent talking to her Adapted Child):* Yes, you really should stay where you are. You know you aren't really up to the job. You may have fooled them at the interview but they'll find out soon enough and then you'll regret it.

SONJA: *(switching to Good-enough Parent)* That is not true. You did a good interview because you knew you had the right skills and experience. You're quite capable of doing this job well. What's more, people like you and you can make friends easily. I understand you're a bit scared. It's natural to be scared when making such a change but you can still go ahead and take this opportunity. Don't scare yourself even more with these negative thoughts. As you say, it's exciting too.

SONJA: *(switching to Natural Child)* Right. It is exciting and I am scared but I don't have to let that stop me by telling myself negative things. That's a relief. But I'm still concerned about my old friends.

COACH: Move back to Adult and see what solutions you can think of to this problem of friends.

SONJA: *(Adult)* Well, let's see. If I want to keep in touch with my old friends once I've moved, I need to organize it. I could make sure that I arrange to go to friends or for them to visit me. This is possible at weekends or holidays or even when I'm doing a late shift the next day and don't have to be 'on call'.

COACH: It seems you could see your old friends quite regularly.

SONJA: *(Adult)* Yes, I think I was allowing my Inadequate Parent to use this as yet another reason for staying put without even looking for solutions. If I listened to that part of me, I'd never do anything.

COACH: Do you want to finish on the Natural Child chair and express your feelings about this?

SONJA: *(Natural Child)* Sure. What a relief. I feel like a whole weight's been removed – I hate that Inadequate Parent that squashes everything. I will accept the job. I'm glad I've dealt with it so well. In fact, I'm really pleased with myself!

Use of the five-chair technique will not always result in such a clear resolution. It will, however, help bring to light the various attitudes being adopted in response to the situation or problem. Bringing these into awareness and clarifying in which mode these attitudes are being adopted can greatly assist in the problem-solving process. Using five chairs and moving from one to another is not essential – your room may not be big enough! But the physical changing of position does assist in identifying our attitude in a particular mode and helps to differentiate more clearly between each mode. If it is not possible to move from chair to chair, it would be useful to adopt a different posture for each functional mode, a posture that your client associates with each particular one. Making a diagram of this, or having the client use objects from around the room to represent the different modes, are other ways of proceeding.

Exercises

Self

1 Think of a current decision you need to make and use the five-chair technique to help in your decision-making process.
2 What do you notice about the responses from your different functional modes? Are some more helpful than others? Between which modes do you experience the most disagreement? How might you use other modes to resolve this?

Working with Clients

When your client presents a decision-making problem or some confusion in their response to a situation, explore their functional modes by using the five-chair technique. Encourage the client to move into all five functional modes to get a total picture. Facilitate your client in moving from one mode to another as and when you or they think it appropriate. Opening up the dialogue between two modes may be constructive and lead to resolution or it may reach a sticking point. If there are certain points when you think moving to another particular mode may be useful, invite your client to move to that chair. You might invite your client onto the Adult chair to provide a commentary on what they see happening between the other modes. Providing an objective overview often indicates which next move might be helpful.

Sometimes you might be working with a client who doesn't know the model of functional modes and you don't want to interrupt the process by teaching it to them. In this case, you can allow yourself to be informed by the concept without trying to impose the terminology into the session. You can say, for example, 'What would you say to a dear friend who was in this position?' (inviting Good-enough supportive Parent) or 'What does the child inside you want?' We have never met anyone who doesn't understand the question ... it seems that we all know what it means to have an 'inner child'.

Application 3: A Macroscopic View

Another of the ways in which this model may be used for oneself or when working with others is as a descriptive overview of how a person is functioning in their lives in order to assess where changes may usefully be made. It can be used to answer such questions as:

Does this person use the whole range of functional modes?
If not, which are lacking? Which might be more usefully developed?
Which mode does the person adopt most? Is this useful?
Does the person use the same modes towards self as well as to others?

We have adapted Jack Dusay's original concept of the Egogram (1972) to produce a pie chart of functional modes (see Figure 5.3): a diagrammatic representation of the spread and adoption of functional modes. The five functional modes are allocated 'slices of the pie' according to the comparative amount of time and energy a person spends in each functional mode. Clearly this is more an intuitive assessment than a scientific one. The best way to draw such a chart for yourself is to assess intuitively which functional mode you adopt the most and draw an equivalent section of the pie chart to represent this. Then assess which functional mode you use the least and draw its representative slice adjacent to the first. The next three sections can then be added by assessing them in relation to these two. You could check this with people who know you well. Technically, if you analysed all your transactions in a given day or a given week, you could get a very accurate picture.

The Constancy Hypothesis

Jack Dusay suggested in his article (1972) that when one *functional mode* 'increases in intensity, another or others must decrease in order to compensate. The shift in psychic energy occurs so that the total amount of energy may remain constant.' Thus it may be that a person, by increasing their time spent in Natural Child mode – by arranging more free time to be with friends, organizing more fun and recreation and so on – concomitantly reduces both their Inadequate Parent mode and their Adapted Child mode. The use of a pie chart shows clearly this redistribution of energy as any change in one section inevitably means a change in another or others.

Let us look at the pie chart in Figure 5.3 as an example. By drawing this pie chart, James realized that he spent a large amount of his energy in both an Adapted Child mode and in Inadequate Parent mode. These two modes were clearly interrelated and mutually reinforcing. In the Adapted Child mode he would obediently respond to others' demands without question. In the Inadequate Parent mode he would fuss around others, offering to do things for them. This, in turn, set a precedent for them to make demands on him which resulted in his return to the Adapted Child mode and so on. The pie chart graphically emphasized for him the lack of Natural Child and Good-enough Parent modes, as well as a much-depleted Adult mode.

In his counselling James decided to focus on expanding his Good-enough Parent mode to others and to himself. To others, he became more appropriate in what he offered to do, waited for others to ask (not demand), let them use their own

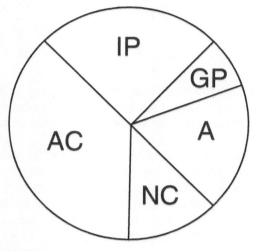

Figure 5.3   A pie chart of functional modes

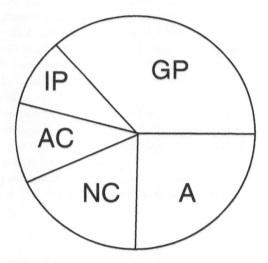

Figure 5.4   James's later pie chart of functional modes

problem-solving skills and contributed his own skills when they were really needed. He realized that a Good-enough Parent allows independence and personal power in others. Towards himself, he adopted a more nurturing attitude, stopped to think what his own needs might be and encouraged himself to ask for those needs to be met when appropriate. In this process, he concomitantly increased the energy in his Natural Child mode and in his Adult mode, as shown in the second pie chart (Figure 5.4).

Exercises

Self

1 Using the five functional mode headings, list the types of behaviours you have adopted during the day. Repeat this exercise over a number of days to get a more general view of how you function and assist in recognizing your functional modes more easily.

2 Draw your own pie chart of functional modes, using the method outlined earlier. It may be interesting to draw a pie chart for different situations in your life. Some people discover a very different pie chart with regard to work-life from a pie chart for when they are at home or in other social situations. Explore these varying functional modes by comparing your pie charts. It can be illuminating to ask others to draw a pie chart of how they see you and compare it to the way you see yourself. If there are discrepancies between the two, see if you can work out why this might be.

Having drawn your pie chart, are there things about it that you want to change? If so, focus on the functional mode that would most usefully be increased.

It may be that you need to increase the frequency of behaviours you already adopt or it may be that you need to adopt some new behaviours. Choose a set of behaviours and make a contract to practise each of these behaviours a specified number of times each day. Remember, the more specific you are, the easier this will be.

Use the pie chart as a measure of change in your distribution of functional modes by drawing another at the end of a two-week period. If you asked others to draw a chart of you initially, ask them to redraw how they observe you now. Having focused on increasing one functional mode, what do you notice about the others?

How does this fit the constancy hypothesis? It may be that you have concomitantly decreased a mode inadvertently which you do not wish to decrease (for example, by focusing on increasing your Good-enough Parent, you may have caused your Natural Child mode to suffer). Are there further changes you wish to make? If so, repeat the steps above.

Working with Clients

1 Use the first exercise above to help your clients familiarize themselves with their functional modes.

2 Together with each client, draw a pie chart to represent a general overview of your clients' functional modes. Invite them to review the previous week.

3 Discuss with your clients what it is they want to change in their chart and make a behavioural contract for change. For example, your client may choose to increase Natural Child mode and make a contract to arrange at least one hour doing a specific enjoyable activity with others each day.

4 Within a specified period, redraw your client's pie chart as a measure of change.

Combining the Structural and Functional Models

We have already pointed out that sometimes people confuse the structural and functional models. As both models are represented by three stacked circles, it is often assumed that one diagram can simply be superimposed upon the other. This is not so. If we do this we are in effect implying that the Introjected Parent ego state solely functions in an Inadequate Parent mode or a Good-enough Parent mode, that the Integrating Adult ego state functions solely in Adult mode and that the Archaic Child ego state functions solely in an Adapted or Natural Child mode. This view is not only restrictive, it is inaccurate. The fact is, we can function from each of the structural ego states in each of the five functional modes.

Our view is that it is simplest and best to keep the two models separate wherever possible, especially in the coaching situation where the functional modes are more likely to be addressed, recognizing one as a structural model of ego states and the other as modes of behaviour. However, there may be times in working with behavioural modes when the client seems stuck, despite identifying the options they have, and it may be helpful to look at where, in terms of structural ego states, a particular behaviour is originating. For example, Shirley, wanting to change her Adapted Child mode of behaviour, found it useful to do a structural ego state analysis and discovered that her adaptation was not to be located in her structural Child ego state but in her structural Parent ego state – it was a way of behaving that she had introjected from her mother. The work then focussed more on her Adapted Child mode of the structural Parent ego state, her mother's way of being, and became much more productive.

In Figure 5.5 we have located all the behavioural mode possibilities within the structural model of ego states. Let us explore this combination using Ramya as an example.

Example

Ramya's Introjected Parent Ego State

Starting with her Introjected Parent, we might identify an ego state that is made up of the feelings, thoughts and behaviours borrowed from, for example, Ramya's mother. In order to further illuminate how she might function in this introjected ego state we can use the functional modes. In other words, we can use these five modes to describe how Ramya may function from this structure. Drawing a functional mode pie chart of Ramya's mother's functional modes would provide further information as to the general levels of these modes.

We might discover that her mother has a high Inadequate Parent mode whereby she is very dismissive of Ramya and of her own Natural Child mode. This may be further substantiated by a low Good-enough Parent mode lacking in nurturing

(Continued)

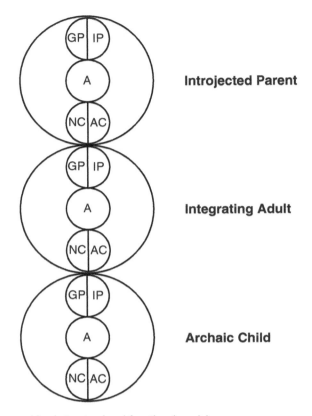

Introjected Parent

Integrating Adult

Archaic Child

Figure 5.5 The combined structural and functional models

(Continued)

skills. Her functional Adult mode may be very poor at problem-solving, which may be reflected in a high Adapted Child mode showing her dependence on others to tell her what to do. Her Natural Child mode may be almost non-existent. All of these functional modes will be a part of Ramya's structural Parent ego state.

Ramya's Structural Archaic Child Ego State

If we turn to Ramya's Archaic Child ego state and explore the functional modes adopted here, we may discover something very different. For example, we may find that in this ego state Ramya has a high Good-enough Parent mode in that she used to look after her inadequate mother much of the time as a child. In this case, her Inadequate Parent mode may be fairly low. She may have a high functional Adult mode, again because from an early age, owing to her mother's inadequacy, she had to be independent and self-sufficient and do much of the problem-solving for herself.

It is likely that her Natural Child mode will be quite low, as clearly she had to take a 'grown-up' role within her family and her Adapted Child will be high as a result of being compliant to her mother's needs.

Ramya's Structural Integrating Adult Ego State

In her Integrating Adult state, when there is no interference from either her Introjected Parent or her Archaic Child, we may find that Ramya is flexible and fluent in her choice of functional modes. She may from this ego state consciously 'draw upon' the more constructive functional modes of her Child ego state, there being little to 'draw upon' from her introjected Parent ego state unless she introjected more positive aspects from her father or from later important figures. It may be that she recognizes a deficiency in her Natural Child mode and, like many clients, is wanting to make changes in this respect. In the Integrating Adult ego state she can usefully model herself on others in her current life and consciously practise new options.

Application

By presenting the above example of Ramya, the application of the combined structural and functional models may be made quite self-explanatory. Basically this combination can be used to explore simultaneously both the content of ego states (structure) and the process (function) by which a person may transact in each ego state. It can appear in some ways over-complicated and we would suggest that it may be more useful to employ part of it (as in the previous example of Shirley) rather than the whole combination. However, there may be times when this sort of detailed understanding can be enormously empowering for the client.

This model combination may also be used to further illustrate the multiplicity of functional options a person has to choose from in any given situation. However, we do not suggest you use a fifteen (or more) chair technique unless you have a lot of time and a lot of space and are the sort of person who can regularly remember the football scores of the entire premier league!

Exercises

Self

1 Choose one of the parents or parent-figures that are now part of your Introjected Parent ego state. Use the five functional mode headings and under each describe the behaviours and attitudes of this person towards themselves, yourself and others.
2 Do the same for one of your Archaic Child ego states. Describe how you function in each of these modes.

3 Repeat this exercise to explore your Integrating Adult ego state. Are there functional modes here which are unique to this ego state? Which ones? Which functional modes do you integrate from your Parent and Child ego states? Are there any functional modes you may need to develop?

Working with Clients

1 Use the exercises you have just done for yourself when working with your clients to explore further the contents of their ego states and the process by which these may be manifested.
2 Use this combination of the two models creatively to widen the range of possibilities when exploring options in a given situation. Discover, for example, what resources they have in their Introjected Parent by asking, 'What would your mother/father/teacher/neighbour have done in this situation?', or explore the resources in their Archaic Child by asking, 'As a child, how did you handle such a problem?' Invite your client to be that person, or the child they once were, and use the five-chair technique to illuminate the functional modes within the structural ego state and discover the potential resources.
3 Inviting your client into her Parent ego state, interview his or her parents (or other figures of authority) to discover the influences that your client is carrying around. Invite the Parent to commit to new functional modes of being in the world.

CASE STUDY: A COACH'S STORY

At the end of the previous session, Anita had touched on the functional modes of ego states – how they manifested in the here and now. Gunther recognized that what was most behaviourally noticeable about his leadership style was a sort of meticulous Adult and Parent – apparently thoughtful and caring but actually an IP mode as it left no room for his authority – nor his own feelings. He thought the model would be useful in understanding his team's behaviour.

The third session saw Gunther feeling positive. He had had individual conversations with all his team members. While not actually showing them the model, he had inquired into their experience of the new organization in the various modes. He had asked them all how they were getting on, what they enjoyed and didn't, what they were finding hard to adapt to and so on. He also asked what their opinion was about how the restructuring had been accomplished – what was useful, what had been badly done. And he invited them to join him in deciding on courses of action that might address the issues. All the team seemed happy that he had consulted them, but Gunther was also pleased that he had been firm (GP and A) about those elements of the new situation that were 'a given' and needed to be adopted.

He had made a special point of talking at length with Joe. He said he had noticed Joe's reluctance to deliver (RC), and wondered what that meant. At first Joe made excuses. Gunther commented that Joe had had a lot of emotional adjusting to do – not just practical. Not only was it a new organization but Joe's move within it had also meant him having to relocate to the UK from the US. Joe just shrugged and said it was OK. Then Gunther took a risk. He asked Joe about his past experiences of major changes – did Joe remember anything about that? Joe began to talk about the time when he was eleven. His father had got a new job and the family had moved from a small town in the Montana countryside to the immense city of Los Angeles. He started at a new high school which was large, noisy and multicultural. Joe knew nobody and felt anxious and lost. He responded by withdrawing and his grades plummeted. For years he developed a persona as a failing rebel. Gunther empathized: his father had moved cities after his wife had died and Gunther too had felt lost. He invited Joe to recognize that he might have brought that child's experience to the present job. Joe felt touched at Gunther's understanding. He commented that he had been 'dragging my feet a bit' and he promised to have the figures on Gunther's desk by the end of the day. He kept his word.

Gunther was very pleased with this outcome. He also wanted to discuss with Anita how he had resonated with Joe's experience of loss. He wondered now how his experience of losing his mother, then moving home and school might have affected his present behaviour with the team. For him this turned out to be another piece of the jigsaw. He recalled that he had made an effort to be quiet, industrious and helpful after the move, in order to support his father and brother. Using the Functional Model, he recognized that when he took this new job – and particularly after the merger, he had tended to close down on his NC mode and use his A and P modes to organize both his team and himself. Together, he and Anita drew up an Egogram and he realized that both internally and externally, his IP, GP and A, were vastly in evidence, followed by his compliant AC. His NC was nowhere to be seen! Anita asked him if he used to have a hobby that he no longer did (in her experience, all busy executives had this experience of giving up an enjoyable activity of their youth). He said yes, that he used to play squash every week but he had not done so for years. He agreed to investigate the local sports club.

He also looked at how he could change his profile at the office by increasing NC activity there. He decided that he would experiment with expressing feelings a bit more with colleagues.

6
Strokes and other Human Hungers

People need other people. Developed and nourished inside a mother for nine months, we are born needing and seeking contact. All through our lives, in one way or another, this relational need and this search for contact continue. Even a hermit had need of parents and probably still seeks regular contact with them (or others) albeit inside his or her head.

In our very early life, if we were left to fend for ourselves we would quickly die. Our obvious need is for food and warmth and protection. Yet, even if we were well provided with these things, without contact with another, though we might not die, our emotional, psychological and physical development would suffer. It has been recognized that those babies who by necessity are kept in incubators for the early weeks of their lives – and thus provided with food, warmth and protection – survive well, make better recovery and show healthier development when they have physical contact with others, even though this may be through gloved apertures in the incubator. At the other end of the developmental spectrum, many hospitals have introduced animals onto the wards of elderly patients, having recognized that the stroking involved (both ways) has a healing and beneficial effect.

Eric Berne used the terms *recognition hunger* and *stimulus hunger* to describe our need for such contact. Later, Richard Erskine (personal communication) uses the term *relationship hunger* which, in the light of neuroscientific research and the centrality of the relationship in the early development of the human brain, is appropriate. However, we consider 'recognition' to have its own nuance of being seen as a distinct and whole being, of being seen in one's separate identity. Berne used the term 'stroke' to describe the contact itself, defining it as 'a unit of recognition' or 'any act implying recognition of another's presence'. All transactions are therefore, by definition, exchanges of strokes. As we grow up, though physical stroking may still be important to us and to the quality of our lives, the frequency of our need for such strokes may decrease (though social and cultural conditioning may account for the extent of the decrease). We learn instead to replace our need of physical strokes with verbal strokes and stroking gestures which will satisfy our stimulus and recognition hunger. A simple 'Hello', a smile or even a frown from a stranger is a stroke and can, however minimally, satisfy our need. At the very least, it indicates that we exist and we can take comfort from the recognition of that fact.

Types of Strokes

Physical, Verbal and Non-verbal Strokes

We have mentioned already the importance of physical strokes. These are any strokes where physical contact is made: a hug, a pat on the back, shaking hands, a massage, a grip on the arm, even a punch in the mouth are all physical strokes. Verbal strokes are those transactions which involve speaking to one another, whether it be a single word, an exciting conversation or a torrent of verbal abuse. Non-verbal strokes are the stroking gestures we use, sometimes independent of words but most often accompanying our verbal communications: a smile, a frown, a toss of the head, a hug (physical strokes being included here too), a dismissive wave, would all be in this category. It is the discrepancy between the verbal and non-verbal communication that may sometimes lead us to question the genuineness of the verbal stroke. Non-verbal strokes are also the common vehicle of ulterior transactions.

Positive and Negative Strokes

Any stroke which is intended as pleasant is a positive stroke. Likewise, any stroke which is intended as unpleasant is a negative stroke. It is the intention of the stroke which defines it as positive or negative, whether it is received in this way or not.

'I'm so pleased to see you,' is a positive stroke. The person receiving this stroke may respond with a similarly positive stroke, 'I'm pleased to see you too.' Or they may respond with a negative stroke, 'Well, you could have come to see me sooner!' and invite negative strokes from the other. You may now recognize this as a crossed transaction. But why should someone do this? When positive strokes are so much more likely to make a person feel good, why should they invite negative strokes at all? Why is it that sometimes people seem to prefer to hear a negative stroke when a positive stroke was intended?

To answer these questions we would need to look back to the person's childhood environment. We may discover that in a particular family there were few strokes given at all. In preference to stroke-deprivation, a child may devise ways of attracting negative strokes. Negative strokes are better than no strokes at all. Being insulted may be preferable to 'being sent to Coventry'. Being punished physically may be preferable to the stroke-deprivation of solitary confinement. Or it may be that we discover that in a particular family, negative strokes were the only currency of stroke-giving. Thus the child grows up in the belief that negative strokes are the only strokes and seems not even to hear the positive strokes; they have become desensitized to them through lack of familiarity. This selective attention in relation to strokes is called the 'stroke filter' (Steiner 1974). Those of you who are teachers in schools are probably well aware of pupils from these stroke-deprived or negative-stroking environments. You may start out with the best of intentions to give positive strokes to them – you know this is what they need – but in the end, your energy depleted by their disruptive behaviour, you give them the negative strokes with which they are so familiar. Changing these stroke patterns can be a tough job. With such pupils it can take a long time and your success will often depend on the supply of positive strokes in your life. If you are positive stroke-deprived it is hard to give positive strokes to others, especially if they seem to be demanding negative ones. This goes for working with clients in counselling and coaching situations too.

Conditional or Unconditional Strokes

Conditional strokes are those strokes which depend upon our doing something. In response to our behaviour we may receive a positive or negative stroke. 'That was a wonderful meal you cooked' is a positive conditional stroke. 'I really don't like your hair-style' is a negative conditional stroke. Unconditional strokes are those strokes which require no action; they are for our being. They are for existing as we are without having to perform in any way. The most obvious and desirable positive unconditional stroke is, 'I love you!' with its negative unconditional counterpart, 'I hate you!' 'You're so good to be with' is a positive unconditional stroke. 'I don't like being near you!' is a negative unconditional stroke.

Of these four types of stroke, three are important to the continued well-being of the human organism, but the fourth, the negative unconditional stroke, causes only harm. It is important to find ways of dealing with the negative unconditional strokes which we are almost inevitably going to meet with in life. We do not have to accept or 'take on' these types of strokes. We may, for example, ignore the stroke or we may explore what seems to be the underlying cause of the negativity.

Reinforcement Through Strokes

Our natural hunger for strokes plays an important part in the development of our life script (see Chapter 7) and the way we live as adults. Because of our need, as children we adapt our behaviours to receive as much stroking as possible. If a child attracts strokes for a particular behaviour, that behaviour is reinforced. The child repeats the behaviour, gets the same stroke and the behaviour is further reinforced. It is likely that in adulthood such behaviour will be perpetuated, so long as it is reinforced with strokes from others – or internal strokes from their Introjected Parent – of similar frequency and intensity.

Imagine a child in a low-stroking family sitting hungry for food and recognition while her parents watch the television. She says she is hungry but receives no response. She feels abandoned and begins to cry. She is ignored. She cries louder but is still neglected. Eventually, she screams. This time one of her parents goes to her, furiously picks her up and shakes her, shouting at her to be quiet. Her physical hunger may still be ignored but her hunger for strokes is satisfied, albeit painfully. The next time she feels hungry or neglected, the child omits to ask for what she wants, skips the crying and sobbing and goes straight for the screaming. Again, one of her parents goes to her and shakes her. Negative reinforcement is in progress. The quality of the stroke is physical and negative, the intensity of the stroke is high, the frequency is becoming regular. This child now knows that if she screams she will get some attention. It is likely that as an adult she will attract negative strokes from others of a similar quality and intensity by being loud and demanding *even when this is inappropriate to the current situation*. She will be perceiving the world through a Child ego state.

Take the same scenario but this time imagine that even the child's screams are ignored and that this situation is repeated several times. She eventually 'gives up' and sits quietly by herself. When her parents have finished watching the television, they perfunctorily feed her and put her to bed. If there is a consistent pattern of non-stroking in response to this child's needs, it is likely she will grow up passive and undemanding, not asking for her own needs to be met but waiting in the hope of others eventually stroking her for her passivity should they even notice her. This person may experience a scarcity of strokes in her adult life *even when this is not the current reality*. Again, we have a Child ego state perception of the world.

Supposing, though, this child's needs had been answered. Supposing she had been fed, or even told she had to wait a while but that she could come and be cuddled while waiting. Supposing she even cried because she had to wait but was still cuddled and told she is a lovable child. Such positive stroking would reinforce this child's asking for her needs to be met. As an adult she is likely to act in the world in such a way: to ask for what she wants, to express her feelings, to deal with delayed gratification at times and to experience herself as lovable.

From these examples, it can be seen that stroking patterns in childhood influence our adult behaviour and that we perceive and experience the world according to these patterns.

The Stroke Economy

In his book, *Scripts People Live*, Claude Steiner (1974) recognized that these stroking patterns in stroke-depriving families have certain rules rather like a financial economic system. These rules control the stroke market by maintaining a scarcity myth. The price of a stroke in the market (family) is thus kept high and the consequent behavioural exchange is often extortionate. In this way, parents control the stroke economy and their children's behaviour: a control that has far-reaching effects into adulthood. Steiner referred to the stroke economy as 'basic training for lovelessness' (p. 137).

A belief that human beings have only a limited capacity for stroke-giving is programmed in childhood. In reality humans have an infinite capacity for recognizing and appreciating the existence of others. The rules of the stroke economy are:

- Don't give strokes even if you have them to give.
- Don't ask for strokes when you need them.
- Don't accept strokes even if you want them.
- Don't reject strokes when you don't want them.
- Don't give yourself strokes.

Let us go through these rules one by one.

Don't give Strokes

Based on the scarcity myth, if strokes are in such short supply, it is deemed better to hold on to them than to freely give them away. We withhold the strokes we could give even though we may be thinking positively about someone or feeling a positive response to someone.

Don't ask for Strokes

This is probably the most familiar to us all. It is based on the belief that, if we have to ask for it, it is going to be worthless. It will be counterfeit in some way. But if we bear in mind the first rule about not giving strokes, we can see that often the stroke we want and could ask for is one which someone may genuinely be wanting or willing to give. By asking for a stroke we may be positively altering the other person's stroke economy as well as our own. If we are not convinced by the stroke, we can always check it in some way or ask for another.

Don't Accept Strokes

This rule again may involve a certain amount of distrust based on the scarcity myth. If someone is freely giving me a stroke can it be worth much? Why would they be giving it away if it was? Or, if they are giving me a stroke, they must be wanting something back from me in exchange. Or, they are just being kind. Or our reluctance to accept a stroke may be based on our perception of ourselves as worthless or undeserving.

A common example of non-acceptance of a stroke is illustrated in the following exchange:

'I really like your jersey.'
'Oh, this old thing. I got it at a jumble sale.'

Here the stroke is not accepted. It seems unheard. The information given by the second person is totally irrelevant to the first person's liking the jersey.

Don't Reject Strokes

This may seem to contradict the above but there are some strokes which we have been conditioned to accept which we might appropriately question, challenge or reject. Women may accept strokes about how they look when really they want to be treated as a whole person with a mind as well as a body. Or men may accept strokes about their physical strength when really they want to be acknowledged for their sensitivity. Rejection of such conditioned stereotypical strokes combined with asking for those strokes which are more valued is a simple way to change the stroke economy.

Don't give Yourself Strokes

The British seem to set a lot of store by this rule: modesty is a virtue, being positive about yourself is 'showing off', self-deprecation is almost applauded while masturbation is a sin. Changing this rule means challenging many of the messages we received as children and which we perpetuate by repetition from our Introjected Parent ego states.

Application

Whether or not we are aware of it, we are giving strokes to our clients and, in so doing, are positively or negatively reinforcing aspects of their behaviour. Instead of Carl Rogers's phrase 'unconditional, positive regard', we could say we are often giving unconditional positive strokes and inevitably conditional ones. Accepting the person as they are without judgment is reinforcing the way they are. For every 'Mm hm' of the most non-directive practitioner we can assume that some reinforcement has occurred. If we take into account every 'yes', 'no', 'I see', every nod, smile, frown, body movement and every time we do *not* say something (which the client may experience as withholding strokes), we can begin to estimate just how much stroking and concomitant reinforcement is taking place. Often unconsciously, we are shaping the client by our interest and apparent approval. If we ask a client, 'How do you feel?' we are stroking their existence, their feelings and their expression of feelings. We are making a judgment that feelings are OK in general and that it is OK for this person to express them. It is not so much a question then of do we or don't we stroke and reinforce our clients' behaviour but of awareness of when, how and why we are doing so. By observing our own and our clients' stroke patterns (see later exercises), we can increase our awareness of how and when we are stroking healthy or unhealthy behaviours. We can also increase our vigilance in being aware of when, how and why we may be using the client to get our own needs met and reduce such behaviours by making sure we get our own good-enough supply of strokes from others outside the client/practitioner relationship.

The TA practitioner utilizes strokes creatively to help the client change. These may be physical, verbal or non-verbal strokes: a hug, a 'that's great', a smile in response to some thinking, decision, behaviour or feeling that may be a step towards autonomy for the client. The TA practitioner will also be aware of the need not to stroke those thoughts, decisions, behaviours and feelings which may perpetuate the client's problems. Clients, outside their awareness, may attempt to induce the practitioner to enter their frame of reference and seek strokes for their conditioned and unhealthy behaviours. As examples, a client may say something negative about themselves while laughing and an unthinking practitioner may join in the joke (known as a *gallows transaction*); they may be passive and wait for the practitioner to ask what they want or arrive consistently late expecting sympathy, or negative strokes.

Example

In a coaching session, Robert tells of a recent job interview where he was not offered the job:

ROBERT:	(*laughing*) I was terrible! A two-year-old could have done better!
COACH:	(*not accepting the invitation to laugh*) In what way do you think you were terrible?
ROBERT:	Well, you know, I was just stupid.
COACH:	No, I don't know. I don't think you're stupid, you're very bright. So what happened?
ROBERT:	I got scared. They asked questions I didn't know anything about.
COACH:	Not knowing something is not stupid. What were you scared about?
ROBERT:	I don't know. Yes I do! My father always expected me to know everything. I was terrified when he asked me questions I didn't know the answers to because I knew it meant a beating.
COACH:	That sounds terrible for you.
ROBERT:	Yet, it was. He said I was stupid. And that's what I tell myself now.
COACH:	I think you've made a good connection there. I respect the way you think things through.
ROBERT:	Yes, I know I'm not stupid really.
COACH:	That's true. So what do you need to do about the next interview?
ROBERT:	Well, I know I don't need to know all the answers but I do need to do a bit more research.
COACH:	OK. That sounds like a good idea. Anything else?
ROBERT:	(*laughs*) Yes, I won't take my dad with me to the interview next time!
COACH:	(*laughs too*) That's great!

Exercises

We stress the importance of making sure that your own stroke needs are adequately met in order that (a) you do not feel depleted by the amount of attention and stroking your clients need and, therefore, run the risk of giving negative strokes (or inappropriate positive ones) through tiredness or frustration; and (b) you do not rely upon strokes from your clients and therefore seek to extort them for your own ends. This is not to say that it is wrong for your clients to give you strokes, but that you are not dependent upon your clients to meet your stroke needs. The following exercises are to help you to identify your own and your clients' separate stroke needs and plan for healthy ways to achieve them.

Self

1   Look back over your past week and under the following headings list those transactions or occasions where you *received* these strokes:

- Positive physical strokes.
- Negative physical strokes.
- Positive verbal strokes.
- Negative verbal strokes.
- Positive non-verbal strokes.
- Negative non-verbal strokes.

2   Identify those strokes which were conditional and those which were unconditional.

3   What do you notice about your stroke inventory? Are there more positives than negatives? More conditional than unconditional? Are there gaps in your inventory, or types of strokes which are very few? Which are these? Do you want to change this picture? Do you need to decrease the negatives in certain places and increase the positives?

4   Make a plan to change your stroke-receiving inventory to a more positive one. You may need to ask for more strokes. You may need to be more specific in asking for the types of strokes that you want. Write down your specific plan of action. For example: I will ask for positive strokes for each meal that I cook. I will listen to and accept strokes from my boss without turning them into negatives. I will book myself a massage each week on a Friday after work. And so on.

5   Use the same headings to make an inventory of the strokes you have *given* over the past week.

6   Identify the conditional and unconditional strokes.

7   What do you notice here? Use the questions in 3 to survey your stroke-giving inventory.

8   Make a plan to change your stroke-giving in ways that will be positive to you and your friends, acquaintances, colleagues, neighbours and strangers. Make a list of the specific stroking behaviours you will put into operation. For example: I will say hello to my neighbours each time they are in the garden. I will give my partner a ten-minute back rub each evening before supper. I will compliment my colleagues on the work they are doing at least once a day. And so on.

9   Repeat 1 to 3 for the strokes you have given yourself over the past week and make a self-stroking plan now. For example: I will luxuriate in a hot bubble-bath by candle-light while listening to Mozart on Sunday evening. I will treat myself to a meal in town every Tuesday. And so on. Make these unconditional.

10   If you are in a support group or counselling group take it in turns to 'brag' for three minutes each (or more). The listeners encourage the person bragging with a 'strokeful' commentary as they move from one self-stroke to the next. This could become a regular part of the group each week.

11   Make a list of the most important and significant affirmations for yourself. Pin them over the bathroom mirror or around the house and repeat them aloud to yourself each day. For example: I love me. I am really lovable. I am a clear thinker. I like my sense of humour. And so on.

Working with Clients

1 Introduce your client to the concept of strokes and the vital part they play in our lives.
2 Share the rules of the stroke economy with your client and discover which rules your client follows.
3 Encourage your clients to ask for strokes from you and to stroke themselves – you could include the bragging exercise in the counselling or coaching session.
4 To assist your client to accept strokes, ask them what stroke they would like from you. Encourage your client to keep eye contact while you say the stroke – you will need to be genuinely willing to give the stroke and, if not, to explain why – to listen carefully and, as the stroke is given, to take a deep inward breath. This helps your client to focus and hear the stroke as well as 'take it in' on a psychological and physiological level.
5 Use the self exercises to make a plan of action to help change your clients' stroke inventory in ways they want.

Directly introducing or 'teaching' the concepts of strokes may not be appropriate or necessary in some situations. However, we believe it is important for the practitioner to bear in mind the need for strokes when working with clients. Be aware of how you stroke your clients. Avoid colluding with self-deprecation on the part of your clients. Stroke those behaviours which are constructive and healthy changes.

Further Human Hungers

Eric Berne identified six human 'hungers' which we need to meet in order to maintain physical, mental and emotional well-being. Given that human beings are, existentially, always in relationship, these hungers are sometimes seen as relational needs. We have already addressed in some depth the centrality of 'strokes' in relation to stimulus hunger and recognition-hunger. We return to these two hungers here and expand and elaborate upon them, along with the four additional hungers.

Stimulus Hunger

This comprises our biological need for sensory stimulation. Our five senses need contact and stimulation from the environment: in other words, we need to see, touch, hear, smell and taste the world in which we exist in order to adjust to that world with the best degree of accommodation possible. Furthermore, 'the arousal system' of the brain needs excitation for the health and continued functioning of the organism. When this sensory stimulus is lacking, adjustment and balance is difficult. Prolonged sensory deprivation can cause people to have delusions and hallucinations, They are unable to retain their mental and emotional stability without stimulation.

Contact Hunger

In some respects this is a subset of stimulus hunger, in that it comprises our need for touch. However, it is different in that this is our hunger for contact with another being's skin (physical strokes). The contact between one human being and another is both energizing and pleasurable as well as healing to the recipient. The contact of mother and baby during feeding, for example, will provide such energy and pleasure as well as food. Neuroscientific research suggests also that this soothing and nourishing contact facilitates the development of the brain and the baby's sense of self.

Recognition Hunger

The nervous system of the human being is so designed that verbal recognition and body language can, to some extent, substitute for physical contact and assist in the development of our self-image and well-being. This need for acknowledgement of our existence and our sense of self may be met in a simple 'Hello' or a long discussion of political views. Each person needs a different quotient of recognition and has a personal preference as to the type of strokes they require. A pop star may hunger for applause from thousands while the person who delivers the post may be satisfied with one householder's smile of appreciation as they receive their letters.

The need for recognition is also a need to be 'accounted' – to have made an impact. It is now well recognized (see, for example, Stern 1985) that the need to have a sense of agency – to make things happen – is part of human development.

Sexual Hunger

Like our hunger for contact, sexual hunger may be seen as a subset of stimulus hunger but specifically involves stimulation and contact of our sexual organs (skin, breasts, genitals and so on) by self or others. Healthy human beings have these needs met by sexual contact with other consenting adults, or with themselves, in a way that causes neither hurt nor harm. People who do not manage to have their sexual needs met in healthy ways may have recourse to inappropriate means of gratification, for example with minors or unwilling partners or by channelling their energy into aggression and certain types of destructive games (see Chapter 8).

Some theorists, for example Freud, suggest that we can sublimate or divert our sexual hunger towards creativity or spirituality (through celibacy) while others would posit separate and distinct hungers for creativity and spirituality. Berne seems implicitly to include these within the other five hungers.

Structure Hunger

How to fill the 24 hours in a day, the weeks and years ahead of us and, similarly, how to organize our personal environment (homes, offices, gardens and so on) preoccupies all of us much of the time. In short, we are concerned with how to provide sufficient certainty and security in our lives for us to feel safe enough to encounter all those things in life over which we have no control. As the previous hungers have shown, our healthy survival depends upon our relationships with other human beings. There is, therefore, in every human encounter the potential for the fulfilment of healthy needs, but there is also anxiety: will we be accepted and what will transpire?

Eric Berne suggests that we manage some of this anxiety, at the same time as attempting to get what we want, by structuring our relationships and our life's time with six possible forms of behaviour.

The first form of time-structuring is *withdrawal,* whereby we are alone or lose contact while with other people and, figuratively speaking, withdraw into ourselves.

The second type is *rituals,* whereby we exchange fairly 'ritualized' strokes with people in a familiar way. The obvious example of this would be 'Hello, how are you?' – 'I'm fine thanks, how are you?' – 'I'm fine too, thanks. In fact, I'm very well.' – 'Good, but it's ages since we met.' – 'Yes, what have you been doing all this time?' And so on.

The third type of time-structuring is called *pastimes*. These are conversations which are less ritualized but still remain within familiar parameters in terms of both content and style. They are the sorts of exchanges we have about our jobs, our hobbies, our children, the state of the roads, the state of the country, the state of the world, and so on. This may sound as if pastimes are sometimes rather a trivial way of passing the time, but they are actually a vital part of human encounter whatever the subject of the pastiming. They are the way we can signal our interest in each other and our shared world, and our goodwill towards each other. They are an important part of our 'warming into' greater closeness with others. They are our means of finding out who has things in common with us. They are a means of exchanging positive strokes in a safe way, thereby fulfilling at least two others of our hungers, stimulus and recognition.

The fourth way of structuring time, *activities*, refers to people engaging together in joint endeavours, be it at the workplace, on the sports field, at home or in the garden. In activity, those involved interact to complete a task. Their common purpose is a source of both strokes and satisfaction.

The fifth type of time-structuring time is *games and rackets*. These are the repetitive patterns of negative behaviour that we engage in with others – in other words, those situations where we end up saying, 'Oh no, how come it's turned out like this again?' usually closely followed by some comment like 'I should have known ...' or 'I *knew* ...'. People who have been playing games leave the situation feeling familiarly uncomfortable and unsatisfied despite the high intensity of stroke exchange. Games and rackets will be explored in greater detail later in this book.

The sixth and final way of structuring time is *intimacy*. Intimacy occurs when two or more people exchange their thoughts and feelings, without defence and generously. They behave towards each other in an open manner, fully sensitized to the here–and–now experience. They part feeling enriched by the interchange.

The way in which the two authors interacted while we wrote this chapter illustrates how time-structuring works. The shared task of writing this book was the activity. At times, one of us would go into a daydream or prepare tea (withdrawal) whilst the other continued writing (activity). At other times, we would both stop to recognize the arrival of a friend and exchange pleasantries (ritual) which would often extend into conversations ranging from the weather to the type of pizzas preferred (pastime). There were times when we shared our thoughts and feelings for and with each other, including both funny and poignant moments as we resonated to the material with personal memories of our own (intimacy). At the present moment, we have just had a discussion as to which games we might have been playing and have decided that so far today we have been game-free in our interchanges with each other. If this changes we will let you know later in this chapter!

Healthy individuals structure their time across the above range of options in such a way as to meet their particular needs and proclivities. Different temperaments will require different blends and quantities of the six ways of structuring time. An unbalanced mixture can lead to an unhealthy life-style, for example that of the workaholic's over-devotion to work-activities.

Incident Hunger

This last hunger is connected with the previous one, but where in structure-hunger we look for stability, in incident-hunger we seek to be destabilized. It is the need for excitement, the unexpected and the new. When there is too much predictable structure or not enough stimulus in a person's life, boredom sets in. The hunger for incident may then drive that person to create some excitement in life. This can be constructive, as in choosing to make a successful parachute jump, introducing something novel into daily life or interrupting proceedings to tell a joke, or destructive, as in reckless driving, a violent argument or restructuring the business every two years. People have different incident needs. For some, the celebration of Christmas is more than enough incident in the year. For others, a party every weekend may seem absolutely necessary.

The fulfilment of these six hungers is essential for people's health and survival. It is important for practitioners to recognize the significance and impact of these hungers in their clients' lives and in the counselling or coaching session itself. *If these hungers are not met directly, attempts will be made to meet them indirectly by the use of psychological games – the fifth of the methods mentioned under the hunger for time-structuring.* We return to games more fully later in this book.

Application

As with strokes, identifying how and to what extent clients satisfy their six hungers in their lives can be a useful way into the dissatisfactions brought into the counselling or coaching situation. Though there is no 'right' way, or prescribed 'mix', of hunger-satisfaction, since each client will have their own individual proclivities and needs, it is often illuminating to explore the high and low satisfactions of these hungers, what may be missing, and what may be experimented with as a means for change. For example, Mary, a client who 'felt' there was something missing in her life, identified that, of the six hungers, contact hunger and sexual hunger were by far the least satisfied in her life. She had a stimulating job through which she gained recognition, she thought her time structure was well balanced and she even had a satisfying amount of incident in her recreational life. Though she had a sexual relationship, she recognized a lack of good contact with her partner for whom the emphasis of their sex together was orgasm. Until she learnt of her possible need for better physical contact and strokes, she had accepted that this was enough. Fortunately, her partner was willing for them to explore ways of pleasuring each other which would satisfy both sexual and contact hunger. They jointly attended a massage class, spent much more time holding and stroking each other non-sexually as well as sexually and became generally much more physical with each other.

Clearly, a similar assessment within the area of structure hunger and the six ways of structuring time can help clients discover what is 'missing' in their lives. Are they spending enough time getting positive strokes and satisfaction through ritual exchanges, pastimes, activity and intimacy? Are they spending too much or too little time in withdrawal? Or are they attempting to meet their hungers negatively and indirectly by structuring their time in the script-bound and script-reinforcing playing of games?

Exercises

Self

1 When beginning to experiment with awareness of your ways of meeting (or not) your six hungers, start by reviewing the week you have just lived. With regard to stimulus hunger, think about or list the variety of ways you sought the following:

   a *Visual stimulation:* Perhaps it would be helpful to think of this aspect of your life in terms of colour, distance, contrast, direction and content. As you sit reading this book, take some minutes now to feed your eyes on some variety of colour, distance, lights and range around you.

   b *Aural stimulation:* As you remember or relive aspects of your past week, as with your use of your eyes, think of your awareness of the sounds that surrounded you. As you read this book, a suggestion now is to stop a while and explore listening to unusual sounds, aspects of the world about you to which you do not usually focus your attention.

   c *Tactile stimulation:* How often in the past week did you let yourself touch those things in your world at which you were looking? Can you remember the texture and temperature of the handle of your hairbrush or comb? Feel some of the items near you now. It will probably help to do this with your eyes closed.

    d *Olfactory and gustatory stimulation:* Over this past week can you remember/ re-smell some of those odours and tastes you have experienced? What flavours and consistencies have you experienced? Do you need more variety?

2 An exercise which includes stimulation of all these aspects would be to take a 'trust-walk' with a friend who leads you blindfolded to explore the garden or wherever will awaken, refresh and restimulate your hearing, sound, taste and olfactory senses. Then take the blindfold off and really look.

3 Moving on to contact hunger, what physical contact have you had with other people in the last week? How can you improve the quality or quantity of physical contact with others?

4 With regard to recognition hunger, at what moment in the past seven days did you feel most recognized? Was that special because of the identity of the person who recognized you – for example, someone you admire praised you – or was it because of the content of the stroke, or was it the way it was delivered – for example, a soft and friendly smile?

5 How have you dealt with your sexual needs in the past week – alone, with a satisfactory or unsatisfactory partner, or have you chosen to focus on some other expressive form instead, involving your spiritual growth or your creativity? How, if at all, would you like this to be different?

6 Look at the way you time-structured your last week. Apportion the estimated time you spent alone (withdrawal), in rituals, chatting (pastimes), participating in some activity, playing psychological games, and being close or intimate with others. Do you feel satisfied with the results? Work out how you can change your time structure to satisfy your individual needs.

7 How did you get excited (incident hunger) over the past week? Was your life too humdrum or too exciting? What could you plan, say in the week ahead, to bring the balance you need?

Working with Clients

Some or all of the above exercises may equally be applied to working with your clients in order to bring into awareness their hungers and how they are or are not satisfying them. The practitioner's attention to how their client is or is not satisfying their hungers and structuring their time may provide useful insight into the issues the client is bringing to the consulting room, be they related to the work or home situation.

CASE STUDY: A COACH'S STORY

Session Four saw Gunther and Anita continuing to look at functional modes as they applied in his team and also his division. He had been practising using a clear GP in terms of making demands – clarifying what was negotiable and what non-negotiable in the tasks and responsibilities of the roles. Instead of creating the increased resistance that he feared, the rest of the team seemed to have appreciated his clarity and seemed more energized. Anita shared with Gunther a quotation from Eric Berne about the Parent ego state, which, he said, 'conserves energy and reduces anxiety ... by making certain decisions "automatic" and relatively unshakeable' (1961 p. 76). That made sense to Gunther, as did the notion that his attempts to develop his own Child mode were inviting a similar creativity in the staff. He had noticed more inventiveness, as well as more Adult accountability. Anita asked whether he had commented to his staff on the changes that he so welcomed and she introduced him to the idea of 'strokes'. Luckily this bit of jargon was a familiar concept to him as he had read of the effects of lack of relationship – contact, stimulus, recognition – on orphan babies in Romanian children's homes where well-meaning nurses in charge of 20 orphans were not able to give the relational contact they needed for their development. He also understood the importance of 'feedback' (hearing how others are experiencing us) in learning and recognizing our impact.

Despite this knowledge, he realized that his own stroke profile was rather impoverished. The range of strokes he received (and therefore learned to give) was limited and the idea of expressing pleasure in his team's achievements, their ideas and their responsiveness was a little alien. However, with his now familiar twinkle, he agreed to experiment. Anita suggested that after the upheaval of the merger, everybody probably had a higher need for structure than for novelty. However, the need for contact, recognition and relationship would all be high as people made their way and created a new culture. Now might be the time to try to shape a better organizational PAC in terms of communication and recognition. The team 'away day' was coming up, so they spent some of the session thinking about how Gunther could use the concept of hungers to design a day which would be stimulating and nourishing for everyone as well as help them address some of the issues like differences in organizational culture and what they needed to ensure the smooth running of the division in future.

Gunther also began to talk about his home life a little. Clearly his wife was hugely important to him. She was his childhood sweetheart and he knew that in some ways she filled the gap left by his mother. His two small children were a source of delight to him and he happily shared that he had been enjoying changing the nature of his transactions at home as well as at work. Anita picked up, however, that his wife was not happy living in England and wanted to be able to go back to work. She did not make a comment as it was not part of the contract, but waited to see if Gunther would bring it up again.

7

Life Scripts: the development of a lived narrative

Each of us has a life script. That is, early in our lives each of us makes decisions, in response to our perception and experience of life at the time, as to how our life will be in the future. We tend to generalize from our specific, current experiences and assume these will always be so. As we saw in Chapter 6, if a child experiences constant negative stroking in childhood, this may become an expectation of life: the world is then perceived and engaged with as a negative-stroking place populated by negative-stroking people and this expectation for the most part is fulfilled.

The script is a personal life plan developed mainly before the age of seven under parental, familial, social and cultural pressure. It determines the most important aspects of a person's life. The script is 'written' in early childhood, rehearsed and revised in later childhood and performed in adulthood. (We will explore the means by which the script is fulfilled and, therefore, further reinforced, in later chapters on games and the racket system. For now, we will stay with scripts.) First a word about words! In this, and other TA books, you will find the words 'decisions', 'conclusions', 'meaning making', 'script writing' and the like. This is because it is the most straightforward way of describing the child's process. It is important to stress that the child's 'decisions' are very rarely as cognitive and conscious as the word implies. They are visceral, embodied, emotional, 'limbic brain'; they are adaptations made long before the rational neo-cortex is fully developed. The narrative comes later. It is built on the foundation of the earliest relational experience – what Berne called the *protocol* (Berne 1972; Cornell and Landaiche 2006) as a way of making sense of the non-verbal 'knowing'.

Because of small children's dependence on their caretakers and their overall lack of experience and knowledge of the world and of overall perspectives, they rely on others to define the world, themselves and others. As an example, imagine a child learning to walk. Each time she falls over, as all children learning to walk must do, her parents laugh at her affectionately and call her clumsy. The child, hearing the laughter, stops herself crying and laughs too. Imagine this same child at various later ages and stages falling down the stairs, dropping a plate, cutting herself, tripping over the cat and each time being laughed at and told she is clumsy. Imagine this girl in her teens dressing rather gawkily and clowning about in her peer group to maintain some popularity. This girl is not only receiving verbal and non-verbal *strokes* each time she does these things, she is also receiving an *attribution* that she is clumsy. Further, the nature of the non-verbal stroke, laughter, also carries with it the suggestion that this girl's pain is not important. In response to such experiences, this child may decide upon a script which involves some or all of the following:

'I am clumsy.'
'Being clumsy gets attention.'
'Being clumsy makes people laugh.'
'Being clumsy pleases people.'
'I'd better do clumsy things or I'll lose others' attention.'
'No one in the world really cares. Even when I hurt I will laugh.'
'My hurt feelings are not important.'
'Being hurt gets attention.'
'If I hurt myself I will get attention.'

From her specific experience with her parents and later rehearsal with her peers, the girl has generalized such experience into a life script which involves beliefs about herself, how others will respond and how the world is. It is now likely that as an adult she will behave clumsily, find people who laugh at her even when she hurts and experience the world as an uncaring place.

Now it may be that if we question the parents in this example, they will have a totally different perception. They may say they really cared about their daughter, that when they laughed it was out of sympathy with her, that they did not want her to hurt herself and so on. Their intentions, as far as they were aware of them, may have been well-meaning. What is important here is that it is the child's perception of her experience, however skewed, mistaken, misinterpreted or misinformed, and her response to that perception that form the basis of her script decisions. This is not to release the parents or caretakers from their responsibility to be aware of the possible impact of their behaviour on their child. It is a grown-up's responsibility to attend to their own behaviours and unresolved issues, not the child's responsibility. However, it is emphasizing that script is a person's own meaning making, the unique way their experiences sit with them. It is, in effect, co-created.

Children begin developing a script instead of following their own autonomous nature as a result of their vulnerability and dependence, attributions, their developmental stage, their suggestibility, the modelling they receive from caretakers and older siblings, trauma, verbal and non-verbal messages, and in response to fantasies and dreams.

Script Messages

In light of the above, when we write of 'script messages', we mean the messages received from parents or other figures in childhood *as perceived by* the child. Many of these messages, however they are delivered or received, will contain the parents' fears, ignorance, unresolved conflicts and unmet needs which give rise to these *injunctions* to the child. In other words, many of the child's received messages will be the script messages of the parents. Let us take a look at the way such messages may be conveyed.

Verbal and Non-verbal Messages

These will be familiar to you from Chapter 6, where we pointed out that verbal communication is often accompanied by non-verbal communication, the verbal message being corroborated or not by the non-verbal message. In transactional terms, the non-verbal communication carries the psychological message of the ulterior transaction beneath the social level transaction. It is the ulterior transaction that carries the significant message at the psychological level. For example, a busy mother picks up her crying child and holds him close to comfort him. She may even say soothing and loving words to him. But if she is tired and tense, it is likely that her face is tense too, and her voice tone strained. She may hold him too tightly or rigidly or, conversely, hold him loosely, with little energy involved. The social level message may say, 'I love you and I care about you. I like holding you. You are safe with me', but the psychological level message may be, 'I don't want you. You're too much for me. I don't really care. You are not safe with me.'

Modelling

The general behaviour of parents and other authority figures in childhood is another vehicle for the communication of script messages. Telling children to 'do as I say, not as I do' is pointless. The way children see people behave is much more influential than imploring words. In a family setting, seeing father get what he wants from mother by shouting at her, Tom is likely to conclude that this is how to behave when he wants something, despite any lectures about the rudeness of shouting. Or seeing little brother get more attention from mother for being dyslexic, Christine may decide it is better to fail than succeed at something despite the verbal homage paid to success.

Another form of modelling is that found in story books, radio and television stories, films, songs, nursery rhymes and so on. For example, Monica is very impressed at the age of four by the story of Tarzan and begins to model herself and make decisions in line with becoming strong, wild and very involved with animals.

Commands

Direct instructions or commands to children may also be taken on as script messages, depending upon the frequency and intensity of them. If the verbal message is matched by an equivalent non-verbal message, clearly they will be doubly potent. 'Just go away and don't pester me!' if repeated often enough, loudly enough or if accompanied by physical gestures of dismissal may be received as 'Your needs are not important' or 'You're not wanted.' 'Pull yourself together' or 'Don't cry' may be received as 'Your feelings are not important' or 'You're weak if you show your sadness.'

Attributions

In the earlier example, the child who was told she was clumsy grew up to be clumsy. Similarly, a child told he is stupid may decide this is true and grow up acting stupid in response. A child told, 'You're just like your Uncle John' may connect this with their uncle's ineptitude in social situations and construe that they too must be socially inept in response to this message. Often in families different members are given different roles and proceed to live up to them. An example of this would be one child being deemed 'the clever one', another child 'the practical one' and yet another 'the musical one' and so on.

Even more potent, in some ways, are the attributions by a parent or parent-figure made to a third party about you in your hearing: 'Oh, he's such a naughty boy' or 'Julie's the quiet one in the family' or 'It's no use asking Ann for a sensible answer' may carry more weight by 'going public' in this way.

Trauma

Although the repetition of certain negative experiences and their associated perceived messages could be taken on as part of the life script, one traumatic event may be enough for a child to make momentous script decisions about themselves, others and the world unless these traumatic experiences are responded to sensitively and respectfully. Death of a parent, loss of a sibling, physical and sexual abuse, accidents, illness and surgical operations are but a few of the shocking and terrifying experiences a child may suffer. As a consequence, he or she may make far-reaching decisions about themselves being worthless, shameful, sick, non-sexual, crazy, unlovable or undeserving of life; about others being malevolent, untrustworthy, unloving, sadistic, violent or (perhaps justifiably in the child's mind) abusive; about life being pointless, dangerous, desolate, chaotic, cruel or not worth living. These are just some of the possible messages a child might perceive and decide upon in response to trauma. Sadly, for many of our psychotherapy clients, even these shocking experiences were repeated and the subsequent decisions further reinforced.

Positive Messages

So far we have given examples of negative script messages when discussing how these messages may be conveyed and perceived, but positive script messages can be given and conveyed in the same ways. A child attributed with being 'like Aunt Florence', who happens to be a very successful career woman, may take this on as a message to be successful too. A child who overhears a parent proudly singing the praises of their achievements may similarly take this as a permission to achieve. A child genuinely, consistently and warmly hugged by a parent and told 'I love you' is likely to believe and grow up believing they are lovable. A child whose parents listen to and respect each other's needs and wants is likely to model their own behaviour on such attentive respect. Again, the intensity and frequency of such messages will determine their potency.

Just as a single, traumatic experience may influence a child to develop a negative life script, so too an isolated, positively dramatic incident or intensely satisfying peak experience may promote a positive life script. For example, Susie wins the final race of the day which wins her house the school trophy. She is treated like a heroine. From this incident, part of her script is devoted to winning the day on behalf of others. As mentioned earlier, even positive scripts may be limiting to the person's individual potential, being based as they are on the premise that the individual is *only* OK if they are achieving X, Y or Z. It may be, therefore, that Susie has to win for others in order to feel OK.

Depending on their perception of the message, children receiving positive messages are likely to develop mainly positive life scripts. In the same way, children receiving (or perceiving) a lot of negative messages are likely to develop negative life scripts. Most of us have a mixture of messages and experiences and we develop equally mixed scripts. In a sense, scripts are essential. They are our way of learning about, understanding and managing the world. Without them we would be helpless to navigate our way through life (see Cornell 1988; English 1988, 2010; Summers and Tudor 2000). However, whether positive, negative or a mixture, they are all scripts; they are life plans based upon our response to our experiences as children and, as such, may be helping or interfering with our autonomy as adults. Receiving the attribution that you are like your successful Aunt Clarissa, the actress, is all very well and positive, but if, at the end of drama school training and ten years 'treading the boards', you realize you have never really wanted to be an actress at all, then this could be a problem. Similarly, modelling yourself on your father's lifelong dedication to his work may be fine, but if you would be happier living cheaply and working less, there doesn't seem much point in being like him. Clearly, many people may never even realize they have lived their script rather than their life. If it is a happy, exciting, creative and fulfilling script, which does no harm to others, maybe this does not matter. If awareness of their script would enhance life further, maybe it does.

Autonomy

In the present context, the opposite of script is *autonomy*, a word that Eric Berne used in a particular way: to describe our capacity for awareness, spontaneity and intimacy. In response to perceived messages and subsequent script decisions, we may lose touch with these three qualities, if indeed we ever had a chance to touch them. Autonomy means living our life in Integrating Adult. Any moment lived in a structural Child or

Parent ego state is inevitably script, unless it is Adult-monitored or Adult-integrated (here we are referring to the *structural model of ego states* – see Chapter 3 – not the functional modes described in Chapter 5, all of which are a necessary part of human functioning). Put another way, our script is expressed through the contents of our Child and Parent ego states. If we automatically replay the contents, we are in script. The way out of script, then, is through our Integrating Adult awareness which, as we stated earlier, involves choice and, with choice, responsibility.

Given this, perhaps it will not surprise you to learn that we have yet to meet a human being who is totally autonomous! Living a script-free, autonomous life is an ideal towards which we can only aspire, and indeed it may be impracticable if we are to live in the world. As practitioners, our task is to help others in this process of increasing autonomy. Whether this is in one particular area of their lives or in many, will depend upon the goal and timescale of the agreed contract, but whatever these may be we will find it useful to the process, to explore and work through those perceived messages and subsequent decisions which detrimentally affect our clients' lives.

Exploring Script Messages and Decisions

Script messages start out in childhood as external transactions. The resultant decisions are perpetuated by internal transactions between Parent and Child ego states and will most likely be reinforced by 'projecting' one or other of these ego states onto someone else, returning to an external transaction. Here is a much simplified example.

Example

External Transactions

Script messages often contain the unresolved issues of parents. Sarah's mother, as a result of her own script, is a very dependent, clinging woman who is scared of responsibility. She has a lot of support from her husband when Sarah is born but, even so, struggles to cope with the newborn baby, finding her needs almost unbearable. Sarah is regularly left to cry alone. When she is attended to by mother, the attention is perfunctory and tense. The perceived messages here – the external transactions transmitted non-verbally at this early stage – could include, 'My needs are more important than yours', 'You are too much for me', 'I don't care about you' and 'Don't be a needy baby, grow up quickly'.

When father dies some years later, mother becomes even more helpless, but by this time Sarah is able to take on the nurturing role father had played. The external transactions, now transmitted verbally as well as non-verbally, could include such messages as, 'You are so good to take care of me', 'What a big girl you are', 'I'm so pleased when you stay at home', 'You were such a demanding baby but look at you now', as well as the repetition of the earlier, non-verbal messages. In this way, some of Sarah's need for strokes is fulfilled. Sarah responds by taking care of mother.

Decisions

Sarah makes her script decisions in response to these messages. She decides that her acceptability (OK-ness) is conditional upon her looking after others, that others' needs are more important than her own, that if she looks after others they may care but that really she is too demanding. She also decides that children are too demanding. Though we are focusing here for simplicity on the decisions in response to mother, Sarah is also making decisions in response to father. This may include the decision, based on father's early death, that the only way to cease looking after others is to die.

Internal Transactions

The original external transactions are now internalized within Sarah's Parent and Child ego states. In her Parent ego state she has introjected a helpless and demanding mother who shows pleasure when Sarah neglects her own needs to look after others. In her Child ego state are her experiences and responses to such a mother and her consequent decisions. Now, whenever she feels needy, Sarah replays the internal dialogue (the script) whereby her Parent – now not simply her mother but a generalized defining voice – admonishes her for being needy and exhorts her to look after others if she wants to feel OK, and thus reinforces the script decisions. In a subtle twist, Sarah has added a few stern accusations of her own, to keep her from straying from the script path.

It is most likely that the script decisions are so fixed that the internal dialogue is somewhat redundant and totally unnoticed. However, it is important to remember that behind each decision lies an internal dialogue which once was an external dialogue containing the kernel of the script message and consequent decision. Sarah will most probably need to bring these dialogues and messages into her awareness if she is to challenge and change them.

Externalizing the Internal

The process now comes full circle as Sarah, in her grown-up life, projects her needy and demanding Parent onto others. It may be that she subconsciously 'selects' people who, like mother, appear helpless and demanding but, even if they are not, she will perceive and respond to them *as if they are* in order to fulfil her script decisions involving looking after others and keep herself OK. If she finds someone who deeply loves her, such as her own children, then she may externalize the internal in a different way by repeating similar transactions with her own children from her Parent ego state. Thus she experiences them as too demanding and gives them messages that invite similar script decisions to her own. So the script may be passed on to the next generation, just as it was probably passed on to Sarah's mother.

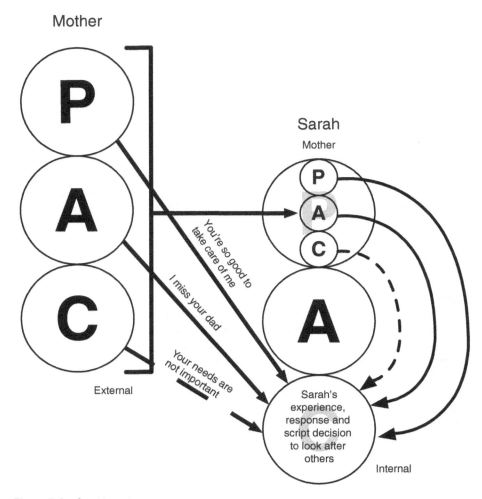

Figure 7.1 Sarah's script process

A Script Diagram

Using the structural model of ego states we can illustrate Sarah's external to internal script process as in Figure 7.1.

Here we can see that the messages originate in the three ego states of mother and are sent to Sarah's Child ego state. Sarah experiences these messages in her own individual way, responds to them and makes her script decisions. Simultaneously, Sarah introjects mother's messages into her Parent ego state. Her responses and decisions are later further reinforced by the same messages being sent internally from her Introjected Parent ego state to her Child ego state.

You will notice that the messages from mother's Child ego state are drawn with the broken line of psychological level or ulterior transactions. This is because, for the most part, these are the type of messages a parent would not consciously give to a child. They are the covert expression of the unmet needs, adaptive responses or restrictive script decisions of the parent's Child. The mother does not intend to send them, but because they represent her own script adaptation to the world, she knows no other. We will refer to these as *psychological level messages*. (For simplicity here, we have not referred to the mutual influence between Sarah and her mother but will do so later under the Script Matrix.)

The messages from the mother's Parent ego state are drawn with an unbroken line. This is to show that, for the most part, these are the type of overt messages a parent probably would not think twice about giving to a child. In fact, they may be quite proud in saying, for example, 'I always told my kids that honesty is the best policy' or 'If you don't take it for yourself, no-one will give it to you'. Such messages are often the identical messages they received from their parents and their parents before them. We will refer to these as *social level messages*.

Some TA writers refer to the messages from the parent's Adult ego state as the 'programme', the 'here's how to' messages which often support the script, but we believe that these messages, if they directly support the script, will not come from an Integrating Adult ego state but from the Introjected Parent or Archaic Child of the parent. If we had shown Sarah's father's messages in diagram form, the 'here's how to look after mother' would have been drawn from either his Parent or Child ego state, not his Adult. We see the Adult messages as more those Integrating Adult messages which, though appropriate to the here-and-now reality of the parent, may be interpreted differently by the child. In our example, from her Integrating Adult, Sarah's mother sends the message 'I miss your dad'. Sarah may (and most likely will, in the light of the other messages) interpret this to mean she must take the place of her father in looking after mother. Often these Adult messages, by their definition as appropriate responses to the here-and-now reality (their being overt is indicated by an unbroken line), will be the more positive and constructive messages of the script and provide a buffer or alternative to the more restrictive aspects. We will refer to these messages simply as *Adult-intended messages*. If they are not Adult-intended, they belong in either the Parent or Child ego states.

The Script Matrix

There are several versions of the script matrix in TA literature based upon the original matrix devised by Claude Steiner (1966). Basically, the matrix opens out the structural diagram of ego states, usually showing both parents but, sometimes, other figures from the past, to illustrate the origins of the contents of ego states. Figure 7.2 is our amended version using the labels we have described above and showing the introjection of the message-giving ego states of the parents into the Parent ego state of the offspring from whence the script may be replayed and reinforced. The messages from Child to Child have a broken line with a double-headed arrow, to indicate that these relational patterns are an unconscious and often non-verbal interplay – a co-creation between child and parent. We also include Berne's aspiration arrow, to which we will refer later.

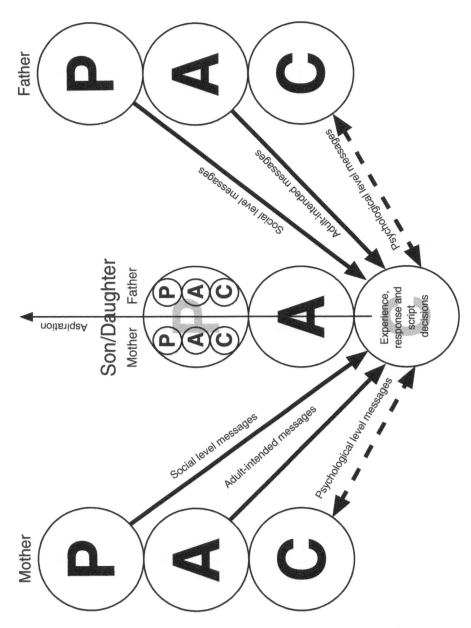

Figure 7.2 The script matrix

Social Level Messages

These messages, which parents give to their children in an overt manner, are probably familiar to all of us. They will have been given often and in many and various situations in our childhoods and further reinforced by other grown-ups. Getting in touch with social level messages from the past is often easy: we 'hear them' internally even now. Such messages may include such shibboleths as 'Be a good girl and do as you're told', 'Now do your best', 'It's rude to grab', 'Boys don't cry', 'Always look smart', many of which may prove socially useful as we grow up and as adults make our way in the world. However, not only may some of these messages not be useful but their automatic and unquestioning use may be restrictive and dysfunctional. For example, a child told to 'Always look smart' may take this in as an all-pervasive rule of life and consequently spend much time and energy on achieving a smart appearance. They may go to great lengths to avoid entertaining or creative activities which involve looking anything less than smart. They may miss out on the fun and relaxation of such activities and, as a result, appear cold and aloof and thus find difficulty in making friends and good relationships. 'Smart but lonely' may be the outcome of such a response to the original message.

There is a driven quality to the way people respond to these social level messages. This is because, implicit within the message, there is some positive but conditional stroking. The message often becomes, 'If you are like this, only then are you acceptable' or 'You're OK only if you...'. As children wanting strokes to satisfy our recognition hunger we readily adapt to such conditions. As adults we continue the adaptation, believing that our being OK is conditional on behaving in certain ways. We feel 'driven' in search of recognition and acceptance. Kahler and Capers (1974) recognized that these driving, social level messages could be categorized under five headings. For obvious reasons, they are called *drivers*:

- Please People
- Be Strong
- Be Perfect
- Hurry Up
- Try Hard

Tudor (2008) identified a sixth driver that has emerged in the different world of the twenty-first century:

- Take It (meaning 'go for it' or 'grab what you want')

We all carry these drivers around in our Parent ego state in one form or another and respond to them in our Child ego state. However, because of our different family environments where a different emphasis was placed on what are important ways to behave, we prioritize them differently and each of us is likely to have one or two 'favourite' ones. Recognizing someone's most-used driver behaviour will give some clue as to the script messages they were given (see Table 7.1 for some guidelines for recognition, although everyone has their unique version).

Table 7.1 Driver spotting

Driver	Verbal patterns	Gestures	Facial cues
Please People	Would you ...? Could you ...? Is that OK? Sort of .... May I ...? If you don't mind ... Can you understand me?	Lots of head-nodding, reaching towards the other, head tilted, placatory movements.	Raised eyebrows, horizontally wrinkled brow, looking upwards if possible, tense and persistent smile.
Be Strong	Few, if any, feeling words. Rarely uses 'I' statements. Separates self from feelings and thoughts by using generalizations: One should always ...; It's better to ...; People are ...; or over-detailing: The six major points here are ...	Rigid, stiff, hardly moving. Posture tight and closed; arms or legs crossed and close to body; energy and strength in chest and shoulders.	Flat and immobile. Either hard and cold or sometimes constantly kindly and caring.
Be Perfect	Of course ...; possibly ...; most probably ...; one might even say .... Tends to list the points in a conversation by numbers or letters: Firstly, secondly, etc.	Sits upright; looks smart and flawless. Counts off points on fingers while talking or 'steeples' fingertips while listening. Scratches head or strokes chin while thinking.	Looks upwards and sideways as if scanning a prompt screen for the right (perfectly right) words. Stern and serious. Or 'perfectly (sometimes excessively) attentive'.
Hurry Up	Interrupts others. Finishes others' sentences but often not their own! Quick speech. Expressions like: Quick; let's go; come on; let's just quickly ...; pop and ...; hurry up ...; don't be long. For alternative, see under Facial Cues.	Taps fingers, agitates foot etc. Looks at watch.	Darting glance. Frowning. Mouth tense and moving. Alternatively, slow and closed-off expression, repetitive, overly thoughtful and halting speech as resistance to 'Hurry up' message.
Try Hard	The word 'try' used frequently. Goes off at tangents. Over-detailing, but often not finishing. It's hard to ...; I can't ...; I don't understand; What did you say? What I'm trying to explain is ...	Leans forward, elbows on legs, hands to cheek or ear, straining position; straining to understand or make self understood.	Looks perplexed or confused; screws up face in an effort to understand.
Take It	Tone abrupt and certain; low growling bullying or high whining and defensive. Words: It's mine; I want it *now*; I'm certain ...; there's no doubt ...	Hands held out, either pointing or clenched fists. Posture square on, one foot in front in boxing stance ready to threaten or sway back if defensive.	Open face with eyes forward but focused beyond the other. Persuasive expression: eyes narrow, lips pursed.

There is nothing intrinsically wrong in the six types of driver behaviours. On the contrary, they often turn out to be our greatest strengths. Striving to be perfect while doing a graphic design may be fine, as may hurrying up to deal with the situation at the scene of an accident. Remaining steady under stress can be a positive quality, as is kindness to others or determination and doggedness. It is, clearly, the more persistent and driven aspects that may be dysfunctional, the belief that *we are only OK* if we are achieving one or more of these behaviours. When we go into driver behaviour without thinking, feeling or choosing, these patterns become unproductive.

Coaches and consultants who work in organizational settings will notice that often one or more of the drivers becomes part of the organizational culture (the organizational script). One organization seems to thrive on 'Try hard' for example, and the habit of working late, and its employees have a style of producing lots of great ideas and lots of paperwork, analysing problems but not changing anything. Another organization is perfectionist and much success is thwarted through obsessional attention to detail, or through people not daring to have creative or spontaneous ideas. Often these patterns are instigated by the 'Parent' figures in organizations (the founders or the CEO) and can also be handed down through the generations. Sometimes it is the nature of the organization itself that creates particular driver behaviour and it can be useful, even when working with an individual client, to invite reflection on the sort of product or service offered by the business, as well as the norms: what gets rewarded round here? What gets frowned upon? It is easy to imagine that an accounting firm might develop a 'Be Perfect or Try Hard' culture, a theatre company might develop a 'Please' culture, a hospital could practise a 'Be Strong' culture and so on. (For more on working styles and drivers in organizations, see Hay 1992.)

Psychological Level Messages

These covert messages are communicated for the most part non-verbally at the psychological level. While social level messages from the past are easily available for examination because of their verbal content and the words still playing inside our heads, the psychological level messages are experienced more physiologically and thus may take more time to acknowledge. That churning of the stomach each time we are close to someone, the banging heart and racing pulse when we are expecting criticism or the blushing that occurs when we are given attention: all may be signs of response to a psychological level message.

These messages usually originate in the Child ego state of the parent. As we know from the discussion in Chapter 3, Child ego states may be positive and constructive; in which case, these psychological level messages may be experienced by the receiver as encouraging and life-enhancing. For example, a mother playing with her child may transmit the joyful and carefree experiences of her childhood to her own child in the manner in which she plays, the tone of her voice, the laughter she shows, the open look on her face and so on. The psychological messages perceived by her child could include 'Life is fun!', 'It's OK to be close', 'You're fun to be with', 'You can express yourself openly' and the subsequent decisions be positive and life-enhancing. Such messages are referred to as *permissions*.

On the other hand, we know that Child ego states may also be negative and destructive. They may contain the restrictive experiences and decisions, the unresolved issues and unmet needs of the caretaker's childhood, the unmanaged affect of powerful feelings. For example, a mother who was not allowed to play as a child may go through the motions of fun and laughter with her own child, yet at the psychological level be transmitting negative messages from a jealous and resentful Child ego state. The third rule of communication applies here: the child perceives the psychological level communication rather than the social level. The messages may be experienced and perceived by the child as 'Life's a struggle', 'You aren't really wanted', 'You shouldn't take up my time like this', 'Don't be close to me' and the subsequent decisions be negative and life restricting. Such messages are referred to as *injunctions*.

Bob and Mary Goulding (1976) categorized these negative, inhibiting messages into twelve injunctions each of which describes a limitation to full, healthy living:

1 Don't exist
2 Don't be you (for example don't be the way you are or even don't be a separate person)
3 Don't be a child
4 Don't grow up
5 Don't make it
6 Don't (do anything)
7 Don't be important
8 Don't belong
9 Don't be close
10 Don't be well (Don't be sane)
11 Don't think
12 Don't feel (Don't express what you feel)

Clearly, this list of injunctions can be turned into a list of permissions or freedoms by deleting the 'don'ts' and substituting 'You can'. Allen and Allen (1972, 1982, 1999) have elaborated a list of permissions that are related to the developmental tasks of growing up and living fully. They range from the permission to exist and make an impact in the world, to experience one's feelings, thoughts and sensations, to the permission to be in relationship with mutual love and care, and the permission to succeed in sexuality and in work and finally to find and make meaning in one's life.

As with drivers, this categorization of messages into a list of injunctions (or permissions) can be a useful shorthand for further exploration. It is important, however, to work with the client's own experience and the particular messages – and wording of those messages – that are unique to each client.

Adult-intended Messages

These are the messages that originate in the parents' Integrating Adult ego state. If a parent is responding to their child with feelings, thoughts and behaviours appropriate to the here–and–now reality, it is likely that they will be perceived in this way by the child and taken in as constructive and positive. These may provide a counterbalance to the Parent and Child ego state messages and, depending upon the intensity, frequency and potency of these messages, be taken in rather than the more negative script messages. However, as in our example of Sarah, the child may perceive even Adult messages in a way that fits the restrictive Parent and Child ego state messages where these are more potent and pervasive. What is more, an incident that involves strong, perhaps painful or confusing feelings has the likely effect of 'decommissioning' Adult in the recipient and having a more lasting impact on script conclusions.

Self-created Injunctions

Sometimes the Child will design and impose on himself his own injunction. He does this to help him control himself and follow what he believes will be the only way of keeping himself acceptable in the eyes of his parents. Humans will do almost anything to stay in a needed relationship. Often, these self-imposed injunctions are more vicious and critical than any real parent could be, because they are made without Adult information and assessment.

Decisions

In response to the perceived messages from parents, the child makes decisions about themselves, others and the world. When working with clients, the coach or counsellor can inquire into the client's core beliefs about himself in the world as well as the decisions that can be inferred from his attitudes, body language, metaphors and so on. It is important to engage in a process of discovery in relation to a client's individual and specific decisions, as often these are more complex than may at first appear.

Example

Sonny, for example, in exploring his script, discovers that he spends a lot of time in a 'Please People' driver. He decides he wants to change this and begins to say 'No' to people, to look after his own needs and to let others do things for him, all appropriately and consciously. Contrary to his expectations of feeling better about himself and enjoying his life and his friends more, Sonny feels depressed, out of touch with others and has suicidal thoughts. He reverts to 'Please People' behaviour and feels better and close to his friends again.

(Continued)

> *(Continued)*
>
> In his counselling sessions, he further explores his script and discovers that the most potent psychological level messages he perceived were 'Don't exist' and 'Don't be a child with needs'. An unplanned pregnancy and a difficult birth, he arrived in an already large family, an unwanted child among much older siblings, and his needs were very much marginalized. In order to survive as best he could in this family, Sonny made a script decision which could be expressed as: 'I can stay alive here if I grow up quickly. Then I can get some attention if I please others in my family by putting aside my own needs to look after theirs.' Thus it was that, when Sonny attempted to change his driver behaviour of pleasing others, he ran up against the other components of his script. If his own needs came to the fore, he was a child with needs, and as a child with needs he found it difficult to exist. Hence his subsequent depression, distance from others and thoughts of suicide. In his counselling, Sonny needed to address first his issues about staying alive, then those of being a child with needs, and finally his driver behaviour.

In this example, Sonny 'does a deal' in response to the perceived messages, one component being conditional on the next. It will always be the case that, where decisions contain more than one component, the psychological level message will be defended by the social level. Put another way, driver behaviour will be used to defend against injunctions. In this case, Sonny used a 'Please People' driver to defend against a 'Don't be a child with needs'. This part of the decision was, 'I can get some attention if I please others in my family by putting aside my own needs to look after theirs.' Another deal was made at the psychological level, one injunction being used to defend against another. In this case, Sonny defended against the more severe 'Don't exist' injunction by agreeing to the less severe 'Don't be a Child with needs' injunction. This part of the decision became 'I can stay alive here if I grow up quickly'. When we consider injunctions, they will need to be addressed in the order of their severity.

If we draw a script matrix for Sonny we may discover that the perceived 'Don't exist' message came from mother and the 'Don't be a child' from father. The decisional 'deal' may then be in playing off one parent's message against the other. In this case, 'If I grow up for dad, I don't have to die for mum.' As long as Sonny obeys his father's injunction, he is protected from his mother's more destructive injunction. In each of these examples, Sonny complied with the directives of his script messages. He could equally, however, have rebelled against them – if this could have ensured his survival – and stayed a child, stayed needy, refused to do anything that might please others and so on. But he would still be in script. He may have a sense of autonomy but it is false. His defiant decisions have still been made in adaptation to the parental messages. His life plan is dependent upon his disobedience of these messages. This type of script response is called an *antiscript*. It is often experienced during adolescence in an attempt to break free of the script.

This example describes some of the complexities that might be involved in working with script. It is the sort of work that might be undertaken with a counsellor or psychotherapist, or perhaps a social worker or child therapist. Normally a coach or team leader is not going to work with this type of situation. The sort of script beliefs and behaviour that will be identified in a coaching situation will usually be related to the client's work identity and focus on more accessible patterns, often those that were developed during school years. If, as a coach, you and your client begin to discover some deeply rooted issues of the type we have described, you may want to invite them to reflect that this sort of work deserves more regular support than can be offered in, for example, monthly coaching sessions. You can offer to help the client find some therapeutic support.

As we have already mentioned, a child may be given positive messages and permissions and make positive script decisions in response to such messages. These are still part of the script and may be usefully explored in counselling in order that the client may now assess, amend, keep or discard these decisions from their Integrating Adult ego state. They may also be explored and utilized creatively in the service of undoing the more negative script decisions. Bringing a client's strengths and positive decisions into awareness may sometimes be forgotten in the script exploration. Such an over-emphasis on negative aspects of the script and an ignoring of the positives is disadvantageous to the client in its neglect of important resources.

Whether our script decisions are compliant, defiant, seemingly positive or negative, creative or restrictive, we need to respect them. Though they may now be inappropriate to our grown-up lives, they were made by us in order to survive as best we could in the circumstances of our childhood. Whatever changes we may now undergo, whatever new decisions we may now make, the Child within us deserves to be given acknowledgement, understanding and gratitude for bringing us thus far.

Aspiration

There is one arrow of the script matrix diagram (Figure 7.2) that we have not yet discussed. This is the arrow that diagrammatically begins in the heart of the Child ego state, forges up through the Adult and Parent ego states and continues upwards beyond the ego states to infinity. Berne includes this arrow in the script matrix shown in his book, *What Do You Say After You Say Hello?* (1972). It is the arrow of aspiration.

Whatever our script messages, we each have our own autonomous aspirations, the creative yearnings and dreams of what we may be, of what we may do and the ways in which we may achieve such longings. Berne referred to these aspirations as our secret gardens. To continue the analogy: the garden of our aspiration may be weathered by the downward elements of the script, the storms, the drought, the sun, wind and rain of our parental messages yet survive, grow, thrive and blossom nonetheless. Berne sees that the object of script analysis is to free our clients 'so that they can open the garden of their aspirations to the world' (1972 p. 131). As practitioners, our task is to help release our clients from the restrictive and sometimes destructive elements of their script, to release their potential and achieve their aspirations.

In his first book, *The Mind in Action* (1949) and many of his later writings, Berne referred to the pre-Socratic concept of *Physis* – 'the force of nature, which eternally strives to make things grow and to make growing things more perfect' – to describe the natural tendency of human beings towards health and growth. This creative force for change may be seen as the energy or power that is drawn upon by practitioners and their clients in the quest for the fulfilment of their aspirations. Our colleague, the late Petruska Clarkson, wrote more extensively about the concept of Physis in many of her writings, in particular her book *Transactional Analysis Psychotherapy: An Integrated Approach* (1992).

Application

In this chapter we are dealing with the exploration of the life script and its formation. The emphasis is upon discovering and exploring the life plans that our clients have made as an aid to making changes. This is known as *script analysis*. In analysing the script many clients already make changes. By bringing into awareness the underlying messages, responses and decisions that are now inappropriate and restrictive in their lives, clients have new responses and make new decisions while in the process of exploration. Thus, in itself, script analysis opens up the opportunity for choice and the possibility of change.

Example

George came to counselling at a time when David, his lover, was threatening to leave the relationship after they had spent two years together. George, like his father, was a successful architect. At 32, after several short-term relationships, he had met David, bought a house with him and thought that all was well until David threatened to leave. George was shocked by this sudden announcement. He wanted to save the relationship. David's complaint against George was the lack of time they spent together. George worked in his office in the city each day, often until late in the evenings, and brought work home at weekends. The solution seemed apparent: work less, spend more time with David, save and enjoy the relationship. In practice, however, it was not so simple. Like many 'solutions', it was really a goal. In fact, the solution became the counselling contract. Using it as a solution before entering into counselling, each time George determined to spend a weekend relaxing with David he would somehow pick an argument, and in response to David's angry retaliation would storm off to do some work. George told his counsellor that he really loved David and wanted their relationship to work, but that 'Sometimes, I seem to pick a fight in spite of myself. I know I don't want to fight but I still do it! I seem to be sabotaging the relationship even though it's the last thing I want to do.' The counsellor suggested they do a script analysis. She asked George to tell her what it was like to be a child in his family, what his parents were like, what their relationship was like, what expectations they had of him, what the family sayings were, what the family values were and so on.

The life story that emerged was as follows: George's father had become a successful architect when George, an only child, was quite young, setting up his own firm by working long hours at the office and at home. George had many recollections of sitting quietly, watching his father working meticulously at his drawing-board, tearing plans up and starting again at the slightest error. Sometimes his father would teach George the skills of drawing and design and was supportive and encouraging of his efforts, for which he certainly seemed to have a natural aptitude. But these times were rare owing to the pressure of work. His mother supported her husband's career and seemed quite happy to play a background role. George thought she was never happier than when his father was working in his study and he was doing his homework in his bedroom and she busied herself in the kitchen. At times when he wanted attention, he remembered that his mother would get very angry and tell him that he could not have what he wanted until all his work was finished. If he cried, she would tell him to pull himself together, that boys don't cry and that if he wanted to get anywhere in life, he should be like his father. He could not recall seeing his parents spend time together except at meal times and these were often very tense, usually ending up with his mother getting angry with father over some trivial matter and his father storming off back to his work. Thus George's early experience of life and how it is lived involved his parents' modelling of relationship and work, the command to be like father, positive messages about his drawing skills and many experiences of neglect of his need for closeness and attention.

George and the counsellor drew a script matrix (Figure 7.3) to summarize some of the perceived messages relevant to his current problem. In response to these social level, psychological level and Adult-intended messages perceived by George as a child, he made the following script decisions: 'To survive in this life, I must be strong and work hard like my dad who says I'm good at this anyway. If I have any needs, others will get angry. I can hide my needs by staying away from others and I can do this by working. Others will love me if I'm out of the way.'

Through analysing these aspects of his script in this way, George could see the interconnectedness of these compound decisions. It was not just a case of cutting down on his work. If he simply did this, as he had attempted to do, he was not just going against the decision in response to the social level message to be like dad and work hard, he was also coming up against the decision in response to the psychological level messages not to get his needs met and not to be close, which he had covered by going away and working hard. Thus, with David, simply organizing more time to be with him was not enough. Out of Adult awareness, he would sabotage the attempt by inviting David to be angry with him. This way, he obeyed his decisions not to be close and not to get his needs met, which at the same time, paradoxically, he believed would mean David would love him. The counsellor gave encouragement to George by pointing out to him that he was already moving out of script in coming to her to explore his needs, which inevitably involved being close to her. Her empathic and accepting interest also gave permission for him to have his needs met and be close to David. David, too, was only too pleased to give

(Continued)

(Continued)

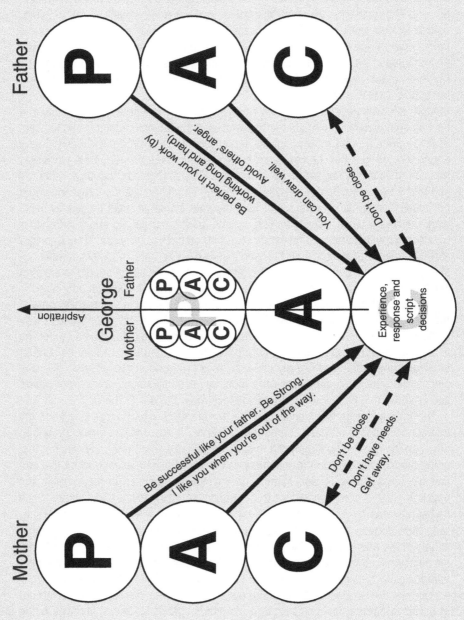

Father

P A C

Be perfect in your work (by
working long and hard).
Avoid others' anger.

You can draw well.

Don't be close.

George

Mother   Father

Aspiration →

P A C   P A C

A

Experience,
response and
script
decisions

Mother

P A C

Be successful like your father. Be Strong.
I like you when you're out of the way.

Don't be close.
Don't have needs.
Get away.

Figure 7.3   George's script matrix

him this permission. This did not mean that David would never be angry with George again but that George would not hide his needs (especially his need for closeness) from David by running away to work. His awareness of how he might 'set things up' to get David angry with him was all that was needed for him to avoid doing this.

You can see from the above example that full script analysis entails the conceptualization and amalgamation of many variables extrapolated from the client's history. However, just as it is possible to use a précis, a trailer or a fractal to understand the essence of a book, film or a picture, so too the basic essence of a person's script may be seen in the mini-versions of it that are played out, for example, in the counselling situation. At one point in the counselling, George went through a period of cancelling his sessions at the last moment. The counsellor noticed herself becoming irritated and impatient with him and knew there might be a danger of her becoming less committed to her client. This experience showed them both the power of the script.

Organizational Script

At the organizational level, ask yourself:

- How old is this organization? (metaphorically; e.g. infant/adolescent/old)
- What gender? What animal? What sea creature? (drawing the team in a fish tank with colleagues and yourself as sea creatures can be interesting – but make sure there is the safety for that sort of revelation)
- In a sentence, what is this organization about?
- As a visitor, what might strike you within the first five minutes?
- What are the unwritten rules?
- How would you describe the leaders? (What role do they take?)
- What happens to the organization under stress?
- How do things get done in this organization?
- What's rewarded? How could you really mess up?
- What are the symbols of power?
- What do people wear? What do they not wear?
- Who are the heroes and villains?
- How does the organization have fun?

Then at the individual level, the client might ask himself:

- How do I personally get things done in this organization?
- How does the organizational script fit or not fit with my individual familial/ cultural script?
- Might any incompatibility be linked to the issue that brought me to coaching?

Exercises

Self

Script Themes

Fairy tales, legends and myths are stories of universal life scripts. Their themes of quests, love, relationships, tasks, hopes and fears, success and failure, and the conditions and environments in which they are set reflect the themes of human life. In particular, they often reflect a child's-eye view of the world: a world populated on the one hand by giants, ogres, witches, monsters, dragons, kings and queens, gods and goddesses (for all of which read 'parents' or other authority figures), and on the other hand by seemingly powerless beings, poverty-stricken offspring, ragged and downtrodden stepsons and stepdaughters, defenceless and ill-treated animals (for all of which read 'children'). Two of the ingredients that so often bring about a change of fortune in these stories are magic and royalty! Through magic, Cinderella goes to the ball, through royalty she leaves the family and lives happily ever after. How wonderful for us, as children reading these stories, to feel our powerlessness change to power. How sad, however, that we often go on believing them and, as adults, spend our lives waiting for the magic or the rescuing prince or princess and keeping ourselves powerless.

One way of exploring our own scripts and their general themes is via the route of these universal scripts. It is likely that those stories that attracted us most as children, or which stick in our memories, are those which contain the major general themes of our own particular script. It is also likely that the films, plays, novels or stories we are attracted to today are connected in some way with the script that we are still playing out. To help you begin to identify aspects of your own script, first choose a favourite early childhood fairy story, or TV programme, nursery rhyme or song, myth or legend and write down the story as you remember it. Now choose an influential story, play, film, poem or song from your primary school years, another from your teenage years (this may be from a pop song or TV show) and a current one. Write these down as you remember them and then ask yourself the following questions for each story. (We suggest you write the stories now before looking at these questions, which otherwise might influence your natural response.)

- What themes does your story express?
- With which of the characters do you identify?
- How does this character play their part in the story?
- What do they do and how do they do it?
- How does the story begin and how does it end?
- What part do the other characters play in the unfolding of the story and its development?
- Which of them do you admire most, or despise?
- How would you describe the story: is it hopeful or pessimistic, constructive or destructive, magical or pragmatic, funny or serious (and so on)?

Look for the themes of the story that may in some way reflect your own life script. Having written notes on the themes and aspects of each story, what do you notice? Do they remain the same in each case? If not, how do they differ? Is there some general development from one to the other? Are they totally different? How do these stories reflect the themes of your own script that you identified from the first story? How do you account for the similarities or differences at different ages of your life? How do they reflect the decisions you have made? How do they reflect the aspirations you have fulfilled or would like to fulfil? What are the negative and positive aspects of your script that are reflected in the stories?

Script Messages

Draw a script matrix for yourself and use the following as a guide to complete it. For the social level messages, ask yourself how you most often behave towards others, and in accomplishing tasks, in a way in which you feel driven by the belief that, if you did not, you would consider yourself to be unacceptable in some way. You may find it helpful to refer to the later exercise for identifying driver behaviours when working with clients. From the six drivers, Please People, Be Strong, Be Perfect, Hurry Up, Try Hard, Take It, choose the one under which these types of behaviour would come. Which of these would come second? Is there a third or fourth driver behaviour which you persistently adopt in your life?

Enter these on your script matrix on the social level arrow according to which of your parents or caretakers you think sent such messages. These might be from both or one of your parents. Remembering that these are useful shorthand phrases, see if you can identify the more specific messages that they are describing. Think of the modelling, the commands and attributions of your parents or caretakers. How did they, for example, encourage you to please people? You may be able to remember the actual words they said. What are the words you still hear in your own head? Add these to your script matrix.

Injunctions

At the psychological level, because these messages were received much earlier and are mostly pre-verbal or non-verbal, some of the injunctions may be more difficult to identify for yourself. They may be usefully explored in your own counselling, psychotherapy or coaching. Others may be more apparent to you immediately or, looking down the list provided on page 102, you may identify them from your physiological response as you read them.

One way of exploring what these psychological level messages may be is to deduce them from the messages at the social level.

If you have a 'Please People' driver and messages which support this – 'Put others before yourself', 'What a good child to do that for me', 'Always mind your manners' – it is likely that you might have interpreted that to mean one or more of the following injunctions: 'Don't be you', 'Don't be a child with needs', 'Don't be important' or 'Don't feel (Don't express what you feel)'. Conversely, 'Don't grow up', 'Don't be well' and 'Don't make it' may be pleasing to a parent who wants their child to remain dependent.

Similarly, if you have a 'Try Hard' driver, 'Don't make it', 'Don't (do anything)' or 'Don't think' may apply; and with:

- 'Be Strong': 'Don't be a child', 'Don't belong', 'Don't be close' or 'Don't feel';
- 'Be Perfect': 'Don't be you', 'Don't be a child', 'Don't make it', 'Don't belong' or 'Don't be close';
- 'Hurry Up': 'Don't be you', 'Don't be a child', 'Don't make it', 'Don't belong' or 'Don't think' may apply;
- 'Take It': 'Don't be close', 'Don't belong', 'Don't feel' and 'Don't think (about others)'.

The 'Don't Exist' injunction may well apply whatever the driver. These are only guidelines to help in your exploration. They are by no means the only possibilities. Add these messages to your script matrix on the psychological level arrow and, as with the social level messages, write more specific messages in your own words.

Adult-intended Messages

It is to be hoped that you received many Adult messages from your parents and made many positive decisions in response. These messages could be listed separately as a recognition of the strengths you have as a resource in your life. For the script matrix, however, we are looking at those Adult-intended messages which you perceived as being a further reinforcement of the Parent and Child messages. They may have shared feelings, thoughts and behaviours which were appropriate to the here-and-now reality, such as shouting 'Stop!' and grabbing your hand as you were about to push a knife into an electric socket. Without subsequent explanation, you may have perceived this as going with other prohibitive injunctions like 'Don't explore' or simply 'Don't'. Look at the other messages of your script matrix and see which Adult-intended messages you may have perceived as fitting these. Add them to your matrix.

Decisions

Now you have completed the actual or perceived messages of your script matrix, express in your own words what decisions you made in response to these messages. Remember that these are likely to be compound decisions which often contain 'deals' or 'trade-offs' between injunctions and drivers or sets of injunctions in interplay with your relational needs and psychobiological hungers. At this stage, the four script 'stories' you have already identified in the exercise on page 110 may help to highlight some of these decisions.

Your Script

Having explored your script themes, script messages and decisions, how do they fit each other? For example, how are your drivers reflected in your favourite stories? Where do the injunctions fit? How do your decisions relate to the themes? Use this analysis to clarify your script for yourself.

Changes

What changes do you want to make in your script? What are the new decisions you may need to make in order to make these changes? Write these down along with what you will need to do to make these changes. Remember, if they are compound decisions, you will need to work from the more severe injunctions to the less severe and from injunctions to drivers. What will you need to change first? What were the aspirations you identified for yourself and what are the aspects of your real self that need freeing? Who and what will you need to help you to make these changes? If you are having coaching, counselling or psychotherapy (and if working with clients, we believe this is imperative), discuss these changes first with your practitioner. This cognitive work can be very useful but more profound change occurs through deeper exploration and experience within the therapeutic relationship. In Chapter 10 we will be looking at the process of change in TA which will help you to achieve these changes.

Working with Clients

1 Explain the idea of a life script to your client and use the first exercise on pages 110–11 to explore the general themes of their life script.
2 Driver spotting (using the clues in Table 7.1). Driver behaviour often occurs very briefly for a few seconds as the person experiences stress and feels driven to obey the message. First of all practise identifying them by observing television characters.
3 Explore the more specific messages of your client's script by drawing a script matrix and using the second exercise above.
4 Work through the script matrix with your client to discover how it relates to their presenting problems and issues brought to the coaching or counselling situation. Use the script matrix to discover what changes your client is wanting to make and help them to uncover and encourage their autonomous aspirations.
5 If you are working with a coaching client or as a consultant to a team or organization, the script story exercises can be both fun and revealing. Inquiring into the myths and legends of the organization shows up many of the patterns and culture of its script. You can invite people to discuss questions (developed from a list offered by Lindsey Masson at *Ashridge Consulting*: personal communication) such as those suggested in the box on page 109.
6 Use the questions in the box to help you draw up a script matrix for the organization you or your client is working in, reflecting on Berne's ideas of Etiquette, Technics and Character. How is this organizational script empowering or limiting its employees in the current twenty-first-century context? Could some different conversations be happening? Is your client's script and working style a 'good fit' for the organization?
7 Invite clients to design their own antidote to their particular driver – one that they can say to themselves to support their change. Some examples are below, but an individually designed one is often more powerful:

Driver	Antidote
Be Perfect	You are perfect as you are
	It's important to make mistakes – that's how we learn
Be Strong	Your needs are important
	You can ask for help
Try Hard	Do it EASILY!
	If at first you don't succeed – try something different!
Please	It's important to please yourself
	It's OK to disagree or say 'no'
Hurry Up	BE in what you do
	Go at your own pace
Take It	You can negotiate with others; other people are important to you, and you to them
	There is enough

CASE STUDY: A COACH'S STORY

Anita's sixth session with Gunther took place after his trip to Germany for a family birthday. He showed her photographs of his home in Frankfurt, including pictures of the main square where the birthday dinner had taken place. When she admired the beautiful old buildings, he explained that they had been totally destroyed by the Allied bombing during the war and that the people of the city had faithfully reconstructed their historical centre. Anita found herself uncomfortable. Previously they had talked about the impact of the war on Gunther's father and his generation, and then the influence of that on him. Now Anita was painfully aware that she too lived with a legacy from those times. Her own father also had grown up during the war and afterwards. Her grandfather had been in the Air Force and although he 'flew a desk' as he used to put it, she was now faced with recognizing what had been done by British people to Gunther's home town. Awkwardly, she mentioned how sorry she was. It seemed to open a door for them both. They shared their thoughts and feelings about the war and about each other's country. They swopped 'cultural transferences' – projections about what Germans were like and what the English were like. At the end of the conversation, they had learned a lot and felt close to each other. Their dialogue had co-created a 'merger' between them which led to a very useful and collaborative discussion about Gunther's team. Anita took the opportunity to talk about scripting and transgenerational scripting (Noriega 2004, 2010), and Gunther was interested to think about the cultural scripting (Shivanath and Hiremath 2003) influencing different members of the team. Anita did not go into the minutiae of scripting and the script matrix, but invited him to think also about the script of the two organizations that had merged and the implications of that, as well as the script that was being 'written' in the moment in the new emergent place. In order to explore the organizational script, Anita reminded him of

Berne's ideas of Etiquette: the dynamics, norms, accepted behaviour, traditions and mission statement; Technics: the structure, physical environment, roles and responsibilities, contracts for work, resources; and the Character: the feelings, atmosphere, ambience, how anxiety is managed and what ulterior transactions go on. In order to stimulate both reflection and imagination in exploring this, Anita offered him some creative questions to consider and to use with the team at their away-day that was coming up shortly (see the organizational questions in the box on p. 109). At the end of the session, Gunther suggested that they go for a drink and perhaps a meal, as he was staying in a nearby hotel that evening. Anita thanked him warmly but said that she had a policy to keep a boundary around coaching sessions. In her experience, it facilitated the work better. Gunther at first looked disappointed but then almost immediately happy and relieved. He quite understood, he said, and appreciated the clarity of the contract.

(*Note:* The nature of the coaching contract, as can be seen from Anita's and Gunther's relationship, is a much more social, open one than, for example, that of therapist–client. Consequently, many coaches have more flexible boundaries to the session and the scope of the relationship. However, we find that keeping the time, place and contract boundary creates a more powerful and effective container for the coaching work, and avoids difficulties that might arise as a result of the inevitable intimacy that occurs in the relationship. For example, Anita was probably listening with more empathic and warm attention to Gunther than was usual from his family, friends and colleagues. She was making no demands upon him other than for him to pay close attention to himself and his thoughts, feelings and behaviour. Consequently, it would not be surprising for him – or any coaching client – to develop an attachment that might contain not just affection but dependency or erotic feelings. This can be anxiety-provoking for clients and therefore it can be very useful to clearly keep to the container of the coaching work.)

8

Games: understanding relational dynamics

In his *Games People Play* (1964b), Eric Berne called a game 'a series of moves with a snare'. The use of the word 'snare' is to suggest that, though a particular situation might at first seem ordinary, even pleasurable, it turns out to have a hidden, though predictable, catch in it. He also defines a game more formally as *'an ongoing series of complementary ulterior transactions progressing to a well-defined predictable outcome'* (ibid. p. 44, our emphasis). We would add that this progression to a predictable outcome develops via a negative crossed transaction at the social level.

Berne's choice of the word 'game' is consistent with his proclivity for encapsulating complex psychological dynamics within pithy and sometimes amusing terms. Unfortunately, the term 'game' risks implying a certain light-heartedness towards these repetitious, relational dynamics. In fact, the reverse is true: games, sometimes referred to as 'enactments', are often the ways of being in the world that are the most painful and the most destructive to individuals and relationships.

At the social level, transactions are being exchanged on a particular topic while at the ulterior (psychological) level, *and out of Adult awareness* another series of transactions is going on; a series that is dictated by our script beliefs and which will lead to a script-reinforcing 'pay-off' as the ulteriors are acted upon and become overt. Remember the third rule of communication, that the outcome of communication is determined at the psychological level.

Example

Tim, as the result of his experiences with his mother as a child, has a script belief that he is useless and, however hard he tries to please people, he cannot succeed. His wife, Alice, owing to her childhood experiences of her complaining mother, has an Introjected Parent belief that her needs will never really be met. When Tim says, 'I'll make lunch today', Alice replies, 'Thanks, that's great' and

(Continued)

(Continued)

all seems well. The social level transactions are complementary (Adult to Adult) and pleasant. Meanwhile, however, a different set of transactions is going on at the psychological level. Here, Tim is saying, 'I'm trying really hard to please you' (ulterior Child to Parent), while Alice is saying, 'Hmm! You can try but no one has pleased me so far' (ulterior Parent to Child). And sure enough, Tim somehow 'forgets' that Alice hates scrambled eggs, and this is precisely what he places on the plate in front of her. He is shocked when the eggs come flying across the room at him with the accusation, 'You're bloody useless! You never do anything right for me!' (overt Parent to Child) from Alice. In this way, at the end of the game, they both have a 'pay-off': the script beliefs of both of them are confirmed and reinforced. Tim, familiarly, feels hurt, rejected and useless, while Alice feels outraged that her needs, yet again, are unmet. In other words, a game is not played by one person – it is the co-created dynamic of two complementary scripts. Indirectly, their hungers for stimulus, recognition, structure and, as it turns out, incident have been met. The game can be represented transactionally as in Figure 8.1.

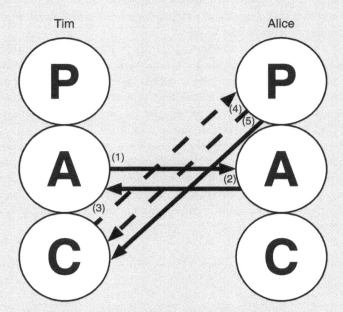

Tim   Alice

(1) Tim (stimulus social level): I'll make lunch today.
(2) Alice (response social level): Thanks, that's great.
(3) Tim (stimulus psychological level): I'm trying really hard to please you.
(4) Alice (response psychological level): You can try, but no one has pleased me so far.
(5) Alice (crossing the transaction at the social level): You're bloody useless!

Figure 8.1 A transactional game diagram

Eric Berne might have put those psychological level messages in a much starker version such as:

TIM: Kick me.
ALICE: I'll get you.

These messages serve to illustrate the idea that games contain our script beliefs and expectations in their purest form. Every time we play a game, we reinforce some limiting belief about ourselves, others and the world and we repeat a pattern of relating. In other words, we fulfil our scripts.

Given how painful and unproductive this can be, one naturally wonders why human beings are drawn to do this. There are many reasons:

- Enacting script has the advantage of being true to our earliest solutions to the problem of making sense of our lives. It repeats a relational dynamic that may be 'hard wired' into our very sense of self. It is an interplay between our relational need or hunger, our early relational experiences and attachments; it is how we found our way through.
- Our script and its manifestation in games enables us to feel that we can make sense of, and manage, the otherwise overwhelming and unpredictable world. Even though it may be painful, we feel in a strange way in charge of things. The familiar can feel reassuring and we can get our needs met at least to a minimal degree.
- Amongst other things, it provides some predictability and structure – the first of our six hungers.
- Further, games involve a high degree of stroke exchange. We have mentioned already that even negative strokes are better than no strokes at all: negative game strokes are sought in the belief that positive, pleasurable patterns cannot be evolved to promote positive stroking.
- As it is played *out of awareness*, the 'pay-off' of a game often comes as a surprise – even a shock. We find ourselves saying 'How have I got here again?' in amazement. So in some measure it meets our need for incident (if not novelty).

But how could this have been any different in the case of Tim and Alice? What are they doing that leads to this familiar outcome? One answer, and a very important factor implicit in all games, is that they are *discounting*: they are, without Adult awareness, ignoring information that could lead to the solution of the problem. At the simplest level, Alice could have told Tim what she wanted for lunch. Similarly, Tim could have asked what she would like. The fact that he 'forgot' that she hated scrambled eggs illustrates another form of discounting. Forgetting, not thinking, acting impulsively, exaggerating, over-generalizing and ignoring our feelings are just some of the ways in which we might discount information that could be used to address issues. Discounting is an unconscious attempt to force someone else to take responsibility for some aspect of our lives without an overt contract so to do. When we are discounting, we ignore our hungers and appropriate ways to satisfy them and are likely to play psychological games instead. If Tim had recognized his hunger for recognition, stimulus and incident at that moment, he could have found positive ways of satisfying those hungers. Likewise with Alice and likewise with ourselves and our clients. The essence of games is that the players are operating 'on automatic' and do not let themselves notice their real needs, which consequently remain unfulfilled.

The transactional diagram (Figure 8.1) for analysing games is very powerful for identifying the ulterior messages in our transactions and the script beliefs that may be driving them. If a client is familiar with the model of ego states, using this diagram to plot the course of a repeating dynamic can be very useful. There are other ways to deconstruct games that focus on different aspects. One of the simplest and most useful ways is to look at the three possible roles we adopt when game-playing, the discounts inherent within these roles and the switch in roles – that often dramatic moment when the covert (and unconscious) becomes overt – which signals that a game has been played. These roles form the three corners of the drama triangle.

The Drama Triangle

The drama triangle was devised by Karpman (1968) as a means of analysing games. Figure 8.2 shows the three possible roles adopted by two or more players.

Victim

Note the use of an initial capital for the game-role Victim. A game-role Victim discounts their own power and perceives themselves to be powerless in situations where this really is not so. An actual victim is powerless in the face of existential circumstances. For example, someone moaning about their lack of space because of their children's untidiness may be adopting the role of a psychological Victim. They are discounting their ability and power to take charge and control the situation. On the

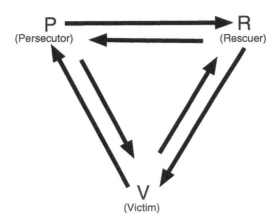

Figure 8.2 The drama triangle (Karpman 1968, reproduced with kind permission)

other hand, someone whose house has just been destroyed by an earthquake would be an actual victim of circumstance. They cannot control an earthquake. The distinguishing feature between these two examples is the level of power they have to change or affect the situation. Even in the wake of an existential crisis such as an earthquake, real victims have the choice of adjusting creatively to the situation by solving the problem of their immediate needs of evacuation, or responding in a Victim role by waiting for others to do all the problem solving. It is the psychological Victim's belief that others are more powerful than them (a 'one-down' position) that keeps them in this powerless role. This is often an I'M NOT OK, YOU'RE OK position. They somehow see themselves as deserving of others taking control of their situation. However, the Victim role can often be the most psychologically powerful of the three roles. Their passivity can be immovable.

Rescuer

Here again, we can make a distinction between an actual rescuer and a game-role Rescuer. An actual rescuer may witness someone being mugged and intervene successfully to save the intended victim. A game-role Rescuer is one who, in order to gain recognition or from a script belief that they must always look after others, uses their perceived superiority (a 'one-up' position) ostensibly to benefit others but simultaneously to keep them powerless. They see the people they want to rescue as NOT OK. They do more than 50 per cent of the work in any situation or take more than their fair share of responsibility. For example, the archetypal Rescuer insists on escorting a blind person across a busy road, oblivious to the fact that the person never intended crossing in the first place. The blind person is left stranded on the wrong side of the road while the Rescuer walks off feeling a little smug and superior. Just as circumstance brings forth real victims, society designates people as real rescuers in the form of social workers, fire-fighters, lifeguards, doctors, coaches, counsellors and so on. Of course, these people may be effective rescuers or ineffective Rescuers.

Persecutor

The Persecutor, like the Rescuer, comes from a 'one-up' position, seeing themselves as OK and others as NOT OK. However, in order to maintain their 'superior' position, instead of 'saving' others, they need to control and belittle them. For example, a white person may make racist remarks about a black colleague in order to secure a 'superior' position and feel OK about themselves. Or one person may order another about, treat them more like an object than a person and criticize them in order to avoid facing their own feelings of inadequacy.

Of course, as we have seen when discussing the Good-enough Parent mode, there is sometimes a legitimate need for one person to control another for that person's well-being or for the safety and well-being of others. Parents, magistrates, teachers, traffic wardens and so on may be required to exercise control of a person's negative behaviour to such ends. Managers and leaders have responsibility for steering their organizations or teams, and may be very conscious of the 'buck' stopping at their desk. It may be, however, that some people in such roles have a psychological need to persecute from a game role in pursuit of their own need to control, not just the behaviour, but the whole person. Describing the Victim role as often the most psychologically powerful may seem a contradiction in terms but, as can be seen, both the Rescuer and the Persecutor are dependent upon a Victim in order to maintain their roles.

Now we have described the three roles involved in the drama triangle, let us see how these are mobilized in the playing of games. We are all capable of playing each role but we will probably have a favourite and predictable role and a pattern in which we move from one particular role to another. We are likely to start a game from one role – probably the one that suits our drivers (the 'I'm OK if I …' script message) most closely – and finish the game in another one. This final role will be the one which produces the pay-off which in turn will confirm the most self-limiting parts of our script. From the complementary transactions which pass between two people (or more), each maintaining their position – albeit subtly – in one corner of the triangle, an unexpected switch in role by one or both players (a crossed transaction) exposes a dramatic conflict of interests or confusion of communication. This may happen within a single set of transactions within a few moments or involve many sets of transactions over a much longer period of time, sometimes years.

The originator of this concept, Steve Karpman, saw how these roles and dramatic switches can be seen not only throughout ordinary human communication but in all forms of dramatization of the human condition, such as fairy tales, plays, myths, legends and so on.

Example

In the fairy tale of Little Red Riding Hood, LRRH's mother could be seen as a Rescuer sending food to LRRH's grandmother. She does not go herself – as is often the case with Rescuers – but sends her daughter, LRRH, to do the deed. In the forest, LRRH meets the wolf who asks where she is going with the food, at which point, LRRH discounts all she ever knew about wolves – as is the case with Victims – and tells all. It is no surprise to us, therefore, that on arriving at grandmother's house, we find that grandmother (Victim) has been eaten by the wolf (Persecutor) who has taken granny's place in bed. When LRRH arrives at her grandmother's, her level of discounting reaches mammoth proportions – as is the wont of Victims – and she fails to notice that grandmother has been replaced by a foul-smelling, hairy creature probably slavering in anticipation of getting his teeth into her – but there we are. She even adds to the anticipatory pleasure of the wolf by remarking upon granny's unusually large ears, nose, eyes and teeth, to show the extent of her discounting abilities; whereupon the Persecutor pounces on the Victim and gobbles her up. Very contented, the wolf falls asleep in the bed. The story illustrates well a sort of sado-masochistic dance that provides the rhythm of game life.

There are several endings to this story, according to which version you were brought up on, but we will use the one with the huntsman who happens to be passing by just at that moment. He (Rescuer/Persecutor) cuts open the sleeping wolf (now Victim) and releases the still-living granny and LRRH. They are still Victims at this point, having waited to be rescued rather than fathoming their own way out. However, they do not stay Victims for long. Soon they switch to being vicious Persecutors as they hit upon the cruel idea of putting stones inside the wolf's gaping stomach before sewing him up again. Once awake, the wolf is destined for a life of heavy indigestion and immobility – probably a very short life indeed. Meanwhile, back on the other side of the forest, we can imagine the Rescuer mother, blissfully ignorant of the bloody state of affairs at Granny's, watching television by the fireside, congratulating herself on the good deed she has done and dreaming of how much she will get in the will.

Leaving the realms of fairy tales, games may, of course, be played within the helping relationship. Although we slightly exaggerate the switches, highlighted by the tenor of their conversation, the following exchange illustrates a not uncommon dance.

Example

A client, Mary, is complaining about her misogynistic and ineffective manager. She shows little emotion as she repeats the same dissatisfactions again and again (Victim). The coach responds with superficial reassurances and messages of sympathy (Rescuer). This continues for some time until Mary, whose hunger for greater recognition, stimulation and incident is not being met by the current transactions, switches role to that of Persecutor by turning on the coach, saying, 'Well, I'm certainly not feeling any better. You're not being any help at all!' The coach, now Victim, vies for the Persecutor role and retorts (in not-so-subtle retaliation), 'I notice that you seem to be expecting someone else to solve the problem. I wonder if you really have any intention to be helped.' Mary switches back to the Victim position, crying, 'Nobody understands me,' but makes a final switch to Persecutor

(Continued)

(Continued)

as she leaves the room, shouting, 'You're no better than my boss!' She ends the game feeling righteously indignant and confirmed in her script belief that all men are useless. The coach ends the game in the Victim position, feeling dejected and ineffectual, as decreed by his script beliefs. The beginning and end moves in this game are shown in Figure 8.3.

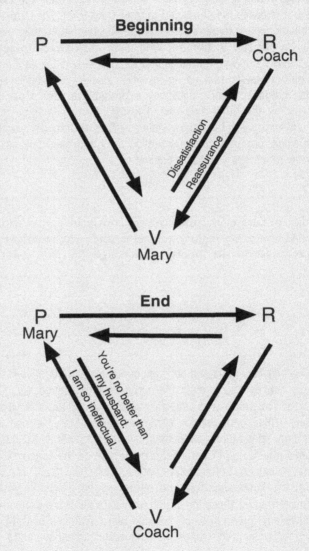

Figure 8.3 Moves around the drama triangle

Degrees of Games

Comparing the story of Little Red Riding Hood with our coaching example, you may realize that games can be played to varying degrees of intensity. Berne suggested that, like burns, there are three degrees of games.

A first degree game can take place in just a few transactions and is signalled by a moment of surprise and discomfort or a vague sense of 'Oh, I didn't mean that to happen.' An example would be the counsellor who plays a brief game of 'Why Don't You … Yes But' with his client, in which he makes two or three helpful suggestions intended to alleviate his client's suffering, to be met by a blank look, a sigh and the comment, 'Yes, I've tried all that'.

A second degree game carries more intense feelings and causes enough pain to ensure an unequivocal confirmation of script beliefs. Berne said that second degree games are those that we would prefer not to play in public.

Example

Harry and Bill arrange to meet in the pub at 7.00 pm each week. Harry consistently comes late. He always apologizes and Bill says it's OK. Bill consistently suggests 7.00 pm and arrives promptly himself, although it is clear that Harry is not going to get there on time. Finally, one night, Bill loses his temper and storms off. He feels abused and disrespected. Harry feels guilty but aggrieved when he later telephones Bill from the pub. He apologizes profusely but cannot understand Bill's 'over-reaction'. It takes them some months to resolve their falling out, a fact they do not mention to their friends.

A third degree game is the most serious and harmful. It ends in an irreversible situation such as a prison sentence, a divorce, a suicide or even murder.

Example

A woman is frequently beaten by her husband. Her friends get to know of her situation and beg her to leave him but she always forgives him. (Here is the standard Persecutor, Victim and Rescuer situation where the roles are genuine as well as part of the game in which the Victim rescues the Persecutor.) However, one night, as she is preparing supper, her husband arrives home violently drunk. As he moves towards her, fists raised, she suddenly feels that she can take no more. Afterwards she cannot remember stabbing him but she supposes that she did.

Naming the Gaming

At the back of his *Games People Play* (1964b), Berne lists 100 games. This is not a fixed list; it can be added to and some in the list may be found to be substantially similar. In fact, many do not contain a switch in game role and should more correctly be referred to as 'racketeering' (English 1976), where two game roles are used to collect familiar strokes by complementary transactions from those roles. Some partners, for example, use racketeering as a basis for their relationship: one person always playing the Rescuer role from an Inadequate Parent mode while the other contentedly or discontentedly plays the Victim role in an Adapted Child mode. Most of the names of the games involve colloquialisms which are self-explanatory and are the words of some of Berne's patients that best sum up the essence of the game. As mentioned earlier, it is Berne's use of such 'down-to-earth' language that has often resulted in his work and TA being seen and rejected as being simplistic, but, as Berne says: 'We prefer playing "Ain't it awful" to "verbalizing projected anal aggression". The former not only has a more dynamic meaning and impact, but it is actually more precise. And sometimes people get better faster in bright rooms than they do in drab ones' (Berne 1976). You will notice that sometimes, identifying the specific game and giving it a name that captures its theme can be a good reminder to oneself. Games typically involve themes of love/care and power. Some of the games overtly concern power and powerlessness. 'Now I've Got You!', 'Kick Me', 'Stupid' and 'Courtroom' could be seen in this light. Other games like 'Now See What You Made Me Do', 'If It Weren't For You' and 'Blemish' have a theme of blaming (often Persecuting from the Victim position), while 'Look How Hard I've Tried', 'I'm Only Trying To Help You' and 'You'll Be Glad You Knew Me' could be seen to contain the theme of dependency and a need to be needed, as the drama triangle tracks the currencies of lovability and caretaking as well as interpersonal power/vulnerability.

The drama triangle is particularly useful in the organizational context for identifying shifts in power, control and competition. Games such as 'Mine's Bigger', 'Now I've Got You', 'Blemish' and 'Courtroom' are fairly common as people fight for power – as well as the more powerless versions such as 'Poor me', 'Harried' and 'Lunchbox'. This last game refers to the phenomenon of bringing your sandwich to the office and working through the lunch hour. We have not explained the other games as we believe that the names themselves – as Berne intended – are self-explanatory.

Application

The notion of these repeating relational dynamics can play a key part in helping people change. Human beings are born in relationship and are shaped and grow in relationship. Relationships are intimately connected to the psychobiological hungers. Therefore, it is frequently our relationships that bring us most joy and most sorrow. Difficulties in relationships are at the heart of many, if not most, issues in the consulting room.

Raising Awareness

The first way that game theory can be useful is in raising clients' awareness about what games are and the place they have in people's lives. What games are they playing? Which role do they take at the beginning and at the end of the games, to what degree are they playing them and how is their script reinforced by such games? These are all areas for exploration with your clients. But, having explored, how do clients stop playing games?

In answer to this last question, given that part of the definition of games is that they are played *without Adult awareness,* by exploration, recognition and naming you are bringing them into Adult awareness. Sometimes, simply being aware of the relational shift through the game roles is the most important thing. However, this does not mean the immediate cessation of game playing. Remember that games are patterns that have been repeated many times throughout our lives (often daily) and are an entrenched part of our script system (see 'The Racket System' in the next chapter), often at a pre- or non-verbal level. It is often only by working through our script beliefs and decisions that we are ready and willing to relinquish our most familiar games. Nonetheless, awareness is an intrinsic and important first step and, in some instances, may be enough to eliminate, transform or lessen the degree of some games.

Working with clients to change any behaviour, including game playing, usually involves three stages (Petruska Clarkson, personal communication, 1981): hindsight, midsight and foresight.

Hindsight

This means being aware after the event that some game has been played, often only when the familiar pay-off feeling or thought is experienced. The game can be usefully analysed in terms of which game was being played and what was its major theme (for example, 'I Was Only Trying To Help', 'Now I've Got You', 'Blemish' or 'Harried') or existential issue (such as power, safety, control, love), which roles adopted, what was being discounted, what hungers were being satisfied and which script beliefs reinforced. It can be given a name – not just one of the standard ones, but a name the client chooses himself because it really sums up the issue for them. It might be useful to draw the transactional diagram and identify the transactions involved in moves of the game and alternative behavioural options can be explored as ways of avoiding future repetition of the game. What could have been said or done differently? How could that particular hunger have been satisfied more constructively (and so on)?

Midsight

At this stage, the client, now familiar with their game analysis, is also familiar with their own 'signals' that a game is being played. They may, for example, recognize their own physiological response at the point the switch is made as 'a sudden sinking feeling in my stomach' and, even at this late stage, avoid the pay-off of bad feeling they usually experience by crossing the transaction with a more Adult response. Better still, they may recognize at an earlier stage that they are playing a game as they experience themselves in their familiar role of Victim, Rescuer or Persecutor and use this knowledge to 'step outside' the drama triangle and, again, address the situation from an Adult perspective, looking at options of the moment.

Foresight

Eventually, the client becomes so familiar with their game patterns that they know how and in which situations they are likely to play them. They can pre-empt playing games by looking, in advance, at creative options for having their needs met or staying out of certain risky situations. By now, they will also be familiar with their 'favourite' game role and can practise the skill for their particular corner (see Choy 1990). The Persecutor needs to become assertive and develop skills of assertiveness and boundary-setting without oppression. The Victim needs to own their vulnerability but learn the skills of thinking and problem solving. The Rescuer learns genuine compassion and caring, for which the skill to be developed is listening.

Game Dynamics in Helping Relationships

The second way in which the theory of games can be useful is their emergence in the relationship itself between practitioner and client. There are several options for responding to games and you will be guided in your choice by the nature of your role and the contract with your client as well as, most importantly, how aware you are that a game is under way. As we have said, games are co-created scenarios that reflect the complementary vulnerabilities and script adaptations of each of the players. Games are the 'here-and-now' manifestations of our relational patterns, often forged in our earliest attachments. The 'job' of the client is to bring himself wholeheartedly to the encounter, with all his proclivities and patterns. The level and degree of the games that emerge will in part be a function of how much the practitioner's vulnerabilities are overlapping. Sometimes, the counsellor or coach is aware of the invitations to racketeering that precede the game, largely because the dynamic is not so familiar to her. Where there is a 'good fit' between client and practitioner, it is often not until after the pay-off that the existence of a game becomes foreground.

We start by looking at instances where the practitioner, perhaps because of how well she knows herself, is aware quite quickly of repetitive dynamics emerging that are skewing the here-and-now meeting. There are many times when it is appropriate to interrupt a game as soon as possible, when the practitioner begins to feel the pull to engage. For example, if the game seems to be a defence against feeling a relational need or hunger, you may decide that identifying that need and helping the client find a way to meet it is most important. Doing something, or inviting your clients to do something, *out of the predictable sequence* will interrupt the usual game pattern and may result in more direct and positive stroke fulfilment. No game can proceed if accounting replaces discounting.

With clients who have some awareness of games and a good working relationship with the practitioner, it can be effective to 'play with' the game and exaggerate the required role in order to 'tease' the client into awareness of the game and where it is going. For example, a client playing 'Ain't It Awful' may give an insightful laugh and move out of the game if the coach plays an extreme Rescuer to their Victim by saying such things as 'My word, that really is awful. In fact, I think that is the most awful story I've ever heard in my life ... and to such a nice person too ...' and so on. Clearly, this response should be used carefully and discriminatingly and only when such 'teasing' will be received constructively as a move out of the game and not as a shaming Persecution.

A practitioner may also choose to play the game in awareness, in order to understand the dynamic better and to see what the pay-off is. This is most likely to be in the early stages of the work in order to identify the game and provide useful current information that can then be analysed. The practitioner, working from Adult, can provide the client with feedback about her feelings at the end of the game, what was going on at the Child level, what switches occurred, and invite similar awareness and reflection in the client. Thus, by the playing of the game, material for exploration and consideration is elicited, whether it be to then work on the game at the behavioural level of looking at options or on the script level of tracing the origins of these familiar roles and feelings. It is vital that this is done in an accepting and compassionate way – 'This is human. This is the best way you know at present of getting your needs met' – rather than a Persecution.

One way of exposing the game (or the invitation to a game) is to confront the discounting always present in games. For example, if someone playing 'Stupid' replies to a question with 'I dunno', the counsellor may move them to accounting for their knowledge by saying, 'And if you did know, what would you say?', which often gets a smile of recognition and a reply to the question. Or, as was once said to one of the authors, 'Well, I'll tell you what to do, but you have to promise in advance that you will follow my advice' (this paradoxical intervention naturally elicited a robust Rebellious Child state).

Similarly, grandiosity and other types of contaminations may be confronted and the game element exposed. Words like 'never', 'always' or 'impossible' can often usefully be reflected back – 'What, never?' – or confronted – 'Wasn't there that time when you...?', 'Have you ever had a similar situation that you managed differently?'

Where clients are familiar with their games but are still at the hindsight or midsight stage, the exposing of the game invitations they are giving can be achieved by such questions as 'If you continue transacting in this way, how will it end?' or 'What is it that you're really wanting when you do this or say this to me?' or 'Just pause and be with yourself at this moment ... what is really going on for you.' The option of being straight about asking for needs to be met may well be served by such interventions as 'Do you have to play "Ain't It Awful"? You can ask for the support you're wanting.', or 'Instead of attacking, could you tell Neil just how angry you feel with him?'

When a client seems really entrenched in a game and where other interventions may not be taken notice of, it may be appropriate for the practitioner to switch roles within the game in order to heighten what is going on. For example, Samantha is again playing a game of 'If It Weren't For Him' (her CEO). In order to emphasize the passive role she is taking and the lack of 'owning' her responsibility, the coach widens the game by adding, 'And that team of yours too and, of course, the terrible way the finance department treats you – how on earth can you be expected to get somewhere in your life with troubles like that?' at which she begins to laugh and eventually to think.

An example of a counsellor switching roles within the game involves Dave, who frequently plays 'Do Me Something' – a Victim in search of a Rescuer. Rather than Rescue, the counsellor chooses to compete for the Victim position by saying, 'Well, I don't know what to do right now, Dave. I'm feeling a bit stuck. I don't know what to suggest.' Dave's efforts to induce the counsellor to Rescue are frustrated by this response and he soon moves into a constructive, problem-solving mode.

Until now, we have been exploring options for addressing the game as the practitioner finds himself aware of the pull to respond to an invitation. This is not always, or even often, the case. In the helping relationship, games emerge and reflect script vulnerabilities of both people. The most interesting moments – sometimes called 'critical moments' (Day et al. 2008) occur when we find ourselves unexpectedly in a mess. At those times, it can be tempting to become very self-critical, but frequently this enmeshment in a game with our clients can be our richest source of information. Some relational patterns are deeply embedded and are not accessible immediately to conscious awareness; our only way of discovering them is as they unconsciously emerge in game dynamics. Our first task is to reflect on how we have got 'hooked' into the game; we need to be aware of our own game moves towards our clients, hence the need for our ongoing supervision and personal counselling. However, the nature of this particular hook is going to tell us something about the nature of the client's vulnerable spots also. What does it mean for the client? How come this particular game has emerged between us with this particular client? Reflecting on what is happening between you through collaborative dialogue is likely to offer two important gifts to the client. One will be a very immediate understanding of the experience of how they bring their script patterns into the present. Exploring the co-created nature of the dynamic helps to deepen understanding and here can be a completely new experience of inquiry and interest rather than blame. The second gift is in the potentially reparative nature of the dialogue. Instead of the game's pay-off leading to script reinforcement and the repeat of old relational patterns, both people stay engaged and committed to repairing and rebuilding the relationship. The client's sense of the coach's or counsellor's open and non-defensive exploring can have the effect of putting a new meaning on an old pattern. In addition, the practitioner's modelling that he can own and survive falling into an old game can be a huge release for the client.

When it becomes evident that a switch has occurred or about to occur, the counsellor or coach will notice in herself the build-up of strong feelings or agitation. She can use this as a signal that a game is going on and inquire into the client's experience; for example, 'What does that mean to you?' or 'You looked very serious then, how are you feeling about what I said?' or 'What just happened between us?' Alternatively, she can take the risk of sharing her own feelings and experiences in order to invite a here-and-now exploration; for example, 'I notice that I'm beginning to feel anxious. I wonder if that is a clue to us about the importance of what you are talking about' or 'I feel frustrated. I wonder if we are getting into something that happens between you and the CEO'. Using these 'parallel processes' or 'out there – in here' dynamics can be very fruitful.

Exercises

Self and Working with Clients

1 We offer here the John James (1973) 'Game Plan' which provides us with a structure to explore the development and playing of a game.

   What keeps happening over and over again in my relationship with X?

   - How does it start?
   - What happens next?
   - And then?
   - How does it end?
   - How do I feel?
   - How do I think X (the other person) feels?

   Using a series of transactional diagrams, plot these transactions sequentially using your answers to the questions according to the originating and receiving ego states respectively.
   At which point did you, out of your awareness, probably send an ulterior message? What was it?
   At which point did you probably hear or receive an ulterior message? What was it?
   How do these messages at the psychological level relate to your script?
   What themes have emerged in your exploration of these transactions?
   In terms of the drama triangle, which role did you start in and which did you end in? Where did the switch of roles occur and why?
   How do your feelings in answer to the last two questions relate to your early childhood experiences? We will be exploring such feelings in the next chapter on 'Rackets'.

2 As another way of becoming more aware of potential game dynamics, practise (with a colleague or client) noticing your inner feelings and responses and the client's body language and metaphors, and commenting on them so that your interventions are solely restricted to the here and now of the consulting room. Notice the dynamic that is created between you.

3 Once you have become familiar with your most common games, you will start to notice your 'favourite' game role (and help your clients to do so). Practise the skills of your corner identified by Choy (1990), described above.

CASE STUDY: A COACH'S STORY

Before their sixth and final session, Anita reflected on some of the tasks she wanted to address. In addition to continuing the coaching, she planned to spend some time on the process of ending: accounting for the work that had been done and the changes made, acknowledging the loss of the coaching relationship and all that would mean in terms of the supportive space for reflection, planning for future problems and discussing where Gunther could get support from colleagues.

However, Gunther started the session immediately by talking about his personal life. Privately Anita wondered whether he was empowered to do so by their restating the boundary of their relationship at the previous session. Gunther had noticed that with his children he had the habit (Inadequate Parent mode) of giving too much leeway until sometimes he exploded in anger and then felt enormously guilty. Also, his wife sometimes complained that he left the boundary-setting to her and didn't support her. Anita helped him think about that pattern. They diagrammed it first using ego states and then the drama triangle. With the latter it was easy to see that he switched from Rescuer to Persecutor (passing briefly through Victim as he felt unrecognized and impotent). The ego states diagram was not quite so easy to plot. It was clear that, like with his team, he started in IP mode – being overly accepting when his children pushed over the boundaries. But the anger he felt and expressed afterwards, while it was Parent mode, did not feel like Parent ego state. It felt like Child. Gently Anita explored exactly how he felt when he began to get angry. He answered 'disrespected, impotent, not important'. She pushed for a word to describe his emotions. After some inward reflection he said 'Furious. Absolutely furious – and humiliated – and scared'. He became slightly tearful as he began to recall some painful incidents from his schooldays when he had not known how to stick up for himself and his 'Always act kindly and correctly' Parent messages were no help to him. He re-felt his old emotional conclusion that he was on his own and that he would never 'make it'. Then suddenly a light began to dawn on his face as he realized that he was projecting the faces of school bullies on to his two little girls – aged five and four! It was the twenty-first century and he was reacting as if he was a thirteen-year-old. He realized that with his children – and indeed, he reflected thoughtfully, with his colleagues and reports – he not only had actual personal power, he had positional power. He was the father and what he said was law!

Anita explained the idea of 'missing skills' relating to the game roles (see above) and Gunther identified two things. First, what had been missing from his Rescuer role was listening to the ideas, thoughts, feelings and needs of his team and of his children and wife – listening and then negotiating. Second, what had been missing totally from his repertoire – other than in a Persecutory outburst of temper – was the Potency of the third corner. This is what he had been working on so effectively over the previous months. They began to discuss what really effective assertive leadership looked like. Anita shared the findings of Suriyaprakash (2009), whose research on transformational leadership showed a need for all functional modes of ego state, whereas traditional leadership tended to involve only the controlling function of the Goodenough Parent and the Rebellious mode of the Child. Gunther saw that he needed both transformational and traditional styles in his leadership. He did some role plays with Anita, practising what he could say in Adult to Adult mode when he wanted to assert his authority, while being ready to employ and listen to the other modes. They discussed the sorts of creative behaviour he would like to see in himself and the team.

Before they left the subject, Anita stressed the importance of using his nurturing GP function internally. He needed to develop the habit of listening to and speaking kindly to his own Child feelings also. Gunther felt touched at this and willingly chose a couple of phrases to say to himself (in his mother tongue, German) when he was getting scared or upset.

Then the time came to begin goodbyes. They were to meet once more in a 'three-way conversation' with the HR director, who had asked Gunther to join Anita and her in discussing how the merger had been going generally, and what further might be needed from HR. The date had been planned some time earlier, and Gunther smiled at her as he said that there was no need for discussion from his point of view. Ladli had said that she had already noticed a difference in the way his team was performing. He thought maybe that Ladli wanted to make some contact with Anita.

Together, they named the insights and changes that Gunther had made. Anita was careful to let him do most of the talking – sometimes even disingenuously asking questions like 'Oh, and how did you manage that?' so that he could fully own and put into words what he had learned. Gunther described his increased confidence and options in his leadership style and said that he saw this more positive energy mirrored in the team, who were working more boldly and effectively together. The merger seemed to have gone well.

Coach and client exchanged appreciations for each other, and then Anita asked him to think about what he would be losing when the coaching came to an end – not just the coaching itself, but other things. It was important to account for the significant things, and think about other ways of meeting the needs in the future. Readily, he identified how much he appreciated the 'time out', the opportunity to reflect and listen to himself. It was so rare to have that these days. And he realized that he had also really enjoyed the learning of new ideas and models. It took him back to his early days of doing the MBA. Spontaneously he asked for some suggestions of books he could read or courses he could attend. He was also happy to think about ways he could set up a network of colleagues for peer support and action learning – as well as some games of squash.

Warmly and with regret, they finally said goodbye and agreed to see each other again at the three-way meeting.

9

Rackets: maintaining scripts in the internal world

'Racket' may seem a strange word to use to describe what is, in fact, an intrapsychic or internal process linked with behaviour. Eric Berne, with his penchant for colloquial terms – in this case borrowed from the criminal underworld – coined the term because of its connection with the expression 'protection racket', a system whereby a person pays in order to be allowed to preserve the relative safety of their situation. A psychological racket works in the same way. It is the means by which we support our script, which feels like self-protection, a way of keeping safe. In other words, we maintain the beliefs about ourselves, others and the world despite evidence to the contrary. In this way, we preserve the status quo and, in so doing, pay for it by limiting our lives.

When Berne and his colleagues first talked about a racket (see e.g. 1964b) they usually described it as a feeling. This feeling may be summed up as the adapted, negative feeling which is most common to us at times when we are feeling bad about ourselves or life in general. We all have a familiar and adapted bad feeling which we tend to 're-run' whenever we experience stress or difficulty. You have probably been in a stressful situation where you cannot understand why others are not responding with the same feeling. If your racket feeling is, for example, fear, you will respond fearfully to the situation. But others have their own racket feelings, so Bob responds to the same situation with anger, while Pavinda responds with sadness. These are their familiar bad feelings and they will perceive them as justifiable and appropriate to the situation just as much as you perceive your own.

Reading the above, it may seem as if we perversely choose to cling to limiting, possibly destructive attitudes and ideas, but, of course, we do not do this deliberately. Much of what we believe is not properly in our conscious awareness. It influences our lives without our realizing. There are many reasons why we might seem to want to confirm our scripts, however negative they may be. As we have already seen, scripts are decided upon under great pressure from our childhood environments and experiences. They usually seem to us to be inescapable if we want to stay in our needed relationships. Furthermore, as we mentioned in Chapter 6, human beings have a great need to provide structure and order to their world and scripts fulfil this need. If we can maintain our script we may feel safer; life is more predictable and secure if we repeat the same situations again and again. At a very deep level, we can feel extremely frightened at the thought of change. A racket, therefore, is the active, internal process of feeling and thinking along with external behavioural manifestations by means of which, outside our awareness, we screen out anything that does not fit our script beliefs, re-experience feelings we have had many times before and confirm for ourselves that our beliefs are true. It is the here-and-now moment-by-moment repetition of script experience.

Example

Part of John's script belief, based on his experiences as a child, is that the world is a bad place where people are out to 'get' him. When he sees someone passing his front door he feels suspicious and scared. He thinks, 'I bet that man has come to check whether there's anyone in before he tries to burgle me.' He spends the next few hours feeling nervous as he looks out from behind the curtain, having somehow failed to notice that the man, finding the right number, calls at the house next door, to be greeted like the long-lost brother he actually is. In this way, John 'protects' his beliefs and feelings about others and the world and, though suspicious and scared, paradoxically, feels 'secure' by making both people and life predictable. His filtering out of information that contradicts his expectations is called '*redefining*' (see, for example, Schiff et al. 1975), which has several elements. John *discounts* (ignores or minimizes) the existence or significance of some aspects of the situation, such as the stranger's approaching the next-door house, while exaggerating the significance of others – his looking up at the house numbers (in TA this exaggeration is called *grandiosity*). At the same time John's fantasies and imagination run wild as he over-generalizes his script beliefs.

Example

Mary's script belief is that she is incompetent and, therefore, that others do not respect her opinions. When she receives an invitation to present her ideas to the executive board, she tells herself that no one will listen to her and ends up feeling so miserable that she decides not to go. She calls in sick that day, feeling a mixture of anxious and resentful. Thus, at the price of a day of misery, Mary 'protects' her script beliefs about herself and others without having to risk their being confirmed or disproved by actuality.

These two examples illustrate how it is what we think and feel that determine and reinforce our beliefs, not what actually happens around us. Our beliefs, in turn, create a 'frame of reference' within which we interpret or *redefine* what happens around us and repeat our familiar thoughts and feelings, leading to behaviour that feeds back into our frame of reference. Thus the racket involves feelings, beliefs, sensations, memories, imagination and behaviour, all of which create the expected outcome.

Rackets and 'Real' Feelings

In an article entitled 'The substitution factor: rackets and real feelings', Fanita English (1971; see also 1972) added considerably to our understanding of rackets. She describes clearly how a person might learn to choose any particular feeling as a racket. She suggests that in every household there are some feelings that are allowed and encouraged and others that are forbidden. Gradually, the child will learn to feel the ones that seem acceptable. Different feelings may be encouraged or discouraged in girls and boys even within the same family. For instance, Bob in his high-chair throws his food on the floor in a rage. His parents smile and say, 'Oh, that's it, Bob, show it what for!' However, when Bob falls down, hurts himself and cries, his parents say, 'Come on Bob, big boys don't cry!' If this sort of thing happens often enough, Bob will learn to feel anger whenever there is a difficult or stressful situation and repress his sad feelings. He maintains his own version of a 'Be Strong' driver by substituting anger for sadness.

Pavinda, on the other hand, receives lots of cuddles and stroking for crying. 'Come on, come and sit on daddy's knee. Daddy's little girl is sad, poor little thing,' says her father. But it is a different matter when she is angry or shouts for what she wants: 'That's not nice,' she is told. Thus Pavinda learns to feel sad as a response to any difficult or stressful situation, even when anger would be more appropriate. This gender-bound scripting of feeling rackets is common. You probably know men who find it difficult to show if they are sad and several women who, when they start to be angry, seem inexplicably to dissolve into tears. These rackets are often visible in the work place and can interfere with a person's ability to demonstrate all-round leadership skills.

Another way of developing a racket as a substitute is through the sort of attributions we talked about in Chapter 7. Whenever Nigel showed strong feelings as a boisterous three-year-old, his parents said, 'He's tired'. Often they would put him in his room for a rest. His mother often complained of being tired – and no wonder when you think of all the energy she was putting into not showing her feelings either. Nigel grew up having his experience labelled 'tired' and he began to label himself as 'tired', too, whenever he felt upset about something. Pretty soon he really started to feel tired. Now he is the man who often gets on your nerves by answering your question 'How are you?' with the inevitable, 'Absolutely exhausted at the moment'.

English's article therefore highlights the way racket feelings can be learnt to replace what she calls 'real' feelings. Of course, racket feelings are real, too, and hurt every bit as much. What English means is that we do not express the original feeling but cover it with a more acceptable familiar feeling. So how can we tell the difference between racket feelings and original feelings? For instance, what is the difference between 'real' sadness and racket sadness? There are some clues. The 'real' original feeling will be associated with something that is happening (or has just happened) in the present. This may seem an obvious thing to say, but, if you think about it, you will realize how much time we spend feeling about things from the past or in the future rather than feeling what is happening in the present. Racket feelings are almost always associated with a thought that links our present moment to the past or future. That thought will go something like, 'Oh, I expect it will all go wrong' or 'Here we go again' or 'Why am I always so ...' or 'It just goes to show that ...' or 'I wish that ...' and so on. The original or 'real' feeling is not associated with any thinking or belief about self in the world, other than an awareness of an event: for example, 'Tom isn't here for my presentation to the board and I feel sad' or 'Patrick forgot to buy the sausages and I feel annoyed'. On the other hand, a racket feeling might be associated with thoughts such as 'Tom isn't here for my presentation. I expect he doesn't want to be here because he thinks I'm boring. I feel sad because nobody appreciates me' or 'Patrick forgot to buy the sausages. You can't rely on anybody to do things for you. Nobody will ever look after me. I feel cross.'

In these last two examples, the racket feeling is the same as the 'real' feeling, but the *quality* of the feeling is different. A 'real' feeling is usually felt quite intensely and, once expressed, dissipates as the person moves on to the next present moment of living. This is not to say that feelings only last for one moment. If somebody I love dies, I will be sad quite frequently for, perhaps, the next several years. However, this sadness will come in waves as I think about the person and how much I miss her. I will feel sad, cry for a while and then feel better for a while, until the next time. Racket sadness, however, seems to 'drizzle on' and is not relieved by its expression. Your client who comes along to the session and weeps quietly from beginning to end is very probably demonstrating racket sadness.

Another indication of a racket as opposed to a 'real' feeling is the response of others. In the case of 'real' feelings, witnesses feel relief as they observe these feelings being expressed, whereas, in the presence of another's racket feelings, they may well end up feeling manipulated and/or frustrated. Anger as a 'real', here-and-now feeling will be clear and probably quite brief, while racket anger will tend to be associated with ongoing resentment, bitterness, comparison, bullying or blaming. Similarly, 'real' fear will be connected with the present moment and bring about action to face and deal with the danger, while racket fear may take the form of anxiety, depression or nervous exhaustion and persist for long periods.

As a rule of thumb, 'real' feelings tend to be wetter and hotter than racket feelings! When a person is experiencing 'real' sadness, tears flow, their body temperature rises, their face colours and they often have a runny nose. Racket sadness, however, tends to leak out damply in a much cooler way. Similarly, 'real' anger tends to be hot and sweaty, with an increase in saliva, while racket anger may take the form of cold resentment devoid of any noticeable rise in temperature or wetness.

Happiness, of course, can also be a racket. If it is developed in the same way as any other racket, a person can learn to 'look on the bright side' of any situation and deny their sadness, anger or fear. Pollyanna is a classic example of someone with a happy racket. 'Real' joy is, as with the other feelings, related to something in the here and now and often manifested in heightened skin colour and other physiological signs, such as a brightening of the eyes. It also tends to be infectious. A racket happiness may seem just as loud and expansive but has an empty quality. When it is being used to 'rise above' something, it will be accompanied by many rationalizations and platitudes: for example, 'Everything is for the best in the best of all possible worlds', as Pangloss assures the eponymous Candide in Voltaire's story (1759).

Again, this is not to say that what the person is feeling does not feel very real to them. The term 'racket' should not be used accusingly or pejoratively but rather as a means of understanding to help clients get to grips with their 'real' feelings. Clients may need to have their racket feelings heard and understood before they are ready to risk uncovering the 'real' feeling that was not allowed in their family when they were young. This, of course, is our eventual aim and a vital part of the process if the client is to get 'out of script'. It thus becomes important for the practitioner to ask herself, 'Which feeling might this be replacing?' and inquiring of the client 'What else might you be feeling?' in order to find ways of safely encouraging and allowing that original feeling to be expressed.

Stamps

Eric Berne (1964a) writes of collecting racket feelings like emotional 'trading stamps': rather like the stamps that used to be given at shops or petrol stations (nowadays we might talk about 'loyalty card' points). With actual trading stamps, the idea is that, for a certain amount spent, a stamp is collected and stuck in a book. When the book is full it can be exchanged for a small gift; or many books full of stamps can be collected for a larger one. Berne suggests that we have a similar psychological book or collection of books. Every time something happens in life that we feel upset by, we repeat the script-associated beliefs to ourselves and collect one racket feeling to hold on to like a trading stamp. When our psychological book is full, after days, months, sometimes years of collecting, we can 'cash it in' by doing something that will really further our scripts and invariably hurt ourselves.

As in shops, where the sooner you exchange, the smaller the pay-off, so it is with psychological trading stamps. A few stamps may be traded in for an argument or a sulk, whereas volumes being cashed in may result in an industrial tribunal, a divorce, suicide or murder: in other words, our final script pay-off. Stamps may be cashed in with the person who is seen as the major source of their collection or might be deflected onto an unsuspecting victim. For example, a husband may have collected many angry and resentful stamps from games played with his wife, yet, having had a further row with her over breakfast that day, cashes them in by having a shouting match with the traffic warden who has booked his illegally parked car or a staff member for a small mistake in her report.

Example

Henry had a belief that to be angry was 'wrong'. When he was a child, his mother sent him to his room for hours any time he was cross or demanding. He would sit in his room feeling resentful and abused, but he soon learnt to be outwardly compliant. Later in his life, at work, his boss frequently undermined his position by contradicting him in front of the staff and by making decisions over his head. Each time this happened Henry thought, 'I'd better not make a fuss' and experienced his racket feeling of silent resentment. After this had happened 50 times and Henry had collected 50 stamps of smouldering resentment, he 'cashed them in' by losing his temper with his boss, shouting at him publicly and calling him abusive names. He was fired instantly, which confirmed to his own satisfaction that he should not express his anger as this leads to punishment.

Example

Dolly's racket was guilt, which helped to support her script belief that she should never get her needs met as others' needs were more important. Thus she never asked for what she wanted from her partner. This meant that she rarely got to choose the film they saw, the food they ate, the furniture they sat on and so on. Each time she put up with something she did not want, she felt a moment's crossness, but then felt guilty for being so mean and selfish. After a year of collecting guilt stamps she was ready to 'cash in'. In her case, it was for depression.

Clearly, there are many different rackets and many different ways of 'cashing in'. For one person it may be having a row, for another a sulk and for another an anxiety attack. A really big 'cash-in' could be leaving a relationship or getting ill or even committing suicide. Again, it is important to remember that we do not do this deliberately and consciously. Our drive to confirm our scripts is not in our awareness. The work of the helping relationship is to bring into awareness the means by which we may be maintaining our script, our racket feelings and the stamps we may be collecting, in order that we may make more autonomous and life-enhancing decisions. In our work as counsellors, coaches or health professionals we can also bear in mind that while rackets and stamps are descriptions of intrapsychic processes – in other words, how someone maintains his script beliefs in his inner world – they are inevitably relational. Originally the internalization of external transactions, people are moved to recruit others to be involved. Consequently, we as practitioners may get drawn into games and racketeering in our work – especially if we have a complementary vulnerability in our scripts. Holtby (1979) describes interlocking racket systems where couples' script vulnerabilities provide the trigger to each others' rackets.

The substitute nature of the racket means that we can be useful to our clients also by monitoring carefully our responses to our client's behaviour and narrative and using them as a signal for where to inquire more deeply into their experiences. Not only might we find ourselves unaccountably unmoved by a client's distress, which may indicate a racket, but alternatively we may find ourselves feeling a strong, unfamiliar feeling, which may mean that we have 'picked up' our client's denied feeling.

The Racket System

Richard Erskine and Marilyn Zalcman (1979) developed a way of understanding how people maintain their rackets. We have made additions to Erskine and Zalcman's original theory, which are included in Figure 9.1. This illustrates in diagrammatic form the way in which a person, in script, enters into a self-reinforcing, closed system of beliefs, feelings, perception and behaviour.

On the left of Figure 9.1 are listed the beliefs and decisions formed in child-hood and at later, stressful moments in life. At the bottom of this column is written 'Repressed feelings/needs'; we think that it may also be a whole experience that is repressed, including thoughts, feelings, needs and – an area which is often overlooked – actions (there is evidence that the 'interrupted gesture' of repressed action process (see for example Ogden et al. 2006) can be hugely script forming). The arrowed line shows the self-reinforcing nature of this part of the system, the beliefs maintaining the repression and vice versa. As a result of these beliefs, a person thinks, feels and behaves in a particular way at any moment, shown in the central column as observable behaviour, reported internal experiences (feeling and sensation) and scripty fantasies (of what will happen). From this position, the person is likely to bring about a real or imagined repetition of the original experiences which caused them to take on these beliefs in the first place. But even if the person does not have the reinforcing experience, they can achieve the same effect by remembering all the times in the past when they did. These 'reinforcing memories', including those misinterpreted by discounting, are shown in the right-hand column. The arrowed line around the diagram shows the self-perpetuating nature of the whole system.

So when does a person get into their racket system? It is to be hoped that we are not in self-limiting script all the time. However, when something happens in our lives which touches on the 'forbidden area' of denied feelings, thoughts or memories, we can escape from the forbidden into the familiar and permissible area of the racket. We can then stay in our racket system until something happens to interrupt or interfere with it. In offering a helping relationship, we are, more awarely, aiming to interrupt or interfere with our clients' racket systems in order to help them out of their script. We will now, in the section on application, look at ways in which a practitioner can help a client interrupt their racket system in order to live more autonomously.

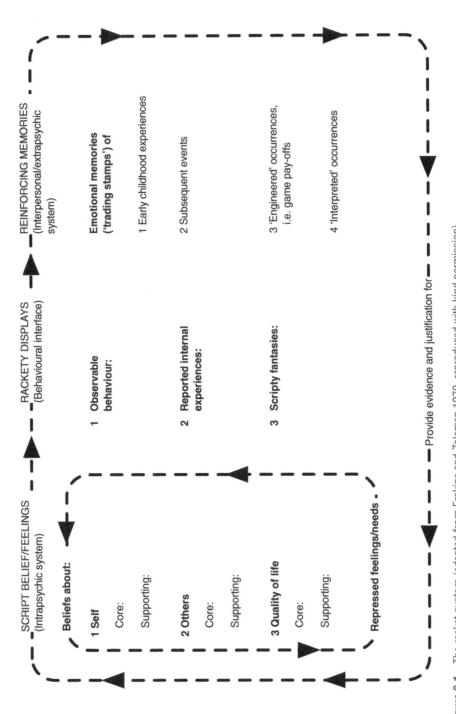

Figure 9.1 The racket system (adapted from Erskine and Zalcman 1979, reproduced with kind permission)

Application

One of the encouraging aspects of working with a client's racket system is that changing just one element of the system can have an effect upon the whole. Consequently, there are many ways of intervening in the here and now, at any point in the racket system, which can invite clients to change the way they are experiencing their lives. This may bring about a change in their script. However, to ensure script change, a person must actually change the beliefs about self, others and the world and, for this, deeper work is sometimes necessary. This section first outlines some ways of intervening; in the second part, some work with a client will be described in which the origins of the racket are explored as a means to more profound and lasting change.

As you start to be aware of your own and your clients' rackets, you will notice that different people tend to emphasize different parts of the system. For instance, when they are 'in their racket', some people are most aware of the emotion they are feeling, while some are more aware of fantasizing about what is going to happen or remembering similar past occasions. Some experience most strongly a body sensation like a sinking feeling in the pit of their stomachs. Others manifest a typical piece of behaviour, such as pacing, increased smoking, and so on. The first task is to raise awareness of the link between this figural 'symptom' and the other components by inquiring into the client's experience. Then he can be invited to change something.

Often the most useful place in the racket system to intervene is not that which is the usual focus of the client's attention. Those who are most aware of their emotion – sadness, anger and so on – may be best helped by being asked to think about what their feeling means and what they need to do about it. Those who are aware of a bodily sensation or a typical behaviour can be invited to plan ahead. What outcome do they want? How will they be when they have achieved it? How can they get there? People whose racket is experienced chiefly in thinking about what has happened may be most usefully invited to be aware of their feelings. For example, they may be asked to breathe deeply, notice their sensations within their body and to express the feelings of which they become aware. Those who are fantasizing about the future may need to be brought back to the present. For example, they may be asked what they are doing right now to bring about the situation and what they could be doing differently. They may be asked to sit differently or act differently at that moment. For example, the floor-pacing client may be invited to lie down on the floor and think from this position. We invite the reader to be flexible in finding ways of intervening, always remembering that the system can be altered by a change at any point. With some clients, it can be useful to draw up a simplified version of their racket system with them in order to better understand their contribution to the present circumstances and invite them to choose which element they could, in the first instance, most easily change.

The following example shows a counsellor working with a client to explore her racket system and underlying feeling. Some 'trace-back' work, where the racket is traced back to its childhood roots, is also undertaken.

Example

During a group session Liz withdraws and loses touch with the other group members. When questioned about this, she says that she thinks everyone is cross with her and she does not want to take up their time. Everyone reassures her that they are not cross and ask her why she thought such a thing. She explains that earlier on she made a comment to which no one responded. She immediately started to tell herself that she had 'taken too much time' and that they were cross. She cheers up at the reassurance and starts to join in again. However, this is not an isolated incident. Liz's withdrawal becomes a regular occurrence. Liz begins to understand that it is a pattern. The triggering factor is her not receiving attention when she wants it. Very often, this is when she has not said or done anything to indicate that she needs something. The counsellor begins to explore Liz's internal process with her by gentle questioning.

COUNSELLOR: What are you saying to yourself when you withdraw like that? (*Here, though the counsellor could have started to work with any part of the system, she first explores the thought process behind the rackety display.*)

LIZ: I'm not thinking anything ... yes, I'm saying, 'I'm not here.'

COUNSELLOR: And how do you feel saying that?

LIZ: I'm empty, I'm ... I'm not feeling anything. Somewhere over there is someone that feels (*points away from her*) but I don't. I'm empty. I don't feel anything. I'm dead inside (*her eyes fill with tears as she contacts, quite spontaneously, a repressed underlying feeling*).

COUNSELLOR: You look as if you are very sad about feeling dead inside.

LIZ: I am ... (*cries*).

COUNSELLOR: You're hurting so much that you have to go dead inside.

Liz cries for some time. She is already interrupting her racket system by expressing her really sad feelings and not replacing them with numb withdrawal. It is only later that the counsellor continues the exploration.

COUNSELLOR: So we have learned that, when you withdraw like that and think that people are cross with you, you are really deeply sad.

LIZ: Yes, I'm astonished. I thought I was empty and out of touch but I realize that I really hurt when I think people want me to shut up.

COUNSELLOR: You think they want to shut you up?

LIZ: Yes, I'm a nuisance. I'm in the way.

COUNSELLOR: So you believe you're in the way. And what about other people, what else do you believe about them? (*Exploring beliefs.*)

LIZ: (*long pause; eventually, in a monotone*) They hate me. They wish I wasn't here. I take up too much time.

COUNSELLOR: So what do you decide to do when you're thinking all that?

LIZ: Nothing. I do nothing. I just go dead.

COUNSELLOR: Have you ever felt like that before – dead and empty, not looking at anyone, not moving? Do you remember being like that when you were little? (*Exploring the reinforcing memories.*)

LIZ: (*stares at counsellor*) I've always been dead.

COUNSELLOR: But when you made yourself go dead ... can you remember times ...?

LIZ: So often ... so often ... I say to my mother ... but she is so ... she says, 'Get out ... shut up', she says, 'Oh, go away do just go away' and she is so sad ... I say, 'I'm sorry mummy, what can I do for you? I want you to be happy (*Liz cries*) ... What can I do?' (*cries deeply*).

COUNSELLOR: And mummy?

LIZ: She's angry. She says, 'I SAID GO AWAY DIDN'T I ... I TOLD YOU ... GO AWAY!' (*she begins to tremble, then stops*). So I go.

COUNSELLOR: You go. You leave quiet and empty.

LIZ: That's right. That's what I did. That's what I do now. When I want something, when I want someone to like me, I just switch off and think that I shouldn't be here or, sort of, that I'm not here. And I go dead and empty.

COUNSELLOR: When really you feel very sad.

LIZ: Yes.

COUNSELLOR: So do you think you could do something different in those moments when you start to switch off?

LIZ: (*pause*) Well, I guess I could speak to someone.

COUNSELLOR: That would be different. Will you do it? (*Contracting for behavioural change.*)

LIZ: Yes, I will.

Clearly there is more work to be done. Liz needs not only to speak to someone, but also to ask for the attention she needs, to believe that she is wanted and that her needs are welcomed by others. She also needs to change the decision to 'go dead and empty' which she made at the time of her mother telling her to go away. However, this is a very important piece of work for her and the start of major changes in her relationships. At a subsequent session, Liz draws up her racket system (see Figure 9.2). The work links directly to an analysis of her script matrix where the injunction 'Don't exist' from her mother produced the decision by Liz to act as if she was dead in terms of attracting attention and seeming acceptable.

The concept of stamps was not used in the work with Liz but was very useful to another group member.

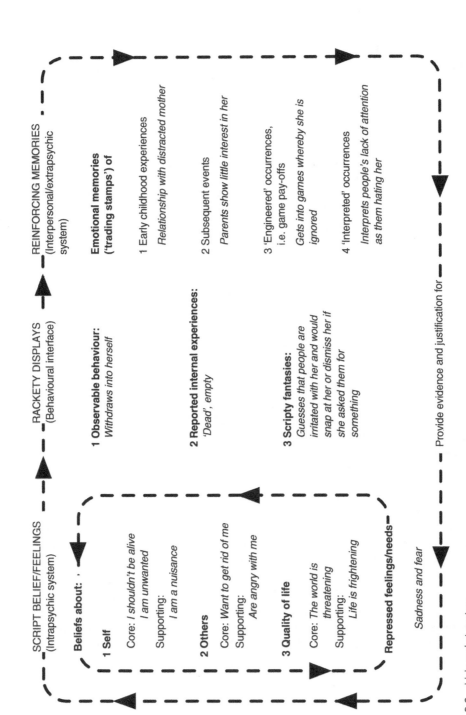

Figure 9.2 Liz's racket system

Example

Daljit was asked by a group member if he would give her a lift home. He agreed. On several further occasions, he gave group members lifts and seemed happy to do so. One day, one of the members was asking for contributions to buy a birthday cake for Chris. Daljit refused and, rather pointedly, said that he spent all his money on petrol. The group confronted him immediately on being mean. Daljit became self-righteous and the group ended on an uncomfortable note.

The following week, the counsellor explored with Daljit his agreeing to give people lifts. He revealed that he actually appreciated the time on his own after groups but that his script belief was that this would be selfish when others had wants and needs too. His mother always told him to 'Please People'. So he had agreed to the lifts and, each time he had done so, he stuck a 'Hard done by' stamp in his book and ignored his own need. After the tenth (or the twentieth or the thirtieth) time, Daljit had filled a complete martyr's book of stamps and felt justified in being 'mean' with his money. This realization helped to identify the work Daljit needed to do in the group on his scripted 'Please People' behaviour and its associated thoughts and feelings, particularly concerning the origins of such behaviour in relation to his mother. However, a temporary solution was agreed upon in the group by Daljit contracting to take time to think whether he really wanted to do something for someone else before responding.

Exercises

Self

1 *Stamps:* remember a time recently when you held back from saying what you were really thinking and feeling.

- What would you have liked to say?
- What did you say or do instead?
- What reason did you give yourself?
- What feeling did you have as you told that reason to yourself?
- After you have collected enough of those feelings, how might you 'cash in' your stamps?
- How might you justify doing it?
- Now work out what you need to do differently to avoid 'stamp collecting'.

2 *Racket feelings:* imagine that you are looking for a gift for a close friend whose birthday is tomorrow. You have been searching for some time for that special gift. In the window of a shop that sells hand-made articles, you see something you know this friend would really enjoy. It is expensive but, as it is such a perfect gift for your friend, you decide to go ahead with the purchase. The shop has just shut,

but you have so fallen in love with this birthday gift that you are determined to return tomorrow, as soon as the shop opens, which will still leave time for you to wrap it and take it to your friend's birthday breakfast. Picture the next day: there you are hurrying to the shop and, now you have arrived, you go inside. The article is still there. You lift it up to see it more closely. On the back of the article is a label saying, 'Sold to M. Smith. To be collected'. How do you feel? What emotions and sensations to you experience? Is there another feeling later? If you had two feelings, it is likely that the first was your natural, spontaneous feeling that was quickly repressed and replaced by the substitute racket feeling. Was this second feeling (or the first if there wasn't a second) one that you commonly have when things 'go wrong'? Notice how this feeling is accompanied by thoughts and fantasies. What do you say to yourself about life, about other people, about yourself? What do you do? Using the blank racket system framework (Figure 9.1), see how much of your racket system you can complete from the answers to these questions.

3   *Further exploring:* remember a recent time when you believed the worst about yourself and imagine yourself there. How do you experience your racket most vividly – by a feeling, thoughts, bodily sensations, actions or fantasies? Go through the following questions and notice which you find the most useful when you are in this racket:

- What are you doing to contribute to the situation?
- What could you do differently?
- How are you feeling (emotions)?
- What do you need?
- How could you get what you need?
- What has been helpful to you in the past that you could use now?

4   With a colleague or friend (with their permission) practise listening to their story 'from your ears downwards'. In other words, pay attention not to the story but to the feelings, bodily sensations and resonances it evokes. Notice when you feel strongly and when you feel disengaged, when you are curious and when uninvolved. Experiment with sharing your responses with your partner, as in 'I am feeling very sad as you say that', 'I don't feel so engaged now and I wonder if there is something else you are feeling', 'I am noticing a tight sensation in my stomach'.

5   Extend the previous exercise by noticing your partner's body language and feeding back what you have noticed. For example, you may say, 'As you spoke about your boss, you sounded flat and deflated but I noticed your fists were clenched' or 'As you talk I notice that your shoulders are slumped and your voice low'. You may discover bodily script signals or alternatively the trace of a repressed underlying feeling.

Working with Clients

1   Explain to your client what a stamp is and invite them to do the first exercise above.
2   Choose a client you have known for some time. What is their racket feeling? (You will probably be able to answer this quite easily.) If it is appropriate, next time they

are feeling it, invite them to remember when they have had the feeling before. Can they remember feeling it when they were a child? What are they believing about themselves when they are feeling it? Gently ask the questions that will elicit the racket system and help the client to notice the reinforcing nature of the pattern. It may be appropriate to draw a diagram of the racket system.

3   Experiment with the list of questions in the third exercise above.

4   If your client likes models and ideas, draw up the racket system with them, when they are talking about a stuck situation at work or at home.

5   When you have practised nos. 4 and 5 above with a partner, integrate this sort of here-and-now commenting into your work with clients. Be aware, this can be both exciting and immediate and also quite challenging to clients, so be ready to be empathic to their reactions.

6   When an organization is involved, reflect on what might be its 'racket'. Sometimes the character of the whole organization can contain a common racket feeling – blaming, feeling over-worked, getting hysterical, being resentful – and so on. Help your client to design an antidote phrase to counteract it whenever she starts to express it – or hears a colleague. The word 'yet' is a surprisingly good interrupter, as in: Worker A (in resigned resentful tone): 'I suppose they haven't fixed the light'; Worker B: (brightly): 'Not yet'.

CASE STUDY: A COACH'S STORY

Despite the rich conversation at the last coaching session, Anita found that – in a rather familiar way – she was approaching the meeting with HR with some anxiety. She often felt like that when she was in situations where she thought she might be evaluated. It felt to her like a meeting with the headmistress – being called in to discuss the report of the science teacher, who had complained of her inattention in class. Wryly Anita recognized that here again was her familiar racket. It seemed to 'kick in' particularly at times of endings, when she would begin to worry that she hadn't done enough, hadn't been good enough and was going to get a 'telling off'. Taking her own advice of ensuring an internal nurturing voice, she soothed herself by reassuring herself that, in reality, the work had gone well. Not for the first time, she wondered why that particular memory plagued her at times like this. She could remember the name of the science teacher and how he had shouted, and the cold frostiness of the headmistress as she predicted that Anita would 'never come to anything'. She even remembered going back to her friend's house and ... with a shock she suddenly understood why that particular racket feeling was associated with endings. That morning, so long ago, she had got a message that her best friend was never coming back to the school. She had got sick and was in hospital until the end of term. Then they were to go to different schools the following year. Anita had been in a state of loss and mourning when she had been staring into

(Continued)

(Continued)

space during the science lesson. 'How complex we humans are,' she murmured to herself as she allowed herself fully to see the link between her loss and her experience of being so criticized and diminished. She felt again the feeling of sadness – and for the first time another feeling: outrage at the meanness of the headmistress. 'What a way to treat a young girl!' she thought, and she imagined writing an angry note to the bitter woman. However, that would have to wait. She had arrived at the company's building and she was pleased to find she felt ready for the meeting.

Anita and Gunther met with Ladli in her office. Their conversation started with Ladli and Anita getting to know each other a little, and then turned to Gunther and what he had got out of the coaching and, more broadly, what his impression was in the organization about how the merger was going. Gunther explained to her a bit about what he had been learning about his leadership style and the changes he had been making. Ladli was quick to agree that there was a marked improvement both in the atmosphere and also the performance of the whole division. She had heard some very positive reports from the board's chairman. Anita talked a little about the importance of paying attention to an organization's feelings at times of big change or challenge. Ladli said that she had been talking to Gunther about this and that it sounded as if Anita might have some important ideas for all of them. She asked if Anita could stay for a while after the meeting.

After Gunther had gone, Ladli turned to Anita. She thanked her again for her help and then asked whether she thought she could offer something to the HR department as a whole. She had realized that the merger had stirred up a lot of personal feelings and 'dynamics' in the organization and she realized that she and her team should be doing more to support people. Gunther had suggested that Anita offer some sessions to her and her team – perhaps some teaching input to talk about the challenges of major change and then some of the concepts of transactional analysis that Gunther seemed to find so useful. Anita was happy to agree!

10

Assessment and the Process of Change

In this chapter we will first look at general considerations of the assessment of clients' problems and the process of change and then, more specifically, address these issues from a TA perspective. So far this book has been addressed to anyone engaged professionally in a 'helping conversation', and indeed most of the ideas and concepts can be useful for the general reader. However, this chapter is intended for more formal engagements such as with a coach and, especially in the later sections with a counsellor or therapist who is actively committed to working longer term with a client within a contract for more personal and relational depth.

When clients come for counselling or coaching, they usually present problems which fall into three main categories of disturbance: confusion, conflict or deficit (Clarkson and Gilbert 1990). Though one of these may be the major focus for the client, it is common for all three to be playing a part in the client's problems. It is important, however, to make an assessment of where, how and to what extent these areas of disturbance are prevalent in order to help the client make changes. Let us take a general look at these areas.

Confusion

Many clients are aware of wanting help, but do not really know what it is they are looking for in the coach or counsellor. They may know that something is not right or clear in their lives, or areas of their lives, but have little idea of what the problem is or where or how to begin to address the situation. They may also be distressed and additionally disturbed by having only a vague notion as to why this may be so.

'I have a good job, a loving relationship, a busy social life but I feel so unhappy and I don't understand it,' says one client. 'I know there's something wrong but I don't know what it is,' says another. Many clients are confused by the strong feelings they are experiencing: intense anger that seems unrelated to the situations they are describing, deep sadness that seems to have no cause, or severe anxiety that is way out of proportion to current events. Others are disturbed by recurring thoughts that seem muddled and out of step with the actuality of their everyday lives. Coaching clients may be confused by the situation in which they find themselves or they may be experiencing some only half-recognized dissatisfaction with their jobs or unacknowledged confusion about the direction their career is taking.

For these confused clients, the contract will fall on the left side of the contracting matrix (see Chapter 2). The area of focus, at least in the initial stages of the work, will be to understand and clarify their states of confusion. In general terms, this may be accomplished through forming a trusting relationship with the client, providing a safe and protective environment, accepting the client's thoughts and feelings and allowing time and space for exploration and reflection.

Conflict

There are two types of conflict which clients may present: interpersonal and intra-psychic, closely interlinked. Here clients often know of the dilemmas, arguments, pros and cons of the situation but seem stuck and indecisive within themselves or 'locked' in unresolved conflict with another person.

'I want to stop having rows with Jim about the house being untidy but I keep nagging him like I'm his mother,' says one client. 'I know I can keep a job longer than I have but I seem to screw it up every time,' says another. Many clients are aware of conflicting internal dialogues that go on relentlessly without resolution: 'I wanted to meet her on Saturday but then I thought she'd think I was too pushy. I told myself she might like me being more spontaneous but then I thought I'd better wait and see 'cos she might feel it as a pressure. But then again ...' or 'Part of me felt so sad but another part kept telling me to pull myself together.' These sorts of difficulties are easily recognizable in organizations where the risks and challenges of making impor-tant and often financially significant decisions create the field for the client's internal dialogue to interfere with his clear thinking. At the level of the organization itself, a conflict may be 'We need to diversify to other activities, but our whole identity is built on this world famous brand; it's not selling anymore but the world won't see us as anything else ...'. And so on.

These clients are experiencing either internal or external conflict (or both) and, clearly, the area of focus in the counselling or coaching situation will need to be a resolution of these conflicts. The contracts on the right side of the matrix are likely to be appropriate here. The feelings and thoughts that lie beneath the conflicts and the purpose they may be playing in the client's life will need to be explored. Two-chair techniques either to role-play the external dialogue or to clarify the internal dialogue may be useful here in bringing about a resolution.

Deficit

Many clients may appear to be neither confused nor experiencing conflict yet still have difficulty in making changes in their lives. Some know what they want and they are motivated to do something about getting it, but somehow they are not succeeding. A contract in the top right-hand side of the matrix is relevant here. 'I want to make more friends and I've been socializing much more, yet I don't seem to make friends easily,' says one client. 'I've decided to be more assertive at work but I'm just being ignored,' says another. Something is missing. That 'something' may be information, skills, experience or permission. It may be that the person wanting to make more friends is lacking social skills, the experience of being close to people and the permission to do so. The person wanting to be more assertive may be lacking in information as to how people can be assertive without being aggressive, as well as the skills and experience of assertive behaviour. Somewhere in their development there has been a lack of adequate teaching, modelling, permission or direct experience of the intended new behaviour. Counselling or coaching can be used to make up for this deficiency. To this end, the relationship between client and practitioner can be used reparatively by providing a protective environment for exploration and experimentation, skill learning, the provision of information and permission to do things differently. A deficit in skills or knowledge may be very important for the coaching client who, for example, is making a transition to a new role. The coach may not necessarily have the knowledge himself to provide what is needed. Indeed that would be more the job of a mentor rather than a coach. He helps the client to think through and understand what are the particular areas of lack and make a plan about who he could talk to or where he could go to find out what he needs.

Other clients' deficit is of a different nature. Perhaps in childhood they lacked the sort of relationship that is needed in order to develop a sense of self and identity in the world. This has left them with little ability to think about their feelings or experiences, make plans for themselves and take charge of their lives. For these clients the reparative experience of a counsellor's empathic attention can help them begin to build what was missing. Contracts in the lower right of the matrix may be more relevant here.

We believe that, indirectly, all three areas of confusion, conflict and deficit – which, of course, interweave and overlap – are likely to be generally addressed by the helping relationship. For many people, the opportunity to talk, to be listened to and to be respected by another is, in itself, likely to facilitate clarity, resolve conflicts and be a reparative experience. However, making a more direct and aware assessment of client needs in these three areas provides a useful diagnostic map for facilitating the work with clients and can assist greatly in the process of change. While it is not always the case, and movement across and between these areas may often be important and necessary, it is generally likely that work will proceed from addressing confusion, through conflict resolution to repairing the deficit. Many clients, for example, avoid experiencing their internal conflicts by becoming confused. It is only in the course of addressing the confusion that these conflicts may be clarified and worked through. It is often in the working through of these conflicts that the developmental deficits may come to light. The contracting matrix offers a container to support the journey through these areas, while TA provides specific concepts which enhance the assessment and process of change. It is to these concepts that we now turn.

The illustrations here are largely of counselling and therapy. While they may be of interest to the coach, except for decontamination they are likely not to be a regular part of his work. Some of the exercises, however, may be interesting to any helping professional.

Transactional Analysis and Confusion

TA provides us with two important concepts of confusion. One is the confusion brought about by the interference with one ego state by another, the working through of which is known as *decontamination*. The second is the confusion often found within the Child ego state, the working through of which is known as *deconfusion*. Decontamination usually precedes deconfusion.

Decontamination

To write of a process called 'decontamination' clearly implies that there must be a state of 'contamination'. This may not seem a very appealing description but it certainly captures the essence of the concept. Contamination suggests impurity caused by the leakage of something into something else, and this is certainly what is meant when the term is applied to ego states. It is the Adult ego state which can be contaminated by either the Parent or Child ego states or, more often than not, both. When Introjected Parent feelings, thoughts and behaviours interfere with the Adult ego state, we speak of a Parent contamination. When Archaic Child feelings, thoughts and behaviours interfere with the Adult ego state, we speak of a Child contamination. If both sets of historic ego states are interfering simultaneously, we speak of a double contamination. Figure 10.1 shows these types of contamination, the overlapping of the circles indicating the contaminated areas.

When we transact internally or externally from a contamination, we consider ourselves, erroneously, to be in Adult. We may make statements about ourselves or others *as if* they were Adult statements. For example, Jane's first words to her coach are, 'I'm sorry I'm late. I really am incapable of doing anything right.' Jane, at this moment, believes this to be a statement of fact. It is as if this is a here-and-now reality

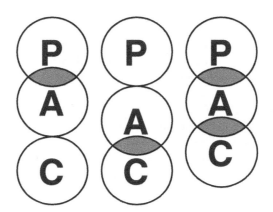

Figure 10.1   Contaminations

of the Adult ego state. Jane is, in this instance, responding from a Child contamination of the Adult. Tom begins his counselling session by saying, 'I know counselling's a bit of a self-indulgence ...', as if this is an indisputable statement of reality. In fact, this is a Parent contamination of his Adult ego state. He is repeating the exact words of his father.

We all have contaminations. We are unaware that some of what we are saying, thinking, believing, doing or feeling comes from historic ego states. Many of our prejudices towards other people or about certain aspects of life have their roots within the area of Parent–Adult contamination. For example:

'All red-heads are quick-tempered.'
'The [particular race or minority group] are stupid.'
'Keep yourself to yourself.'
'Never trust a stranger.'

An organizational Parent contamination may take the form of a manual outlining formal processes and procedures (our colleague Bill Critchley calls them 'conversations in aspic'), which are outdated in our fast-paced changing economic climate.

Many of our delusions and fantasies about ourselves, others and the world have their roots in the area of Child–Adult contamination. For example:

'I'm really hopeless.'
'I'll never come to any good.'
'I can't stop drinking.'
'I just get in people's way.'
'Spiders/cars/people are frightening.'

And in the organizational context, a Child contamination might be:

'Mistakes aren't tolerated around here.'
'I must make decisions quickly.'
'I must know what to do.'

Understandably, when clients first come to counselling, they experience their feelings, thoughts and behaviours as, 'This is me. This is who I am. This is my experience of myself.' And, of course, this is still true. Historic ego states are a part of ourselves, but while their origins remain outside our awareness, they are likely to be interfering with our effective Adult functioning in ways which may not be useful or appropriate, supporting and reinforcing our script beliefs.

The process of decontamination is the identifying and separating out of historic ego states from the Adult ego state in order to allow for more autonomous choice. As we have mentioned in previous chapters, we may actively choose to draw upon historic ego states in order to enhance the present moment. While the present moment is contaminated by historic experiences perceived as Adult reality, this is not possible.

Application

Decontamination is clearly an ongoing process which begins in the early stages of the work and continues throughout and beyond it. Once clients are familiar with their ego states, the concept of contaminations can help to make sense of their experience of themselves, their beliefs, thoughts, feelings and behaviours. Gradually, by identification of particular ego states and their contents (structural analysis), the clients separate what is here-and-now reality from what is there-and-then experience masquerading as a current reality. Many opinions, for example about themselves, others and the world, are discovered to be outdated and out-moded beliefs from childhood. Similarly, behaviours and feelings seen to be inevitable responses to current situations are rightfully placed back in history where they belong. Script, game and racket analysis are all part of the process of decontamination. In the course of following the exercises with clients at the end of previous chapters, you have largely been facilitating your clients in the process of decontamination.

Let us take a closer look at the way in which decontamination may be facilitated in counselling.

Example

Hal is having problems in his relationship with Julie.

HAL:	I'm just so anxious all the time. I want to do things right.
COUNSELLOR:	What does it mean to 'do things right'?
HAL:	Well, to please her, I suppose. You know, to do things for her.
COUNSELLOR:	And if you do things for her to please her, what then?
HAL:	Then she should know that I love her and she'll be happy.
COUNSELLOR:	It sounds like you're saying that loving is doing things to please people?
HAL:	Yes, that's right. But it's not working.
COUNSELLOR:	Have you had other experiences of trying so hard to please someone and it not working?
HAL:	Oh yes, I could never get it right for my mother.
COUNSELLOR:	In what way?
HAL:	I tried so hard to make her happy. She was always wanting me to do things for her. She said that I didn't love her if I didn't.
COUNSELLOR:	You must have felt very anxious a lot of the time trying to prove to her that you loved her.
HAL:	I can't remember not feeling anxious around her. She was never satisfied so I had to go on trying. And I kept failing and getting more and more anxious.

COUNSELLOR:	So you tried and tried to please her. In the process you denied your own needs and, what's more, it didn't even work and you felt you failed.
(Pause)	
HAL:	I shouldn't have had to prove that I loved her. I shouldn't have had to keep doing things for her. That's not love.
COUNSELLOR:	Say more ...
HAL:	That's not love! No, that's not love at all. Love is being with someone and enjoying them. It's giving and taking, not just one or the other. I don't have to keep on proving that I love Julie. It gets in the way of our really being together.

In this example, in a few transactions, the counsellor has helped Hal to separate the historic ego states from Hal's Adult. The belief that love is doing things for someone else belongs both to the Introjected Parent, his mother who told him this, and his Archaic Child, the young boy who believed her and acted upon this belief in a constant state of anxiety. Hal's Adult is now more able to make his own decisions about what constitutes love in a relationship and can choose to act upon these decisions.

Deconfusion

In the process of deconfusion we are dealing mainly with the Child ego state. The term 'deconfusion' means allowing the Child to express the feelings, thoughts and behaviours that were not allowed expression during childhood and sorting out the confusions brought about by such repression. This process is made clearer after decontamination has been achieved, so that the Child ego state can be easily distinguished from the Adult ego state. However, conversely there may be times when deconfusion must come first as it may be an essential part of the decontamination. For instance, in the example in the section on application after this, Deborah needs to feel and express her Child's anxiety about upsetting her mother before she can fully understand just how she has been quashing her anger.

As we have already seen in previous chapters, our current transactions, strokes, games and rackets are all influenced by our past, often our childhood, experiences. These experiences and the consequent (largely unconscious) decisions are replayed from our Child ego state most often with pressure from, or with the reinforcement of, our Introjected Parent. These decisions about ourselves, others and the world were the best possible adaptations we could make within the influence of our particular childhood environment. In the course of deconfusion, we are encouraging our clients to get in touch with and express their feelings, wants and needs, freed from their dysfunctional beliefs. In this sense, deconfusion can be seen as expressive decontamination within the Child ego state, the original needs having been 'contaminated' by interference from the childhood environment. The expression of repressed feelings – catharsis – and the discharge of these feelings may be an important step towards bringing about a positive change in the client's experience of herself and in her script.

Application

The application of the process of deconfusion is here illustrated by the example of Deborah.

Example

Deborah entered counselling because she had been depressed for as long as she could remember. She had no close friends and spent most of her time working or reading. In the course of counselling, Deborah talked about her childhood experiences in a middle-class family where feelings were frowned upon and not expressed by anyone except her mother, who suffered from 'nerves'. If Deborah expressed her feelings in any way, including her delight or excitement, her mother would get upset and take to her bed, whilst her father responded to her with a rejecting, stony silence. Deborah spent most of her time alone in her room in the safe company of books. This was still the case when Deborah embarked on counselling. As a grown-up, she, not surprisingly, held many Parent- and Child-contaminated beliefs about feelings. She saw no place for them: they were selfish, upsetting for others and could only lead to rejection. By ego state identification and structural analysis, Deborah separated her Adult from her Parent and Child ego states with regard to feelings. We join her now in a session where she is showing her first signs of anger.

DEBORAH:	I don't seem to be getting anywhere. All this explanation doesn't seem to help. I'm just as depressed as I ever was.
COUNSELLOR:	Right now, you seem to be angry about that.
DEBORAH:	No, no, I'm just depressed by it all. There's no point feeling angry.
COUNSELLOR:	What would happen if you felt angry?
DEBORAH:	I don't know. You might get upset.
COUNSELLOR:	And then I might take to my bed and leave you?
DEBORAH:	No, I know you wouldn't do that.
COUNSELLOR:	But it sounds like your Child might think that. It's exactly what your mother did. How about letting her speak directly to your mother? Would you be willing to do that?
DEBORAH:	I don't see much point but I'll talk to her.

COUNSELLOR:	OK, just let yourself be little and talk to her (*indicates mother's symbolic presence on an empty chair nearby*).
DEBORAH:	(*to mother*) I don't know what I want to say to you. You never listen to me anyway. You're always talking about your 'nerves'.
COUNSELLOR:	And when she's talking about her 'nerves'?
DEBORAH:	(*to mother*) There's no room for me.
COUNSELLOR:	Tell her how you feel about that.
DEBORAH:	(*to mother*) I don't feel anything 'cos I know you'll get upset.
COUNSELLOR:	So you're responsible for how she feels? Do you want to say that to her?
DEBORAH:	(*to mother*) No, I can't be responsible for how you feel. I'm a child. You're the grown-up. You're meant to look after me!
COUNSELLOR:	And you feel ...?
DEBORAH:	(*to mother*) I feel angry. Yes, that's right, I don't feel depressed, I feel angry! I feel so angry that you can't deal with your own feelings, let alone mine. You just put yourself to bed. You go away from me and leave me alone as if I didn't exist. (*Shouting*) Well, I do exist, do you hear, and I do have feelings! You may not like them but that's your problem, not mine. I exist in my own right and I have feelings!
COUNSELLOR:	And just because she gets upset is no reason for you not to show your feelings.
DEBORAH:	(*to mother*) No, I look after you by getting depressed. That's how I stop feeling things. Well, that's not right. You should be looking after me and my feelings. I have feelings and I need to show them. And I've just done it!
COUNSELLOR:	Yes, you did, and very forcibly too.

In this example, the process of deconfusion begins with decontamination. The counsellor recognizes that Deborah's perception of the current situation is contaminated by her Child ego state. By separating the Child ego state from the Adult (though Deborah initially replays her childhood experience with, for example, 'I don't feel anything 'cos I know you'll get upset') she eventually expresses her anger, which has been 'depressed' for so long. Further, she realizes that her depression of her feelings has been protecting her mother to the detriment of her own natural expression of feelings, that, in effect, she has been 'parenting' her own mother, whose responsibility it was to look after her. Deborah is likely to need to do more decontamination and deconfusion work in the area of feelings and their expression, notably in respect of her father too. She may then be prepared to make a new decision which will liberate her feelings and bring an end to her depression. This process of *redecision* will be addressed in the next section, 'Transactional Analysis and Conflict' (page 162).

Exercises

If you have been following the exercises in previous chapters, you have already started the process of decontamination. You may be well aware of many thoughts, beliefs, feelings and behaviours which you had previously assumed to be appropriate responses to here-and-now reality but which you are now questioning and identifying as intrusions from Parent or Child ego states. You may have noticed that, more often than not, there is a double contamination. For example, a contaminating Parent belief that 'pride comes before a fall' may be echoed by a contaminating Child belief that 'If I express my excitement at my success, I'll regret it', and the consequent suppression of excitement and self-stroking. The following exercises may be used to further identify such contaminations and help to decontaminate your Adult ego state.

Self

Decontamination

1 Write down a list of the sayings and mottoes that were common in your family. Add to this list the things your family said about money, sex, sexuality, race, work, duty and relationships.
2 How many of these slogans do you believe today? Consider the possibility that some of these may be contaminations. Go through the list and pick out any of these beliefs or attitudes that you may have taken in as statements of fact.
3 Against each of these, write down the concomitant, contaminating Child beliefs. You will probably find that many of the contaminating Parent beliefs are prefixed by 'You' and the contaminating Child beliefs prefixed by 'I'. For example, 'You can't trust foreigners' (contaminating Parent) and 'I feel anxious when I am with someone from another country – so I don't trust them' (contaminating Child).
4 Work through these contaminations, question their validity from your Adult ego state, and decontaminate by writing down your reality-based beliefs. For example, you might write, 'Big boys/girls don't cry' (contaminating Parent) with 'I'm a baby if I show my sadness' (contaminating Child), followed by 'Children and grown-ups feel sad at times. Sadness is an appropriate and healthy response to loss or hurt. I can cry and get comfort in healthy ways' (reality-based belief).
5 Do the above exercises verbally with a colleague, counsellor or fellow student.

Deconfusion

The process of deconfusion belongs within the safety of the counselling relationship and setting. Becoming aware of thoughts and feelings not expressed in childhood requires the sensitivity, support, permission and protection of the skilled counsellor who can act as an important ally to the Child. Therefore we do not suggest exercises for you to do for yourself but recommend you work through this process with your own counsellor or psychotherapist in order to create a different relational experience.

Working with Clients

Decontamination

The task of the coach or counsellor in the ongoing process of decontamination with clients is to listen for those thoughts, feelings and behaviours which the client passes off as Adult statements of fact, inevitable feeling responses or inevitable behaviour responses, and to question and challenge them. This does not mean getting your client to ponderously work through exercises with a pencil and paper, nor does it mean engaging in aggressive challenge or persecution. It means that the practitioner, from an empathic position, assists the client in reassessing those aspects of their script which are interfering in the here and now. Such questioning may include:

1   Questioning the origins in order to distinguish and separate the three ego states.

    - Who was it that used to talk of you so dismissively?
    - Did any of your family behave in this way under stress?
    - How was anger dealt with in your family?
    - Did your parents believe that hard work is the most important thing in life?
    - So what happened if you got excited as a child?

2   Questioning the validity.

    - Is it true that people always reject you for showing your sadness?
    - If others are scared, do you label them as weak too? What would you say to a friend in a similar situation?
    - Can you think of an alternative way you might have responded?
    - Have you ever had experiences of being close to people who didn't take advantage of you?
    - Have you ever been in a situation like this that you managed OK?
    - How do you know that others are thinking that about you?
    - That's not my experience of you – can you accept that?

3   Using previously shared information to decontaminate the present (confrontation).

    - That's what your father used to say about you.
    - This sounds similar to the way you felt when your mother scolded you.
    - You were spontaneous when you played with your brother and sister.
    - I remember how angry you said you were when your teacher was absent.
    - That's how your father behaved when things went wrong.

4   *Three-chair work:* using one chair for each of the three ego states, the client moves from one to the other expressing the thoughts, feelings or behaviours that may be contaminating the Adult. For example, the client may explore the belief that they are

'stupid' by moving from chair to chair and separating historic experiences from the current reality. On the Parent chair, they may recall direct remarks and attributions of being 'stupid' from parents. On the Child chair, they may get in touch with their decisions that they were stupid when they experienced themselves as failing. On the Adult chair, they may update this belief by acknowledging their skills, intelligence, creativity and success in their grown-up life.

Deconfusion

As already indicated, the task of the counsellor in the process of deconfusion is to provide a safe and protective environment which will enable the Child of the client to express feelings, thoughts and behaviours that were not received or allowed expression in childhood. Sometimes these disowned experiences have become, in the unconscious imagination of the client, unmanageable and overwhelming – literally dangerous. The client needs time to integrate them into himself and his awareness. This can only be done within the developing relationship between counsellor and client where the genuineness, understanding and potency of the counsellor is responded to with the confidence and trust of the client. We are talking of a relationship between one person and another where meanings can be explored and co-created.

There are times when, once this relationship has been established (as shown in the example of Deborah), the technique of setting up a dialogue between the Child ego state of the client and the relevant Introjected Parent is a useful vehicle for deconfusion. This or other experiments might help to loosen the bonds of repression. However, the release of Child feelings will frequently emerge within the therapeutic relationship itself, much as we have described in the chapter on games where enactments of past relationships occur within the current therapeutic relationship. Here techniques are often not useful. Deconfusion may be achieved through interactions in the relationship itself where a willingness and openness to collaborative exploration and reflection can bring about a different outcome. In this process, the client may be encouraged to express those feelings, thoughts or behaviours which have been repressed, reach an understanding of the decisions they made as children and discover how and why they are maintaining these decisions. This is likely to clarify the internal conflicts and lead to the necessary new decisions to which we now turn.

Transactional Analysis and Conflict

We have mentioned earlier that conflict may be seen externally as between two people or internally as between two parts of the person. Of course, there will always be conflicts between people as part of healthy disagreement. However, when two people seem to be locked in a pattern of conflict that is familiar to one or both parties, we believe that this is usually the external manifestation of an internal conflict. In previous examples we have seen that the perceived opposition of a partner can be the result of the projection of a Parent ego state onto the other. In such cases, the conflict that really needs to be resolved is that between this person's internal Parent and their Child ego states. It is this internal conflict which we will now address.

Impasse Theory

Bob and Mary Goulding, well known for their book *Changing Lives Through Redecision Therapy* (1979), use the word 'impasse' (from Gestalt therapy) to describe the stuck point a person reaches when two ego states are at odds with each other. As we described in Chapter 7, under the pressure of the environment and of parental messages, children will make decisions about who they are and how to live their lives. Sometimes these decisions will involve a wholehearted acceptance of the parental command; for instance, to work hard and achieve academic success. Sometimes the decision will be a compromise based upon the balance between an injunction and the natural drive to grow and blossom. An example is that of the child who perceives father's attitude to contain a 'Don't succeed' message. Naturally, the child also has the instinct to grow and achieve. To satisfy both sides, the child may decide to be successful only in areas that do not compete with or threaten father's self-esteem. An example with even more serious possible consequences involves the child who takes in a 'Don't exist' message. Here the compromise between obedience and survival may be the child's decision to be depressed and thus 'dead' in affect.

As long as these decisions remain firm, and the person manages to function relatively adequately, they experience no sense of conflict. But, as a result of having worked through decontamination, the person begins to experience natural needs and feelings which go against the creative script compromise. As the Adult strengthens, the person allows the needs of the Child to become stronger and, as a result, the inner tussle becomes more vivid. Ultimately, the impasse needs to be broken and a new, healthy decision made. This is called a *redecision*. It requires accounting for the actual needs and feelings of the Child, tempering them only with that part of Parental influence which is appropriate to the current life of the person. There are three types of impasse.

Type 1 Impasse

The conflict here is between the Child ego state and the Parent ego state. The Child is expressing natural needs and is met by a social level message from the Parent which tells them how they ought to be behaving. For example, experimentation, noise and sensitivity are respectively thwarted by such 'advice' as 'It's important to do your best', 'They won't like you if you're noisy', 'Be a brave little soldier'. These are social level messages (drivers) about how to get on in life by being strong or pleasing or hardworking and the like. The Child responds to these demands either by compliance or by rebellion, both of which are adaptations and neglect the natural wants and feelings of the child.

Type 2 Impasse

The second type of impasse also involves conflict between the Child and the Parent. However, here we are dealing with the psychological level messages, the injunctions in their purest form, which were either incorporated by the child or self-created as a survival strategy at an earlier age than the Type 1. Though these messages will, for the most part, have been communicated non-verbally, they may have been embedded, or be perceived to have been embedded, in such statements as 'Get out of my sight!' (Don't exist), 'Oh, don't be such a baby' (Don't be a child) or 'Stop whining!' (Don't feel). In exploring these impasses, a client may experience their parents as being all-pervasively prohibiting, even though, for the parent, their attitude may have been specifically contextual. In these cases, it is the client's experience that is important. They incorporated these messages at a time when their parents seemed very powerful giants to them and they did not have enough information to understand the total context of, for instance, mother's stressful day or father's tendency to get angry when he was worried. 'Type 2' impasses are likely to have a much stronger attendant feeling component both in the Parental message and in the Child response of anxiety, desolation, rage or powerlessness. Fear of annihilation, harm or abandonment is often attendant upon the perceived injunction.

In organizations, coaching clients may experience this sort of injunction in a variety of subtle ways as the (possibly unconscious) pressures of the organizational culture are accommodated by the individual. For example, in Chapter 2 we referred to a charismatic new CEO, Jonathan, who said he wanted to be challenged, but his coach picked up a different message because of his resemblance to her bullying father. Later in the work, she used her own experience to help him understand that his board was in a similar double bind: he challenged them to take initiative and shape the direction of the company, but at the same time they all picked up his strong 'Don't think' and 'Don't be you' messages and were careful not to disagree with him.

Type 3 Impasse

The third type of impasse is different from the first two types of impasse in that the emerging conflict is between two parts of the Child ego state. Using the concept of functional modes, the impasse within the Archaic Child ego state is between a part of the Adapted Child and a part of the Natural Child. The Natural Child has been so successfully repressed by adapted behaviour that certain spontaneous emotions and sensations seem effectively non-existent.

Type 3 impasses are the result of decisions made at so young an age and so deep a level that it seems strange to call them decisions. They are made at a time when our powers of thinking and reasoning are not yet developed. This means that the 'decision' is more of a bodily-affective assumption of a state of being rather than anything that can be said to have been decided upon. Many of our bodily holding patterns originate from the time of such 'decisions'. There is often no awareness of any particular instruction or message from outside the self. There is simply a feeling of having 'always been this way'. For example, a client told his counsellor, 'I just don't really feel very much, I never have. I've always been quiet.' We might guess that this person may have had a mother who, for some reason, needed her child to suppress natural feelings. This could have been due to her own discomfort with feelings, her level of stress at the time, or many other reasons. In fact, the client who said these things was born in a cellar in 1956 in Hungary to a mother who was in the process of escaping during the revolution. From the moment he was born, it was imperative that he remain quiet. But this man was not aware of any internal pressure. He merely experienced himself as a quiet, even person.

The third type impasse might appear in organizations in the strong adherence to 'That's the way we do things around here'. One coach, who had several clients in the same organization, discovered that it was common practice to exclude the Finance Director from strategy meetings. When he inquired, nobody knew why. It was discovered that this practice was inherited; a previous finance director from 20 years ago had been destructive and obstructive in planning meetings and had been excluded. This had become common practice and was now part of the norm.

However, usually the third type impasse is associated with very early pre- or non-verbal adaptations in the Child ego state, and therefore is more the stuff of the therapeutic conversation than the coaching one.

Application

Even when the processes of decontamination and deconfusion have been worked through and the impasses exposed, making new decisions in the Child ego state (redecision) is not likely to be immediate or necessarily achieved in a one-off 'piece of work'. These decisions have been made to please parents, to maximize strokes and, in some instances, to ensure survival. The Child, even with reassurance from the integrating Adult, may be tentative in relinquishing such once-important and neces-sary decisions. It may take time, several repetitions and explorations, much strength-ening of the Adult to provide the nurturing that was not available at the time and a great deal of practising of the new behaviours resulting from the redecision before permanent change is achieved.

We will go on to describe some techniques which may be used to facilitate your client in making redecisions. However, it is our experience that clients can and do make many redecisions in the course of counselling without such techniques. In the safety and trust of the relationship between counsellor and client, developed over time, clients may make new and far-reaching decisions, not only in their Adult ego state but also in their Child ego state. For example, a client with an injunction not to feel may express their feelings and have them received with acceptance and understanding by the counsellor. Over time, the client's Child learns to trust that it is safe and appropriate to express feelings within and outside the counselling setting and makes a redecision to this effect.

Redecision Technique

Whichever impasse is being worked through, the redecision technique requires the client to be in one of their Child ego states while simultaneously being aware of the resources now available in their Adult ego state.

Both Type 1 and Type 2 impasses can be approached in the same way. In practice, we find that, after a Type 1 impasse has been resolved, a Type 2 is usually revealed. (Frequently, a Type 3 will also emerge but, needing a different approach, this will be addressed later.) Broadly speaking, the stages of impasse resolution for these two types involve:

1 An experience of dissatisfaction in the present.
2 The identification of the impasse.
3 The location of the impasse in childhood.
4 The re-experiencing of the childhood situation, including the painful feelings and the decision made, with all its implications – the benefits, the drawbacks and so on.
5 The awareness by the Child that he or she can survive changing the decision and 'defying' the Parent.
6 The redecision.
7 The integration of the new decision into the client's current life.

This simplified list of stages seems to imply that profound change can take place according to a format. Of course, this is not the case. In practice, as we have emphasized, the redecision process will be subtle and take place over time, possibly many months, with much retracing of steps in order more fully to explore, understand and bring about the redecision. Nonetheless, while bearing the above in mind, it may be useful to take a closer look at these stages with the example of Hal from the previous section.

Example

An experience of dissatisfaction in the present

Hal, you may remember, is constantly anxious in his relationship with Julie because he is wanting to please her all the time. This is his current dissatisfaction.

The identification of the impasse

In the course of decontamination and deconfusion, Hal has identified a Type 1 impasse between his Parent and Child ego states. His Parent, the mother he has introjected, is saying, 'Please me to show you love me'. His compliant Child – which up to now has said, 'I'll do my best to please you because then you'll know I love you and you'll be happy' is now saying, 'I don't want to have to please you all the time'. This created the impasse at the root of his dissatisfaction in his relationship with Julie. Recognizing the impasse, Hal decides to stop automatically pleasing others and to look to his own needs. This, however, is not enough. He experiences a great deal of discomfort with this new behaviour and a 'pull' to revert to the old pattern, despite his resolve. Now a Type 2 impasse is identified, which involves the Parental injunction 'Don't have your own wants and needs', which until now has been complied with by Hal's repression of such wants and needs in the service of pleasing others. Tentatively, through his fear of abandonment if he should defy his mother, Hal is now saying, 'I have my own wants and needs'. Here we see why just the Adult recognition of this fact, reached during decontamination, may not be enough to ensure a redecision. Similarly, working through the Type 1 impasse and making a new decision to please himself rather than others, Hal still felt anxious as he came up against the Type 2 impasse where he is instructed not to have his own needs and wants and is threatened with abandonment if he does. Both impasses will need resolution if Hal is to make the changes he wants to make.

The location of the impasse in childhood

Tracing back, from his current situation into the past, Hal remembers the persistent messages from his mother to please her, to do things for her, to look after her, messages which were a continual and all-pervasive 'background' in his childhood experience, and recalls his constant anxiety in his attempts to please her. These are the components of the Type 1 impasse. Further, he recalls a particular scene at an early stage in which his mother had asked him to 'Be a good little boy for mummy' by staying in and sitting with her rather than going out to play with the neighbouring children. Hal remembers feeling torn between his excitement at the thought of playing with the children and his anxiety at the thought of his mother's disapproval. He had hesitated and this mere hesitation had been responded to with a look from his mother. Though she said nothing, this look, to Hal, held sadness – for which he felt responsible – and rage. When the counsellor asked Hal what words he associated with the look, he said, 'If you desert me, you'll regret it. You dare to leave me and I'll leave you, you bad boy.' As he spoke of it in the session, he could feel his stomach churning with anxiety. In the event, all excitement gone, he sat with his mother, whose face now showed benign contentment. These are the components of the Type 2 impasse through which Hal would need to work.

The re-experiencing of the childhood situation

In recounting the childhood scene, Hal is already re-experiencing many of the feelings he had at the time. The counsellor invites him to 'go into' the scene and 'be there'. Talking now in the present tense rather than the past, Hal more fully 'relives' his experience of the scene: his feeling torn, his excitement and his anxiety, indeed his terror, at his mother's almost demonic look, his acquiescence and the dissipation of anxiety once his mother seemed content. He ends by saying, 'I feel better

(Continued)

(Continued)

now. My mother looks happy. I know she will not go away. I think of the children playing outside but quickly push aside my feelings because I mustn't be a bad boy.'

The awareness that the Child can survive changing the decision and 'defying' the parent

While still in the Child ego state, the client has access to his grown-up self in his Adult ego state which can draw upon qualities, skills, information and experiences that could assist the Child in changing the present experience of the past situation. The counsellor helps Hal to be aware of this in the following extract.

COUNSELLOR: What do you want to say to your mother when she looks at you like that?

HAL: *(to mother)* I'm really scared. I want to do what I want but I'm scared you'll leave me.

COUNSELLOR: That is scary for a little boy. If you call upon the resources of grown-up Hal, what can you experience differently as little Hal?

HAL: I don't feel so scared.

COUNSELLOR: And if she leaves you?

HAL: *(to mother)* I know I don't need you around. You can look at me like that as much as you like but I know I don't need you. You don't give me much anyway. It's me that does all the giving, all the pleasing.

COUNSELLOR: And if you don't please her?

HAL: *(to mother)* That's too bad. If I go on trying to please you, I'll be doing it forever! And for what? I've got nothing to be scared of now. I've got nothing to lose.

The redecision

You can probably 'feel' that Hal is about to make a redecision in the above extract. Indeed, it is often the case that, having reached this point of harnessing the grown-up resources in aid of the Child, the Child moves into the redecision spontaneously. Notice that Hal has stayed in his Child ego state throughout this work. The counsellor has spoken to the Child and not invited him out of this ego state, knowing that his redecision needs to be in Child if it is to be effective. Here the counsellor facilitates Hal in making a clear and positive statement of his new decision.

COUNSELLOR: So you could go on forever pleasing her?

HAL: *(to mother)* Yes. If I stay scared of you leaving me I could go on and on. But I'm not scared. I'm really not scared any more. I'm not going to get in a state trying to please you any more. I've done enough of that.

COUNSELLOR:	Will you tell her how you're going to be different?
HAL:	(*to mother*) I'm going to take notice of what I need and what I want, mum.
COUNSELLOR:	And when you've taken notice?
HAL:	I'll do something about them. I don't have to hesitate any more. I don't have to feel anxious. I know I can still give to people but I can take as well.
COUNSELLOR:	So will you tell her what you'll do about your needs and wants?
HAL:	(*to mother*) I'll look after my needs and wants and I'll tell people what they are and get them met.
COUNSELLOR:	And how do you feel when you say that? What do you notice in your body?
HAL:	I feel really released. I feel clear and relaxed. I feel a real sense of solidity in my belly.
COUNSELLOR:	You look it, too! Your whole body looks relaxed. Is there anything more you want to say to your mother?
HAL:	No, I've finished with her. I'm going to go out to play!
COUNSELLOR:	That's great!

Notice that the counsellor checks whether Hal has more to say to his mother at the end of the work. This reduces the possibility of Hal coming out of his Child ego state with a feeling of incompleteness, which may dilute the redecision. After spending any length of time in a Child ego state, it is vital that, before the end of the session or at the end of work, the client is brought back to the here and now and does not leave, for example, to drive home while still in Child. It is therefore important that the redecision work be scheduled within the session with enough time left towards the end for reconnecting with Adult. This process may be assisted by the counsellor asking the client the time or date, what they are planning to do the following day or by asking them to focus on something in the room and describe it. For example:

COUNSELLOR:	Do you think you're fully back in the present?
HAL:	Well, almost.
COUNSELLOR:	What time is it now?
HAL:	(*looks at watch*) It's quarter to four.
COUNSELLOR:	OK, so a few more minutes before you go. Is it your day to pick up Julie?
HAL:	Yes, she's on an early shift, so I'll meet her from work. I'm really looking forward to seeing her.
COUNSELLOR:	Any plans for the evening?
HAL:	I think a meal in town and then a disco. Two grown-ups going out to play!
COUNSELLOR:	Sounds like fun. Enjoy yourself.

(Continued)

(Continued)

The integration of the new decision into the client's current life

However potent the redecision made by the client may seem, if it is to be effective and enduring it will need to be integrated both cognitively and behaviourally into the client's life. The counsellor may have done considerable preparatory cognitive work with the client prior to the redecision, for example, structural, script or racket analysis, or a combination of all three, as well as addressing the desired behavioural outcome. It is still important to discuss and integrate the client's understanding of what they have been dealing with in the redecision process and to find ways of practising and monitoring the resultant new behaviours.

In Hal's case, the counsellor reviewed with him the script matrix they had drawn up earlier. Hal identified the social level and psychological level messages from his mother – 'Please me to show you love me' and 'Don't have your own needs and wants' respectively – and the early decision to please her (and everyone) in order not to be abandoned, which involved negating his own needs and wants. He understood his early need to make such a decision but was now quite clear about his new decision to look after his own needs and wants and get those needs and wants met. For Hal, the most important area in which to practise and monitor his new behaviour was in his relationship with Julie. He contracted to be aware of his needs and wants in his relationship with her and to tell her what they were as he became aware of them. Each week he would monitor his change in behaviour with his counsellor. Once this new behaviour was established and Julie was responding positively to the new 'give and take' of their relationship, Hal contracted to practise this new behaviour with friends and colleagues too.

In this last stage, the client often needs a great deal of ongoing support and encouragement from the counsellor. It is important to remember this and not just move on to something else or relax the focus. After the sometimes dramatic and intense experience of the redecision work, putting new decisions into effect in the outside world can be difficult. Clients are sometimes disappointed by the response of their friends to their new behaviour and need to bear in mind that friends may have a lot of investment in them remaining the way they were – after all, they chose them as friends because of how they were. In Hal's case, he discovered that some of his friends did not like him disagreeing with them, or asking for things for himself. They had been quite happy with him pleasing them all the time. Over time, he let go of such one-sided friendships and maintained those old friendships that could accept the new reciprocity. He then made new and mutually supportive friendships.

The work described above is a classic piece of redecision where the therapist acted as facilitator and supporter of the process. Frequently, the internal conflicts can become externalized in the counselling relationship (as we described in Chapter 8) and the client can experience the counsellor as one half of the impasse. In this case, working through that stuck place between them – discovering, for example, that it is completely acceptable to disagree with the counsellor or express a preference – can start a subtle process of redecision over time.

Let us now take a look at the Type 3 impasse, which is approached differently from the other two. The difference of approach is necessary because, as we said before, the 'decision' is made at such a young, preverbal age and/or at such a deep psychobiological level that there is no conscious memory of adapting to an outside force or repressing a natural part of the self. On the contrary, the Adapted Child mode of the Archaic Child is experienced as the 'real me'. Sometimes, as the counselling progresses, clients come to realize that there may be ways of being which would enhance their lives, even though they seem currently unavailable to them.

Example

Jemma, whose contract is to enjoy her life, would love to be 'the sort of person who goes out dancing'. Her friends go dancing and have great fun but Jemma says she has always been shy and awkward and does not go out dancing. In this case, there were a number of stages in the redecision which were spread over many weeks. The first was for Jemma to heighten her sense of being aware of the conflict between two parts of her self. She did this by enacting a conversation between these two parts – one shy, the other fun-loving and gregarious. In this initial dialogue, Jemma's sense of her real self came from her Adapted Child mode, 'I'm shy'. The other polarity felt very odd and unlikely to her. However, it was the beginning of a possibility.

It is interesting to notice the difference between this Type 3 impasse dialogue and those involved with a Type 2 impasse, in which one side, the Parent, tends to be telling the other, the Child, what he or she should or should not be doing or must not do – 'You must be brave' or 'Don't have your feelings' and so on. With the third type, both sides are talking about 'I', as in 'I don't feel' and 'I want to feel'. Of course, as we explained earlier, the taking of a decision at this level will origi-nally have been in response to perceived outside pressure. It's unlikely that a baby is conceived in the womb feeling shy or unfeeling, depressed or unlovable. Somehow they take on that attitude as a result of their early experience, but so early (even in the womb) that there is no conscious awareness of a Parental mes-sage. Therefore the conflict is between the Natural and the Adapted Child modes of the Archaic Child.

Example

Shortly after Jemma had begun to identify this Type 3 impasse she had a dream about a tigress walking lithely along the streets of a village. There were people about who watched, not in fear but in awe, as the tigress began to run, low to the ground and effortlessly, through the village and into the country, covering the distance at amazing speed. When she explored this dream, Jemma identified the tigress as a powerful and passionate being who could do as she liked. She also stressed how striking she was, and that the villagers had thought her beautiful and arresting. At the suggestion that the tigress in her dream was in fact a part of herself she giggled and blushed, then dismissed the idea. However, minutes later the counsellor noticed that Jemma was stretching on her chair with slow, sensuous and 'cat-like' movements. She chose not to comment at that moment but knew that she was purposely smiling and nodding in admiration in the hope that she was duly playing her part of a villager.

As the weeks went by, the counsellor noticed some tiny and subtle changes in Jemma's manner and appearance. She was dressing in a livelier way. She talked with more vigour. She changed her hairstyle – a sure sign of a change of mind. The counsellor commented on these changes from time to time and Jemma acknowledged them. Then she dreamed about the tigress again, this time playing with other animals in a park. At the following counselling session Jemma agreed to explore the dream by talking as the tigress. On this occasion – feeling protected somewhat by the symbolism – she threw herself into the part, saying, 'I am handsome and impressive. I am playing with the other animals. They like being with me. My skin is beautiful and I am proud of it.' This time, in response to the suggestion that the tigress was a part of herself, she giggled but her eyes sparkled and she did not disagree. At about this time, Jemma was becoming increasingly aware of the negative and destructive things she repeatedly said to herself (injunctions) about her abilities, whether people would like her and what would happen if she 'put herself forward'. She did some Type 2 impasse work in which she began to understand that, whenever she started to do something, she would say to herself, 'You won't be able to do this', then immediately feel hesitant and foolish. Jemma had been the youngest in the family, and she realized that besides her parents, her siblings too would have said those sorts of things to her.

Meanwhile, the work at the Type 3 impasse level was continuing. One day Jemma reported another dream about walking on a beach with a little girl who was splashing and paddling in the waves. She cried as she recounted the dream. She said she felt both happy and sad. Then she did another 'two-chair dialogue' between the Natural and Adapted Child modes of her Archaic Child. From her Adapted Child she spoke about how much safer she felt staying on the sand: the waves could be dangerous and in any case she was 'shy'. She did not like a lot of noise and mess and wetness. She liked calm and staying at home with a book. Her Natural Child, from the heady heights of the waves, replied, 'But I love to play – I love to splash and get wet and laugh and dance in the waves' and then exclaimed, 'I want to dance with my friends'. In her Adapted Child, Jemma wept again and said, 'But what about me?' She felt as if, having discovered a new part of her, she would have to lose the 'me' she knew. A negotiation started between the two 'selves', aided by the Adult, in which a compromise was reached. Jemma decided that she did not need to be shy any more but she could be quiet sometimes and she could certainly make sure she was safe. However, she could also be boisterous, beautiful, noisy, exciting and fun to be with. And most especially, she could dance.

After this, the changes that had been gradually happening over the last weeks and months began to be more evident. Jemma first joined a dancing class. Then she joined a club. Then she and some workmates started going out regularly to have fun and dance. Jemma, initially, said she felt a little awkward at these gatherings, but she got into the swing of them surprisingly quickly. Recently, she and a friend started going to flamenco dancing classes. It was the counsellor's turn to say to herself, 'I think I might like to be as zippy as that!'

We would like to stress that the work outlined above in relation to the Type 3 impasse is not intended to suggest a format for resolving this type of impasse. We believe that there is no such format. The different 'pieces' that Jemma brought to the counselling situation and worked through show the way that the impasse unfolded for her. Everyone is different. The example is given merely to illustrate one approach that can be taken. However, the true resolution of any Type 3 impasse is less a result of TA and more a result of the therapeutic relationship in which the therapist seeks to know, value and accept the client in their entirety and thus invites the client to do the same for themselves. It was in Jemma's willingness to see, to understand and to embrace that split-off part of herself that the healing lay.

Exercises

Self

1   Imagine a situation that you faced recently when a difficult decision had to be made, a situation where it was not easy but you eventually decided what to do. Close your eyes and feel yourself there at that difficult time before you made the decision. Think about the dilemma. Feel the discomfort. Now imagine your mother standing on one side of you and your father on the other. (If you were not brought up by your mother and father, choose two people who were around when you were about seven.) What advice does your mother have for you? What advice does your father have for you? Listen carefully to the voices you hear internally.

Now remember what in fact you did decide to do. Did you follow your mother's advice or your father's, or did you make a compromise between them? Perhaps you made an autonomous decision based on here-and-now information. Whichever you did, it is likely that in that difficult situation you would have been facing an impasse and the exercise could have 'thrown' up some social-level messages that highlight a Type 1 impasse.

2   Stop reading now and listen to the voices you hear internally. Listen carefully. It could be that you are having some Adult opinions about what you are reading. However, along with those opinions, there may be a series of introjected messages in your Parent ego state. Are they about what you are reading or about you? If you pay close attention you may easily become aware of a Parental message undermining you. These internal voices may be reproaching you for all the things you have not done. They may be telling you that reading books is not going to help *you* become a counsellor because ..., they may be telling you that you are stupid and will not remember all this or that the book is stupid and can't teach you anything ... or they may be reminding you that your friend has not called and maybe she does not like you any more. If you cannot hear any voices, that is fine! Breathe in and out and be aware of how you are fully in the here and now. If you can hear internal voices, congratulate yourself on your fine awareness, and tell the voice you are not going to listen any more. If you feel anxious, depressed or hopeless at that thought, you may have reached a Type 2 impasse. You may want to take it to your own counsellor.

3   Put two chairs or cushions opposite each other. Sit on one side and say 'I am ...', followed by an attribution that you have carried all your life that you know is somewhat limiting. (Examples: I am quiet, noisy, loving, clumsy, clever, late, dirty, hysterical, bad, slow, speedy, polite, confident, fearful and so on.) Reel off a few 'I ams' to get into the frame of mind of letting yourself know your self. Then choose one 'I am ...' that still causes discomfort for you. As you say the adjective, let yourself sit and hold your body in a way that suits the word, a way with which you are familiar. Exaggerate a little. Let your voice tone reflect the word. Be aware of how you feel 'being' that word.

Now switch to the opposite cushion. Choose the word that is the complete opposite of your attribution (keep the statement 'possible' however, using an adjective not a superlative like 'the fastest runner in the world'). Say 'I am ...' whatever that opposite is. For example, where you said 'I am cowardly', now experiment with 'I am brave'. Change your body position so that it reflects the new word. Change your voice tone. How do you feel? It may feel very strange indeed. Would you *like* it to be true of you? If not, move off the chair. If, however, you would like to get to know that part of you, you could research ways of building up such an attribute. You may begin dreaming about it, both as daydreams and at night.

Working with Clients

1   Next time your client talks about part of them feeling like this and part like that, invite them to explore those two parts, talking from one side and then from the other. This could be done using two chairs. It can also be done without moving but just mentally exploring the two parts. Some people literally use their hands

to denote the two sides, speaking as if now on the one hand, now on the other. Encourage the client to explore fully the thoughts and feelings of each side. Notice if one side says 'You are' or 'You should' instead of 'I am'. Sometimes, even when it is a Parent message, the person says 'I'. However, you may notice from the tone of voice a critical, scornful or disapproving attitude. On these occasions you can invite the person to say 'You' instead. Later, the client may be able to identify who was the original sender of the message. This should be quite easy if it is a first type impasse message as the words used will probably be the same or similar to the parent or teacher who used them first. If it is a second type impasse message, it may be harder because parents do not usually actually say the things we say to ourselves – we simply perceive and experience them that way.

Also many people feel loyal to parents and do not want to let themselves know how they have been hurt: perhaps, as a small child, they even preferred to believe themselves 'bad' and therefore deserving of ill-treatment rather than face the frightening implications of seeing their desperately needed parent as cruel. It may take some time before clients gradually allow themselves to understand themselves and what happened to them. During this time the counsellor can help the process and give permission for such growth by their accepting attitude of 'I'M OK – YOU'RE OK'.

2   If a client is talking in an animated fashion about something and then seems to interrupt their flow with a 'but', invite them to explore what happened in that interruption, and what message was being repeated subliminally. Highlight the impasse with an enactment of their earlier experience. Invite the client to identify patterns in the way they interrupt themselves.

3   If the client talks about a current situation in which they have repeatedly behaved in a way that has left them feeling 'bad', experiment with going through the steps for making a redecision that were outlined in the application section on page 166. Remember that they do not *all* have to be achieved on the same day, and sometimes the working through of a major impasse can take weeks, months or even years.

Transactional Analysis and Deficit

The word 'deficit' is used in this context to mean some lack of necessary experience – or lack of appropriate timing of that experience – within our development as human beings. An analogy can be made between our development from conception to death and a traveller's journey. A journey requires forward planning and the end of the journey requires anticipation. On the journey itself, there will be different requirements at different stages. So it is with the upbringing of children: their needs warrant anticipation, forethought and the provision of different requirements along the way. Without these, key foundation stones are missed or mislaid, so that many later difficulties may emerge. If factors conducive to normal development – physical, psychological and social – are missing, then the human organism may not be able to continue growing to its full capacity.

At this point it is worth highlighting some of the essential needs that should be met at crucial times in the psychosocial development of a human being. If these developmental tasks are not fulfilled at the time, the person concerned will attempt to fill those gaps as adequately as possible given their present circumstances. Sometimes they may find unusual, and often unhealthy, ways of compensating for the deficit. If the needs of earlier stages remain unmet, the needs of later stages will be detrimentally affected. Counsellors and psychotherapists will benefit greatly from the deep knowledge and understanding to be gained from infant observations, child development studies and a neuroscientific perspective on the complexities of human development and attachment. We recommend such writers as Mahler et al. (1975), Stern (1985), Holmes (1993) and Schore (1994). Here, however, for our purpose of introducing some basic and practical ideas of developmental stages, we draw on the work of Pam Levin (1982), a transactional analyst who has written widely on the cycles of human development. She extrapolates six major developmental themes linked with specific periods in the growing child's lifetime. We here describe these stages, with additional material from the psychoanalyst Erik Erikson (1950/1963).

The Stage of Being

In this first developmental stage, from birth − and, we would suggest, from conception − to approximately the age of six months, the infant requires from the world (and at this stage the world's major representative is usually mother) security, recognition, support and affirmation for being alive. This is communicated by the way in which the infant's body and bodily needs are handled, how the caretakers socially relate to the child and each other, and how they feel about themselves. The latter will in the main be a result of the way the carers in turn were treated as infants. Even tiny babies introject: that is, absorb their caretakers' feelings as if they were their own. Indeed they cannot, in awareness, have a sense of a separate self. So if, for example, a parent feels severely depressed and destructive towards themselves, their baby may well absorb these feelings and then experience them as though those difficult feelings were in fact their own. These are often the experiences at the heart of the Type 3 impasse mentioned in the previous section. If babies are treated with care, respect and love, if they are soothed and mirrored in their carer's eyes, if their emotions are caringly responded to and regulated, they will stand more chance of growing up with a healthy sense of worthiness in being alive than if their bodies and beings are neglected, abused, invaded, or inadequately cared for in major ways by parents or other guardians.

Erikson extends this stage to approximately the age of 18 months and defines its primary developmental task as developing *trust* as opposed to *mistrust*. Infancy is a decisive time for resolving the 'psychosocial crisis' in deciding that the world, mostly represented by mother, is either basically trustworthy or to be mistrusted. In other words, during this stage infants will or will not acquire the psychosocial strength of *hope*. Infants require somatic, Natural Child conviction that responses to their basic needs will be forthcoming and, if they internalize such experiences, they will develop a fundamental sense of appropriate trust and hopefulness about self and others on which they can more positively face their future developmental tasks.

An adult person who has adequately met these earliest developmental tasks will probably have, amongst other attributes, an intrinsic acceptance of their needs, a sense of belonging and a sense of security and optimism. They will feel accepted and accepting of their gender and sexuality, and will demonstrate trust in self and others. A person who, in infancy, has experienced deprivation, unresolved trauma, inadequate modelling, lack of permission or been brought up by emotionally or psychologically disturbed parents will probably exhibit dysfunctional, especially 'needy', behaviours in their adulthood. These inadequacies and difficulties may be generally observable or they may emerge during those periods of an adult's life which most approximate infancy. Such times might include the start of processes such as a new course or a different job, times when they are sick, vulnerable, weary, stressed or hurt, or during traumas such as bereavement or when they are taking care of a young infant.

The Stage of Doing

From approximately the age of 6 to 18 months babies are very involved with developmental needs concerning *acting and doing* things in the world. They require modelling, support and approval of their explorations and experimentations, their proactivity and their curiosity. If the caretakers affirm their children's need to explore, they are likely to develop into adults who have a capacity for uninhibited creativity, motivation and interdependence. If these exploring needs are thwarted at this stage in life – and remember that, although trust issues were super-relevant in the first six months, they are still relevant here and in later stages – as adults such people may exhibit problems such as over-adaptation, lifelessness, passivity, being easily bored, solving difficulties with fight, flight or freeze responses, or being unaware of bodily needs or feelings; they may frequently injure themselves or experience racket fear where anger may be more appropriate.

As mentioned earlier, Erikson includes this stage with the first one as the stage of 'trust versus mistrust'.

The Stage of Thinking

This third stage stretches from the age of about 18 months to 3 years and has as its major focus affirmation of the child's capacity to think. Children meet this developmental task by receiving permissions: to sometimes think things out for themselves, to disagree, to make mistakes in the course of learning and experimenting, to socialize and to experience firm boundaries.

Erikson defines this stage in human development as the *autonomy* versus *shame and doubt* phase. He sees this stage as decisive in the growth of the child's goodwill and willpower. If children at this stage have these psychosocial needs met, they will grow up to have a personalized sense of self and respect for others; will have their memory and thinking ability functioning at an appropriate level for their innate capacity; and will be able to exercise healthy self-control. However, if they are shamed, over-controlled or competed against by adults or older siblings, or spoon-fed with regard to problem solving, then the adults who emerge at the end of adolescence may, for example, be negative, oppositional, over-compliant, dependent, fearful or passive. Equally, someone who was under-controlled and left on their own to make sense of the world might turn out to be obsessive or over-controlling in later life as they struggle to manage their life from an anxious Child ego state.

The Stage of Identity

During the fourth phase of human development, from approximately 3 to 6 years of age, besides reinforcement of their previous developmental tasks, a child's sense of their power and identity needs encouragement, stimulation and recognition. They need guidance and modelling in such things as the ability to think, feel and act simultaneously and appropriately, having their needs met without 'acting' ill, peculiar, confused or stupid, being assertive and knowing what comprises reality and what is realistically achievable as opposed to magical and fanciful.

Erikson names this the 'play age'. Here children will develop their sense of *initiative* or develop learnt feelings of *guilt* in relation to their actions in the world.

Children whose parents are consistent, patient and have respect for their own and their children's thoughts, feelings and attitudes will gain a healthy sense of their own power, will have social skills and will demonstrate a creative and active imagination. On the other hand, if children have inadequate parental guidance at this stage of their lives, for example if they are made responsible for their caretaker's feelings, thoughts or behaviour, encouraged always to please others above themselves or made to feel guilty or inept, they may well, as adults, show symptoms of phobias, manipulate others to take control of their lives, find self-stimulation and creativity blocked, keep trying to make recompense for wrongs they have done or find difficulty in co-operation and healthy competition.

The Stage of Skilfulness

Around the ages of 6 to 12 years children are engrossed with the developmental tasks concerned with skilfulness. Here they need affirmations concerning learning without suffering and with enjoyment, developing personal, integrated ways of doing things, starting and completing tasks, asking for and using positive and negative conditional strokes, receiving and absorbing positive, unconditional strokes and exchanging 'have tos' with 'want tos'.

Erikson sees children in this school-going age group as involved with issues of competence; in his words, *industry* versus *inferiority*.

Now a real sense of the technological ethos of their culture develops. If parents/caretakers are not too pushy, dominating, competitive or alternatively uninterested, if they are not obstructive of, or inadequate in responding to the requirements of this developmental stage and continue to support the tasks of the previous stages which will require practice and nurturing, children, having internalized these relational patterns, are likely to grow up able to take pride in their achievements. They will envisage, begin and complete tasks with satisfaction and feel competent with the technology of their culture. However, if children's progress is blocked or traumatized, they could, as adults, experience achievement anxiety, self-criticism or perhaps a sense of personal inadequacy with regard to expectations from others.

Deficits in the development of primary school-aged children will not only negatively affect the next phase, adolescence, but might be particularly noticeable when, as adults, these people need to take responsibility for managing aspects of their technological world, deal with figures of authority, argue and judge, or take care of school-going children.

The Stage of Regeneration

The final stage to be traversed in childhood is that of the teenage years. During these years, recycling of earlier stages is particularly noticeable. At one moment an adolescent seems like an adult and at another acts like a small child. Youngsters now particularly need affirmation with regard to regeneration. They are learning how to move gradually towards becoming separate from their family while experiencing the sanctuary that home can provide. They also become very concerned with their own individuality and with moving away from parental stereotyping in order to experiment safely with who they are, as different from the older generation yet conforming with certain groups or cliques of their peers. Sexuality becomes increasingly important and requires straightforward and frank addressing without shame, confusion, excitement or disgust on the part of the caretakers.

Erikson describes adolescence as being concerned with developing and integrating a sense of *identity* as opposed to suffering *identity diffusion*.

At this stage, teenagers seek a set of values which they can stand by and, without compromising their essence, live by. It is the stage of developing and confirming fidelity to self and to significant others so that one moves towards self-actualization, autonomy, inter-dependency, spontaneity and heightened self-awareness.

The caretakers of teenagers should maintain their adequate support throughout this sometimes turbulent and revolutionary stage. They should allow their children to separate from them while maintaining unconditional, positive regard for them. If these requirements are met by the caretakers, then the adolescents are likely to have a sound sense of individuality (yet with an ability to be inter-dependent), an internalized value structure, the ability to maintain mutually satisfying relationships and a sense of fulfilment in the way they choose to structure their time. On the other hand, if adolescents are turned free too early or are overly suppressed and protected, they may exhibit such behaviours as escalated game-playing to have needs met, sexual problems, addictions, regression, depression or extreme antisocialism.

You may have noticed that, throughout these descriptions of the childhood developmental stages, it was suggested that children *might* develop into healthy adults as a result of good-enough parental guidance or *might* exhibit disturbed behaviours if such guidance was inadequate. The reason for such uncertainty stems from two elements: one is the degree of psychological and emotional resilience a person may inherently possess; the other is the essential element in all scripting – that of personal choice. Whatever parental influences and life experiences a child is exposed to, he or she makes an individual choice as to how they are going to cope with those experiences. There is the apocryphal story of the constantly over-wrought mother who used to harangue her four children with the statement, 'You'll all end up in a mental hospital!' As adults two of them became psychiatric patients and two became psychiatrists.

Stages in Adulthood

Adulthood, like childhood, has certain readily observable developmental stages. Just as counsellors will need to observe the childhood developmental deficits in clients, they will also need to take cognizance of their clients' present, chrono-logical adult developmental stage. Here, it becomes important also for the coach or other helping professional to think about the likely issues and needs of the client's stage of life.

According to Pam Levin, the six childhood stages are revisited in adulthood in similar cycles, spanning approximately 18 years. However, Erikson, further to his first five developmental stages, delineates three adult psychosocial stages.

He notes that young adulthood is a time of consolidation of the ability to *love*. This is a stage involved with developing *intimacy* instead of *isolation*. Parental caring is replaced by mutual caring for another or others. Sex is no longer part of identity confirmation but should now be part of adult maturity and sexual partners selected out of an aware choice and not compulsively in response to introjected decrees. Full adulthood or maturity is that stage in our lives when we are faced with our sense of *generation* versus *stagnation*. Here we are involved, or not, with *care* of and for the generation to follow. This may involve producing and nurturing children or it may mean being involved in different aspects of making any creative contribution to one's ecological and/or psychosocial world. The eighth and last of Erikson's stages of life, old age, is seen by him as a time concerned with *wisdom*, 'a detached and yet active concern with life in the face of death' (1950/1963 p. 609). Here one encounters *integrity* versus *despair*. If the previous life stages have been well integrated, we can face death as the essential boundary that it is while looking back with a sense of satisfaction and appreciation. If the earlier stages still hold serious deficits, a person might face the last years of their life in depression, hypochondria or even paranoia. An organizational client may want to reflect on the legacy he is leaving for the future of the business or the economy and think about how best to make that transition into retirement.

Application

The major way in which clients make up for their developmental deficits in counselling is through the ongoing *relationship* with their counsellor, and this of course applies to coaching, pastoral care or any other ongoing helping relationship. Having a good-enough experience of a predictably consistent, dependable and caring person involved with one's life is in itself a reparative opportunity for many aspects of developmental disturbance.

Where a counsellor, within the developing relationship with the client, notices certain specific deficits in their client's psychosocial development, they will need to include within their treatment plan some contingencies for addressing or in some way correcting the inadequate caring that occurred during those stages or for helping to create experiences which were absent during crucial times in their client's development. The careful timing of such interventions is essential and must only take place once decontamination has been effected, otherwise the counsellor could, for example, be reinforcing a form of magical thinking in the Child who is still waiting for someone to come and take care of her.

For many clients, the presence of an empathically attuned therapist who listens and responds with understanding can provide enough of a different experience to fill in some of the developmental gaps. However, as in all relationships (past and present), ruptures, conflicts and confusions will at some point occur between the practitioner and the client. We believe that these are equally a part of the reparative work of therapy. It is at these times, when the 'out of awareness' script plays out in the consulting room, that clients not only demonstrate to us their rackets and games but involve us powerfully and deeply in them too (often complementarily engendering our own script components into the arena). What is reparative here is the willingness to acknowledge them, to address them, to be curious about them and to work together to understand them: requiring an open and honest exploration by both therapist and client. It is this authentic, mutual meeting and the recognition of the part played by both parties in the enactment that can bring about the reparative, relational experience that has been lacking in our clients' lives in the past. It can be very powerful (if it is authentic) for the therapist to acknowledge their part in the co-creation of a game, the reinforcement of the client's racket feeling, or the unwitting confirmation of a client's script beliefs.

Example

When Rosa became uncommunicative and withdrawn part way through the session, it became apparent to the therapist that something must have occurred between them in their previous transactions, though he was not sure what. Checking his current state, he realized he was feeling sad. He shared with Rosa

(Continued)

(Continued)

how he was feeling (and his puzzlement over it) and his hunch that something had happened between them. He asked if she was willing to explore what had gone on and Rosa agreed. Together they discovered that earlier in the session Rosa had thought the therapist was distracted when she had been talking of her terminally ill friend. She had interpreted this as a lack of interest on his part, thus fulfilling her script belief that she and her life were unimportant – which had been her decision in response to her experience of her parents. As a consequence, she had become withdrawn. When the therapist tracked back to that point in the session, he realized that indeed he had lost concentration. He had become rather vague and distant, not only from Rosa but from himself and his feelings. He had hardly heard what she had been saying.

THERAPIST: I think I must have begun to feel sad when you were talking of your friend but I avoided my sadness by becoming vague and distant from you and your story. It felt too close to home. Recently, a close friend of mine died. I guess I didn't want to feel my sadness at her loss.

ROSA: It's really helpful for me to hear that. I can understand what was going on for you and I don't feel you were seeing me as unimportant.

Rosa cried copiously at this point and the therapist sat with her giving her his full attention. Later, in further exploration together, Rosa realized that she had skirted over the story of her dying friend in a very matter-of-fact way, avoiding her own sadness and reinforcing her belief that she and her life were not really important. It was her therapist's eventual disclosure of his sadness (resonating with Rosa's unexpressed feelings) that had allowed her to get in touch with her deep sense of grief at the pending loss of her friend.

Extreme or severe deficit, especially associated with physical or sexual trauma, requiring major structural changes and more intensive techniques may need the help of an outside agency such as a psychotherapist or psychiatrist specializing in working with these issues. It is important that, through their training, ongoing supervision and personal counselling or psychotherapy, counsellors can accept and operate within their areas of competency and refer out as necessary.

However, a more simple and less traumatic deficit healing can be achieved by the sensitive and experienced counsellor through the therapeutic relationship as well as by using the TA techniques detailed below.

Building an Internal Nurturing Parent

Part of the Good-enough Parent function is nurturing, both towards others and towards self. When clients exhibit signs of some developmental deficit, it is very likely that this element of their internal self-nurture is missing – at least in relation to that particular developmental task and stage. A client can be invited to deliberately 'design and build' an internal nurturing voice that will gradually support them in taking the risks needed to change.

Example

Raj discovered that the pressure on her to take care of others in her 3–6-year-old stage (initiative versus guilt) had meant that she had stopped listening to what she wanted to do and stopped expecting to have an impact on the world. This was seriously interfering with her ability to be a creative leader. At one session, she expressed a good deal of anxiety as she described her manager's challenge to her to make a presentation to the board. She thought that people wouldn't listen to her and that she didn't have a right to be assertive. Raj did not know about ego states; however, it was easy for her to answer her coach's question: 'If this was a friend of yours who was worrying like this, what would you say?'

RAJ:	(*thinks for a while*) I would tell her 'you'll be fine. Things have changed now. You can have your ideas'.
COACH:	Could you say that to yourself?
RAJ:	(*stares at the coach nervously*) Perhaps …
COACH:	Have a go. Say those things inside yourself. You don't have to say them out loud. (*She watches as Raj seems to go inside.*) How was that?
RAJ:	It felt strange.
COACH:	How about saying it again – this time out loud? Really imagine little Raj, perhaps sitting on your knee ….
RAJ:	(*to herself*) It's fine for you to have ideas and to take them to the board. It's fine for you to be strong and make an impact.
COACH:	How was it that time?
RAJ:	Better that time – it feels good.
COACH:	Notice yourself anchoring that in your body … Would you be willing to keep yourself company in that way, and give yourself that internal support regularly?
RAJ:	Yes I would. I feel good about that.

The Parent Interview

Another TA method of addressing deficit is John McNeel's 'Parent interview' (1976). This is a technique that is suitable only for counsellors and psychotherapists as it can be quite emotionally stirring as well as potentially creating an intense dynamic between practitioner and client. A Parent interview takes place when the therapist talks to one of the internal parents in the client's Parent ego state with a view to helping the client to experience that part as really separate from themselves, and therefore releasing them from the binds of script. The procedure is as follows:

1 A 'two-chair' dialogue is set up between the client's Child and Parent.
2 The therapist talks to the internal Parent as if this Parent were a real person.
3 The therapist asks questions which will elicit the Parent's Child ego state.
4 The therapist facilitates the Parent in expressing those feelings and experiences which are triggered by the needs and requests of the client (the real son or daughter).
5 The client is assisted in experiencing viscerally the Parent from an Adult position and thus seeing the parent as separate.
6 The 'parent' may then give the client permission to live her life differently, or alternatively the client, from her Adult, makes a statement that she is no longer going to be tied by old introjects.
7 The process ends with a discussion between the Adult of the client and the therapist as they discuss and make sense of the experience.

To be effective for, and protective of, the client, the Parent interview needs to be conducted from the frame of reference that the original parent acted from a mis-guided or threatened and not a malicious position. For this reason, we recommend the use of the Parent interview only when the practitioner feels certain that the parents were not actively abusive or cruel; she needs to feel sympathetic to their acting from fear or from their own unresolved issues.

To illustrate the Parent interview here is an extract from Samantha's therapy sessions.

Example

Initially, Samantha is moving between a chair which represents her Child and another which symbolically represents her mother.

SAMANTHA: (*from the Child chair*) You are always criticizing me. Whatever I do or say, you come chipping in telling me how it's just not good enough or how I should be doing it. Why are you never satisfied with me ... oh, what's the use?

THERAPIST: Swap over.

SAMANTHA: (*from the Parent chair*) It's just for your own good, my girl. You need me there. Someone has to look after you, don't you know?

THERAPIST: Change over.

SAMANTHA: (*from the Child chair*) Please leave off nagging me. (*Swapping herself over*) That's right – call 'caring' nagging!

THERAPIST: Can I talk to you a while please, Mrs Williams?

SAMANTHA: (*continues as mother*) All right, but I want you to know that I don't believe in all this counselling stuff. A lot of self-indulgence if you ask me. Samantha would be better off playing a game of tennis or going for a long walk somewhere.

THERAPIST:	Yes, those are certainly ways of relaxing – did you walk or play tennis at all?
SAMANTHA:	Oh yes, especially at Samantha's age.
THERAPIST:	From what I heard earlier, it seems to me that you worry a great deal about Samantha.
SAMANTHA:	Oh yes, indeed. I don't think that she takes enough care in life.
THERAPIST:	I see, and how do you feel when she seems not to be being careful enough to you?
SAMANTHA:	I (*hesitates*) ... I ... well, to be quite honest with you I am terrified that I'll lose her.
THERAPIST:	You are terrified she could die?
SAMANTHA:	(*crying*) Losing one child was torture ... an absolute nightmare for years and years ... and I only just managed, and really only for the sake of Sam, to pull myself back together again. I think that I'd only want to die if I had ever to face that again. (*Weeps.*)
THERAPIST:	I understand. That period of your life sounds unutterably awful. I am sorry.
SAMANTHA:	You know, my father died when I was eight and to this day I can't imagine how my mother seemed to carry on as usual.

Some time is given to helping Samantha's mother's Child release some of her pain. Later the therapist concludes the session:

THERAPIST:	So in a way you show your love for Sam by nagging her?
SAMANTHA:	I suppose so, although I do also buy her presents to show her how much she means to me too.
THERAPIST:	Could you think of any other way in which she might like to know you care?
SAMANTHA:	I could try and tell her, but there's seldom time in her busy life for saying such things.
THERAPIST:	You do find time to nag and choose presents to give her. Would you be prepared to take a few minutes now to tell her?
SAMANTHA:	Yes, I will. Sam, honey, I probably won't say this properly but I do want you to know that I really, really (*cries a little*) love you very dearly ... you are very precious and I'm sorry that I nag you so.
THERAPIST:	OK?
SAMANTHA:	Was that enough?
THERAPIST:	It seems a fine start to me. Thank you for talking to me today despite your initial reservations.
SAMANTHA:	Thank you, too.
THERAPIST:	Samantha, would you go back to the other chair now?
SAMANTHA:	(*from Child chair*) Gosh, I never knew, although of course I must have known to say it all, but I never really took on board just how sad and scared my mother was.

186 An Introduction to Transactional Analysis

Exercises

Self and Working with Clients

With regard to building your own internal nurturing parent, you might want to explore some of the following exercises for yourself and your clients.

1   List positive aspects of yourself and then alongside them list which styles of parenting probably contributed to eliciting them. For example see Figure 10.2.

POSITIVE ASPECTS OF MYSELF	PARENT CONTRIBUTION
• I am attentive to my own and others' needs.	• Modelling healthy interdependence and non-rescuing care to me.
• I am loving to my friends.	• Physically, demonstratively loving to each other and to me.
• I am persistent in my endeavours.	• Permission to take time, be patient and tolerant of mistakes, encouraging.

Figure 10.2   Example of positive aspects and parent contribution list

Similarly, list those parts of yourself which limit actualization, fulfilment, satisfaction and so on, and which types of parenting accompany them. For example see Figure 10.3.

LIMITING ASPECTS OF MYSELF	PARENT CONTRIBUTION
• I hide my anger.	• Equating anger with being 'bad'.
• I don't have enough fun.	• Too much emphasis on work and achievement at the expense of **leisure**.
• I rush my food at meal-times.	• Similar to above. Hurry up to get back to work. Eating is an interruption rather than a pleasure.

Figure 10.3   Example of limiting aspects and parent contribution list

2   Note how you parent yourself in situations of stress, challenge, pleasure and so on. If you find some inadequate self-parenting, suggest alternatives for yourself. For example see Figure 10.4.

SITUATION	SELF-PARENTING
• Partner's illness	• Take good care of myself with weekly massage and asking others for help.
• Giving a speech	• Keep questioning my ability: internal pessimism. Suggest I remind myself of successful past speeches and do some visualization of the next one.
• Playing tennis	• Encourage myself when serving badly and suggest different techniques.

Figure 10.4   Example of situation and self-parenting list

3   Read about childhood needs and development, and about creative parenting. Margot Sunderland's *The Science of Parenting* (also called *What Every Parent Needs to Know*) (2008) is a very good guide that also incorporates some fascinating neuroscience.

4   Take time to be with children of different ages. Observe which developmental tasks a child is involved with and note which caretaking styles promote the child's fuller actualization and which dampen his or her innate individuality. Also spend time watching how parenting styles differ.

5   Gently encourage your Child to list his or her needs and wants while being vigilant not to let a punitive Parent interfere in the process. For a while your Adult will need to be responsible for vetting all negotiations between your Child and the old Parent!

6   Set yourself simple experiments to do each day or week which will promote the caring you require in areas of deficit. An example here could be that you had agreed to give yourself an encouraging remark at least three times daily, so you might now be saying to yourself something like: 'It's good that you are reading and using this book. Well done, Mary.'

11
Relating for a Change

Authors' note: You will notice amongst your own clients that some of them love to be taught the theory so that they can think for themselves and reflect on the implications of what they discover. With these clients, it can be appropriate to do as Eric Berne did: to share the concepts with them, invite them to collaborate in a script analysis, even suggest books for them to read. Other clients are not in the least interested in theory – some are even offended by being 'put into a box'. In this case, the theories and models are there simply for the therapist's support, to help him hypothesize what might be going on and choose his options for intervention. He will ask the client whether this is a familiar feeling, rather than mention a racket, or he will talk about relational patterns, rather than games. In this chapter we tell the story of work with a client, where the therapist overtly introduces the client to transactional analysis. In the interests of describing the TA practice, we have of necessity kept the story short. However, the work actually took its time, and the insights and understanding gained by the client were in the context of a gradual emergence, not a theory-driven protocol.

When Carla telephoned to arrange an initial interview with the therapist, she sounded tearful and distressed. There was a sense of urgency in her voice and yet, the therapist noted, she took quite some time to agree to a suitable time for a meeting – as if other things in her busy life were taking priority. At one point, the therapist was on the verge of offering a time that he wouldn't ordinarily offer as it would mean him rushing back from his supervision to accommodate it. However, he quickly realized that he might be about to initiate a game wherein from an initial Rescuer stance of agreeing to meet Carla at an inconvenient time, he could end up feeling a harried Victim of the situation, and then a resentful Persecutor, blaming Carla for his own decision to arrange an unsuitable time. Instead, he acknowledged to Carla the difficulty they were having in finding a mutually suitable appointment for the initial meeting and that, if they decided to work together, there were only two weekly sessions he had available. It seemed unlikely that they would be able to find a 'fit' so he offered to refer her on to another therapist who might have more suitable times. It was at this point that Carla said she could be available at a time they had previously discussed.

Contracting

Carla, a smartly dressed woman in her early forties, arrived 10 minutes late for her 50-minute appointment. The therapist, aware of his previous urge to rescue his prospective client, reminded them both of the time the session would finish. He asked Carla what had brought her to therapy and what she wanted to achieve through the work. Carla said she was unsure but, tearfully, said that recently she had become anxious, was not sleeping well and felt unhappy with her life. The therapist empathically explored these three aspects to see if he could formulate a more specific contract. He started with 'sleeping' as this seemed the most straightforward to put into a behavioural contract before moving on to the more nebulous 'anxiety' and 'unhappiness'.

THERAPIST: When you say you're not sleeping well, how many hours are you sleeping each night?

CARLA: It can vary but usually I get to sleep at about midnight and wake at about 4 o'clock. Then I feel anxious and can't get off to sleep again.

THERAPIST: (*Staying focussed on his client's sleeping pattern rather than her anxiety*) Four hours, that's very little. That must leave you feeling very tired during the day.

CARLA: Yes, I do feel exhausted. It's not enough.

THERAPIST: No it's not. What do you think would be enough sleep for you?

CARLA: I don't know.

THERAPIST: Well, I notice you said this poor sleeping was a recent thing. How long were you sleeping before?

CARLA: Six months ago, about 7 to 8 hours.

THERAPIST: Was that enough for you?

CARLA: Yes, yes it was. I felt refreshed when I woke and I wasn't tired during the day.

THERAPIST: Might that be a useful goal for us to work towards – to sleep for 7 to 8 hours?

CARLA: That would be great.

The therapist noted that Carla was no longer tearful and that her voice had changed. She sounded enthusiastic and reassured by having a concrete goal to work towards. There were two other aspects to consider which the therapist suspected were very much related to Carla's sleeping pattern as well as inter-related. However, she needed time to introduce herself and some of her story. Carla ran her own internet sales company and was married to Ian, a gardener who was at present unemployed due to a back problem. She had married Ian straight from university despite her parents' disapproval of him not being academic. Her parents were both university lecturers. She was their only child and had been brought up in an environment of material comfort, scholarship and an emphasis on academic achievement.

Time was short and though the therapist asked several questions in an attempt to better describe and understand Carla's anxiety and unhappiness, these remained somewhat general. He did not want to rush his client into finding specifics.

THERAPIST:	There is so much more to discuss and for me to learn about you and I'm aware of the time. We have a clear goal for your sleeping but I think we need longer to explore the other aspects that have brought you here. I suggest we agree to meet for six sessions at this time each week to explore your anxiety and unhappiness and then review and decide where to go from there. Does that sound useful to you?
CARLA:	Yes, that's a good idea but could we arrange another time?
THERAPIST:	Unfortunately, Carla, as I said on the phone, I had only two weekly sessions to offer you, and this is the one you chose.
CARLA:	(*sighing*) Oh, yes I'd forgotten.
THERAPIST:	Do you have a problem with this time?
CARLA:	It's mostly OK but there may be some weeks I have to do a stock check with my suppliers. It could be difficult.
THERAPIST:	Can that be changed?
CARLA:	(*sighing again*) I think it's possible.
THERAPIST:	OK, let's agree to meet at this time and day each week. If you can't make it at this time one particular week, I'll see if I have a space at another time just for that week. If not, we will have to miss that week's session for which I will still charge my usual fee. How does that seem to you?
CARLA:	Well, I don't really want to be paying for missed sessions. I just hope I can make them all.

The therapist clarified more of the 'business contract' of payment, confidentiality and holiday arrangements. He also gave Carla a form on which to give details of her address, contact details, occupation, relationship status, family names and ages, previous therapy, GP, past and current health, medication and her understanding of the agreed contract.

Initial Hypotheses Using Transactional Analysis Concepts

The therapist took particular note of the achievement focus of Carla's parents and pondered the likelihood of Carla's Parent ego state containing an equally demanding quality. In this case, Carla's main driver was likely to be Try Hard (with a concomitant injunction of 'Don't succeed' and probably 'Don't feel').

He also posited an Inadequate Parent functional mode that was controlling and demanding based not just on information about her actual parents but also from his own experience of Carla in relation to arranging the time of the session in which he had felt somewhat controlled by Carla. He was also aware of his own irritation when Carla had 'forgotten' that he had limited sessions available, sensing from Carla's sighs that he was being seen as unreasonable and demanding like her parents.

The therapist wondered if some of this demanding behaviour could be coming from Carla's Child ego state but, though there was an element of demand, he intuited more a defiant quality to Carla's Child. He had felt empathic with Carla's feelings but was also aware that when she cried sometimes he'd felt manipulated. Perhaps this was the 'demanding' quality but it was expressed passively through tears. He noted this as a possible racket feeling of sadness, potentially substituting for her anger.

The therapist had also noted that Carla's anxiety, sleep disruption and unhappiness had begun six months ago at the time her husband had injured his back and was unable to work. However, Carla assured him that her business was doing well and there were no financial problems. The source of Carla's anxiety and unhappiness seemed unexplained by this situation but the therapist remained aware of the timing of her husband's back problem and the recent occurrence of Carla's anxiety.

The First Six Sessions

Though often late, Carla managed to attend the sessions as agreed and told more of her story to the therapist. He listened attentively and empathically though he was aware at times of his irritation with Carla's lateness which he remarked upon and described in terms of her depriving herself of time that was hers. She seemed surprised at this way of seeing her lateness.

THERAPIST:	I wonder if you expected me to be angry with you?
CARLA:	Well, I can tell you're irritated.
THERAPIST:	That's true. I'm sorry, I find it difficult sometimes to be sitting here not knowing when you'll arrive and also that we'll have less time together. I think you deserve your whole 50 minutes.
CARLA:	I'm surprised to hear that. I'd have thought you might be relieved to have a shorter session with me.
THERAPIST:	What makes you think that?
CARLA:	Oh, no one wants to spend much time with me.
THERAPIST:	I'm sorry you think that way.
CARLA:	It's true. It's always been true.
THERAPIST:	I wonder how old you feel when you say that no one wants to spend much time with you.
CARLA:	Little … very little. I think I've always felt it.

The therapist stayed with her sad and lonely feelings as Carla cried in an authentic way, very different from the tears she had shed previously. He felt moved by her rather than manipulated.

Later, he shared TA's model of ego states. Carla understood each of the three ego states and could easily recognize and identify some of her own Parent, Adult and Child states. She realized what the therapist had meant by his earlier question as to how old she felt and she recognized that a lot of the time she 'went into' a familiar archaic Child ego state where she felt either unwanted or controlled.

CARLA:	So when I feel that no one wants to be with me, it's all history?
THERAPIST:	No, I don't think that's wholly likely. But I do think that when in the present you experience that you are alone, and that people don't want to be with you – which could be real or imagined – you move from an Adult ego state into a Child ego state. You seem very small and powerless.

The therapist is aware that he is also talking of her *script* and *racket system* based upon her childhood experiences but does not want to overload his client with more theory here. Ego states seem to be enough to be helping Carla to understand herself.

CARLA: Yes, that's just how I feel. No wonder I feel anxious and unhappy. There was no one there for me when I was a little girl.

THERAPIST: Your parents should have been there for you but they were too wrapped up in academia and achievement. They neglected your emotional and psychological needs. I think that's how you treat yourself at times.

CARLA: From my Parent ego state?

THERAPIST: Does that make sense to you?

CARLA: Yes, it does. I neglect my Child just like my parents did. When I'm in my Parent ego state, I abandon my Child and she feels – I feel – unwanted and alone; anxious and unhappy.

THERAPIST: You've described things really succinctly. I wonder if this helps us in our contracting around your anxiety and unhappiness?

CARLA: Yes, I want to stop neglecting and abandoning myself.

THERAPIST: Can you put that more positively? Rather than stopping doing something, what will you start doing?

CARLA: I'll start to be with me. Does that sound silly?

THERAPIST: No, not at all. What qualities come to mind when you think of being with yourself?

CARLA: Being supportive, kinder, more nurturing – those sort of things. Giving myself good attention.

THERAPIST: Yes, that sounds great. I think you can be all those things in the here and now of your Adult ego state. It's what your Child needs when she feels no one wants to be with her.

CARLA: I really want to do this. I think it's going to take longer than the remaining sessions. Can we agree to work on a more open-ended basis?

THERAPIST: That's fine with me. I look forward to continuing our work together.

Transactions

A few sessions later, Carla arrived upset and tearful. She told the therapist of an incident she'd had with Ian that morning which had left her feeling 'sad and anxious'. The therapist thought it might be helpful to look at the transactions between them in ego state terms. Together, they went through the incident and analysed the components in both structural and functional terms:

CARLA: I was just about to leave when Ian said, 'Will you pick up a catalogue from the garden centre on your way back from the accountant as it's just a few minutes' drive from his office?'

In recounting this to her therapist, at first Carla thought that this seemed to be a straightforward Adult to Adult request but on further reflection realized she'd heard it from her Child ego state as a Parent demand from Ian. She recognized she'd had the Adult option of saying that she had many things to do that day and may not have time for the extra trip. However, in response to the phrase 'it's just a few minutes' drive', she'd ignored her own needs. She and her therapist discussed Ian's phrase as perhaps containing the ulterior transaction: 'It would be churlish of you to make a fuss about a minor errand' (a Parent to Child transaction).

Adding 'collect the catalogue' to her already long list of errands, Carla had responded 'Yes, that's fine'. She could see that this wasn't the Adult response she'd thought it was. In structural ego state terms she had 'gone into' an archaic Child ego state where there was no point in 'making a fuss' in response to her parents' demands. In functional terms, she had complied from an Adapted Child mode.

In the event, in her hurry to get to another appointment with a retailer the other side of town, Carla had 'forgotten' the catalogue. On her return, Ian had been angry with her. Carla had apologized and explained the situation but Ian simply went off into another room. Discussing this with her therapist, Carla realized this was a crossed transaction. Carla had appealed from an Adapted Child mode to Ian's understanding, Good-enough Parent mode but received his angry, Inadequate Parent mode in response. She was left alone feeling sad and anxious.

As she recounted this last part of the story, Carla knew that her being left feeling sad and anxious was an archaic Child experience that had somehow been reactivated. She told the therapist that it was just how she used to feel much of the time at home with her parents. Together, she and her therapist looked at the transactional options that might have changed the outcome. The main one was to have recognized her own needs from the start and made it clear that she did not have time for any extra errands.

In discussing the 'replay' of past events from childhood, Carla remembered many times when her parents, wrapped up in their own research projects and oblivious to any of Carla's needs or preoccupations, asserted their needs as the only priority and demanded her compliance. Carla could see that Ian wasn't purposely doing this but that between them they had 'set up' the situation.

Games

Having already analysed the transactions as involving both ulterior and crossed transactions, and a clear discount of her needs right at the start, the therapist thought this would be a good time to introduce the idea of games, particularly the 'drama triangle' (Berne might have labelled the game here as 'Harried' or 'Now I've Got You'). Carla could see that in discounting her own needs, she had taken the Rescuer position by agreeing to Ian's request. Then, out of her awareness, she had 'forgotten' the catalogue, which could be seen as taking the Persecutor position. In both aspects, Ian had remained the Victim until the end of the game when he switched to becoming the Persecutor and Carla was left as the sad and anxious Victim feeling abandoned.

The reader will have noticed that we keep putting 'forgotten' in quotation marks, as if we did not quite believe it. Carla was also curious about 'forgetting' being seen as a Persecutor position. She didn't like being seen in that way. The therapist suggested that direct anger may not have been allowed in her family and that the only way to express her anger was passively (in later sessions they would explore the likelihood of Carla's sadness being a racket feeling covering her more authentic anger). He gently questioned whether Carla may have been angry right from the start of this exchange with Ian.

CARLA:	Angry? Why would I be angry?
THERAPIST:	Well, you had a lot of things to do this morning.
CARLA:	Yes, I did, but that's not unusual.
THERAPIST:	Maybe not, but it seems to me that with Ian not working and being unable to help much at home, you might well be feeling angry.
CARLA:	I should be able to cope with a few extra things.
THERAPIST:	I wonder where that 'should' comes from. It seems to be getting in the way of your expressing how you really feel.

Carla spent some time considering how she really felt and was surprised to discover that beneath the 'shoulds', even beneath her sadness, she did indeed feel angry.

CARLA:	But it's not fair on Ian. He can't help having injured his back.
THERAPIST:	Maybe not, but his situation seems to remind you of your past experiences with your parents.
CARLA:	But they weren't ill or disabled.
THERAPIST:	... and yet they seem to have been really 'incapacitated' as parents. Their work and study, much like Ian's bad back, left you feeling either abandoned or demanded of.
CARLA:	Yes, that's true. And I think I was angry about that both then and now.

The therapist reminded her that the onset of her 'symptoms' had occurred just at the time when Ian had had to stop working. This was not a financial problem but it did create more work for her and seemed to be reactivating dynamics from her childhood and the feelings she had back then.

A further chance to explore how Carla sometimes discounted her feelings occurred at the therapist's Easter vacation. Since she had explored and discovered some of her deepest feelings, she had been feeling a little disorientated and vulnerable, as if she was no longer sure who she was. Aware that this was their first break since working together and that this may be a difficult time for Carla, the therapist addressed the issue well in advance, encouraging her to express any feelings she may have about the break. He said he would understand if she felt angry about it as it was something she may not choose to be happening at this time, but Carla assured him that she felt 'fine' about the break, that she understood he needed to take holidays, that two weeks wasn't a long time and that she had a lot of work coming up over that period. The therapist was not convinced but decided to wait and see what happened.

Carla 'forgot' her return appointment after the break and was late for the next session.

THERAPIST:	I'd like to share with you how I'm feeling. Is that OK?
CARLA:	OK.
THERAPIST:	I feel irritated by your absence last week and your being late this week because you seem to be neglecting yourself again. At the same time, I feel punished for being away.
CARLA:	I don't like your being irritated with me – but I'm glad you've told me.
THERAPIST:	Because …?
CARLA:	Because you feel genuine and it shows that you care. You aren't walking off and abandoning me.
THERAPIST:	That's true.
CARLA:	I guess the same could be said if I'd expressed my anger with you at the time for going on holiday.
THERAPIST:	Yes, I think you're right. I think you felt I was abandoning you by taking a break.
CARLA:	If I'd not Rescued by my pseudo-Adult 'understanding', I could have expressed my real feelings about it. Maybe then I wouldn't have missed my session.
THERAPIST:	Yes, instead it seems you passively expressed your anger with me – in a way, you sort of abandoned me – and also punished yourself by 'forgetting' to come.
CARLA:	That feels so familiar.

Over the ensuing weeks, Carla paid closer attention to how she was really feeling and discovered that if she expressed her needs and acknowledged her anger – and sometimes expressed it, not aggressively but assertively – she did not feel sad or anxious and subsequently slept well. She also found that Ian responded well to her new assertiveness, was empathic with her needs and took more responsibility for doing things he could manage to do.

In many ways, after six months, the therapeutic 'change contract' had been achieved but Carla was now fully engaged with her self-development, curious to learn more about how her past experiences were influencing the present (her script) and keen to continue in therapy. She also realized that her recent period of symptoms, triggered by Ian's debilitation, was not an isolated one. There had been periods in the past when she had similarly felt unhappy and anxious. She and her therapist made an agreement to continue their work together 'for as long as it took'.

Script

Carla continued to bring day-to-day issues to talk about in her therapy sessions with a view both to currently dealing with situations and to relating them to the 'contents' of her ego states in order to bring about a change in her feeling, thinking and behaving. As a start to this script analysis, together they addressed Carla's drivers and the concomitant injunctions by which she limited her autonomy.

Of the six drivers, Carla identified 'Please People' and 'Try Hard' as her two predominant ones, both clearly related to the expectations her parents had had of her.

She realized her script theme was to please others by trying to get it right for them, much as she had as a child in the hope that her compliant adaptation would get more attention and positive strokes from her parents. As it was, her trying hard to please them always ended in failure and she had to make do with the resulting negative strokes. This was the outcome that happened regularly in her adult life – with Ian, other friends, and even the irritation of her therapist. It seemed, paradoxically, that the only way she could get a sense of power in powerless situations (for example, her therapist's taking a break) was to defeat herself more than she was defeated by others (for example, by missing her therapy appointments).

The main injunctions she identified for herself in relation to these two drivers confirmed her 'defeated' script, notably:

Don't feel. (Don't express what you feel.)
Don't make it.
Don't be you.
Don't be important.
Don't be a child.
Don't exist. (This Carla saw not so much as a self-harm injunction but more as not existing in the minds of others, which resulted in her sense of abandonment and aloneness. Even so, her therapist remained alert to the possibility of a more harmful, even life-threatening, internal dynamic.)

Over the months that Carla explored these aspects of her script, the therapist encouraged her to experiment with them in order not just to understand them but also to change them. In the immediacy and safety of the therapeutic relationship, he confronted her when she 'tried to please' him by getting it right or by putting his needs and feelings first. Their sessions became much more playful and experimental. There was no 'getting it right'; her feelings, whatever they were, were accepted. Even racket feelings were welcomed, explored and transformed into more authentic expressions of what she really felt.

In one session, Carla spoke of the way her father ignored her (as he often did) when she wanted to play with him. She remembered one particular occasion when, busy at his desk, her father had told her he was involved with important work and must not be disturbed. She was expected to sit quietly reading in his study – trying hard to please him by being studious. She did this for what seemed like hours to her but then she crept outside unnoticed. She climbed the apple tree at the bottom of the garden, feeling free and excited, but 'somehow' missed her footing and fell several feet, injuring herself badly. Her father, hearing her scream, came into the garden. Instead of comforting her, he shouted at her and sent her to bed for the rest of the day. The recollection of this event was very painful for Carla and she relived how despairing she had felt.

However, on reflection Carla could see how, even then, her 'defeated' script was in play to the point of risking injury – even her life. Her bid for freedom from her abandoning father ended in a worse defeat. Having wanted him to play with her – and failed – she got his attention (negative strokes are better than no strokes) by falling from the tree. However, the outcome was that she was banished uncomforted to bed and felt even more abandoned. In Berne's pithy naming of games, he would probably have seen Carla's 'accident' as a game called 'Now See What You Made Me Do', passively expressing the anger she felt for her neglectful father by hurting herself. The therapist was concerned that understanding this might cause Carla to pour blame on herself. He was relieved to see that, on the contrary, she truly understood and felt how her whole life had been imbued with her self-defeating script. She felt moved and tender towards the little girl she had been. The therapist also explored with Carla the 'third degree' level of the game in this particular incident that had ended in her physically harming herself. Carla considered this aspect and looked for further evidence of accidents in her life. There had been none. For Carla, the injury had not so much been the physical one but the psychological and emotional 'defeat' of ending up feeling more abandoned, confirming that her 'Don't Exist' injunction was more relationally threatening than life-threatening.

The therapist invited her to take herself in her imagination back to the study and talk to her father (i.e. a Child to Parent dialogue). Initially, Carla found this very challenging, but when the therapist assured her there was no 'right' way of doing this, she let herself fully engage with the experiment. Imagining her father on an empty chair, she spoke to him.

CARLA:	I'm six years old. Six-year-olds need some attention. Six-year-olds don't want to read all the time, they want to play.
THERAPIST:	What do *you* want?
CARLA:	I want to play. I'm trying hard to get it right for you. I'm trying to please you. Please don't ignore me.
THERAPIST:	Tell him what you feel.
CARLA:	I feel lonely. I feel sad. I feel anxious in the silence. It's all cold and silent in here.
THERAPIST:	Maybe you could make more noise?
CARLA:	That's a bit scary.
THERAPIST:	How about putting your Adult on the chair next to you for support?
CARLA:	OK. I want you to play with me (*starts to cry*).
THERAPIST:	He's not coming is he?
CARLA:	(*still sobbing*) No, he's not coming. He won't come.
THERAPIST:	How about talking from your Adult to your Child?
CARLA:	(*moves to Adult*) No, he won't come. He never did. Even when you hurt yourself, he didn't look after you. You tried your hardest – but you don't have to do that any more. You really deserve attention without having to hurt yourself or give up on yourself. You may have to give up on dad. I think he's a lost cause! But you're not!
THERAPIST:	How do you feel saying that?
CARLA:	I feel quite powerful.
THERAPIST:	And your Child?
CARLA:	(*moves to Child chair*) I don't feel sad.
THERAPIST:	What do you feel?
CARLA:	I feel angry!

This two-chair work was one of many experiments in the course of their work together to bring about change in the pattern of Carla's script. Along with the central, relational face-to-face work with the therapist, they were a means of addressing confusion, conflict and deficit. For example, in the above piece of work, decontamination occurred through separating out her Parent, Adult and Child ego states so that Carla could recognize and address each of them distinctly by 'being them' or placing them in the empty chair. Deconfusion, allowing Carla's Child her authentic voice, was achieved through her expressing her grief and anger rather than her racket sadness and anxiety that had been her quieter, creative solution in the past. The deficit of her inadequate and abandoning parenting was addressed through Self-Reparenting where she provided a Good-enough Parent experience to replace the old Inadequate Parent. She could not change the past but she could experience being heard, acknowledged, positively stroked, valued and welcomed in the present.

As part of their work in understanding her script (how to avoid going into it, and how to change it), Carla found it useful to identify her basic racket system – those beliefs, behaviours and memories that maintain our racket feelings and script.

Carla identified the first column of her racket system as:

1 Core Belief about Self: I don't deserve attention.
2 Core Belief about Others: they will ignore/abandon me.
3 Core Belief about the Quality of Life: the world is a sad and lonely place.

Her repressed feeling/needs: anger/positive attention.

From her understanding of her behaviour, she saw her rackety displays as:

1 Observable behaviour: tearful and anxious.
2 Reported internal experiences: tiredness, stomach cramps, powerlessness.
3 Scripty fantasies: if I try hard to please people, maybe they'll love me (but I know they won't).

Her reinforcing memories were:

1 Early childhood experiences: being ignored and abandoned by parents, ending up defeated, e.g. tree incident with father.
2 Subsequent events: continued negligence throughout adolescence, rebellion ending in self-defeat.
3 'Engineered' occurrences, games: Rescues (discounts own needs/pleases) – then Persecutes (from a defeated Victim position).
4 'Interpreted occurrences': feeling abandoned by Ian's back injury, therapist's break.

Carla found this helpful in many ways. On a basic level, when she recognized that she was experiencing herself, others or the world in this way or behaving and remembering in this particular way, she told herself 'This isn't real' or 'This isn't happening now', even 'This is a set-up!' She told her therapist she could then exit the racket system by challenging the beliefs, confronting the reinforcing memories (getting in touch with positive ones, of which she discovered there were enough) and, in so doing, changing her feelings. Sometimes, however, she found the 'pull' of the script too strong to resist and, at such times, with the remaining Adult she had in that moment, gave herself permission to fully feel what she was feeling, even though it was 'rackety'. She discovered that allowing herself to do this 'moved her through' the system quickly. Over time, she could limit her experience of 'going into' the racket system to a few minutes. Mostly, however, she changed her script and her racket system and found a path to autonomy and healthy inter-dependence through her new experiences of authentic relationships with others – her therapist, Ian, friends and work colleagues – acknowledging and expressing her feelings and needs more openly.

Ending

Carla continued in therapy for two years. Though aware of the importance for all clients of the ending to therapy, her therapist realized the particular importance of paying careful attention to the ending for Carla. They mutually decided on a date three months in advance to allow time for processing thoughts and feelings associated with the ending of their work together and the end of their therapeutic relationship. Both recognized the fact that neither of them could pre-empt what they might experience after the event but by grieving the impending loss, acknowledging Carla's achievements and valuing the work they had done together, they were better prepared for the finality of finishing. Carla experienced the work of the last few months as both a deep mourning and a joyous celebration. She felt sad. She felt angry that the therapeutic relationship could not continue into friendship. She felt happy to have achieved things for herself and not for others. She felt positive about her future. She did not feel she was being neglected or abandoned. She knew she had changed her script.

List of TA Organizations

The International Transactional Analysis Association (ITAA)
www.itaa-net.org

The European Association for Transactional Analysis (EATA)
www.eatanews.org

The Western Pacific Association of Transactional Analysis
www.wpata.com.au

The Institute of Transactional Analysis (ITA)
www.ita.org.uk
(The ITA has a list of qualified members and registered TA training establishments
who work under their umbrella in the UK)

The International Association of Relational Transactional Analysis (IARTA)
www.relationalta.com

The Institute of Developmental Transactional Analysis (IDTA)
www.instdta.org
For details of training in organizational and educational TA

Metanoia Institute
www.metanoia.ac.uk
For counselling and psychotherapy training

References

Allen, J.R. (2000) 'Biology and transactional analysis II: a status report on neurodevelopment', *Transactional Analysis Journal*, 30 (4): 260–9.

Allen, J.R. (2009) 'Constructivist and neuroconstructivist transactional analysis', *Transactional Analysis Journal*, 39 (3): 181–92.

Allen, J.R. and Allen, B.A. (1972) 'Scripts: the role of permission', *Transactional Analysis Journal*, 2: 72–4.

Allen, J. and Allen, B. (1984) *Psychiatry: A Guide*. New York: Medical Examination Pub. Co.

Allen, J.R. and Allen, B.A. (1982) 'To find/make meaning: notes on the last permission', *Transactional Analysis Journal*, 17: 72–81.

Allen, J.R. and Allen, B.A. (1988) 'Scripts and permission: some unexamined assumptions and connotations', *Transactional Analysis Journal*, 18: 283–93.

Allen, J.R. and Allen, B.A. (1999) 'On receiving the 1998 Eric Berne Memorial Award for Theory', *Transactional Analysis Journal*, 29: 11–13.

Berne, E. (1949) *The Mind in Action*. London: John Lehmann.

Berne, E. (1958) '"The analysis of games", in Transactional analysis: a new and effective method of group therapy', *American Journal of Psychotherapy*, 12: 735–43.

Berne, E. (1961/1975) *Transactional Analysis in Psychotherapy*. New York: Grove Press. Republished 1975 Souvenir Press Ltd.

Berne, E. (1963) *The Structure and Dynamics of Organizations and Groups*. New York: Grove Press.

Berne, E. (1964a) 'Trading stamps', *Transactional Analysis Bulletin*, 3 (10): 27.

Berne, E. (1964b) *Games People Play*. New York: Grove Press.

Berne, E. (1966) *Principles of Group Treatment*. New York: Grove Press.

Berne, E. (1972) *What Do You Say After You Say Hello?* New York: Grove Press.

Berne, E. (1976) *Beyond Games and Scripts*. Edited by Claude Steiner and Carmen Kerr. New York: Grove Press.

Berne, E. (1977) *Intuition and Ego States*. Edited by P. McCormick. San Francisco: TA Press.

Choy, A. (1990) 'The winner's triangle', *Transactional Analysis Journal*, 20 (1): 40–6.

Clarkson, P. (1992) *Transactional Analysis Psychotherapy: An Integrated Approach*. London: Routledge.

Clarkson, P. and Gilbert, M. (1990) 'Transactional analysis', in W. Dryden (ed.), *Individual Therapy*. London: Routledge.

Cornell, W.F. (1988) 'Life script theory: a critical review from a developmental perspective', *Transactional Analysis Journal*, 18 (4): 270–82.

Cornell, W.F. and Landaiche, M. (2006) 'Impasse and intimacy: applying Berne's concept of script protocol', *Transactional Analysis Journal*, 36 (3): 196–213.

Critchley, B. (1997) 'A Gestalt approach to organisational consulting', in J. Neumann, K. Kellner and A. Dawson-Shepherd (eds), *Developing Organisational Consultancy*. London: Routledge.

Day, A., de Haan, E., Sills, C., Bertie, C. and Blass, E. (2008) 'Coaches' experience of critical moments in the coaching', *International Coaching Psychology Review*, 3 (3): 207–18.

Dusay, J. (1972) 'Egograms and the "constancy hypothesis"', *Transactional Analysis Journal*, 2 (3): 37–42.

English, F. (1971) 'The substitution factor: rackets and real feelings', *Transactional Analysis Journal*, 1 (4): 225–30.

English, F. (1972) 'Rackets and real feelings', *Transactional Analysis Journal*, 2 (1): 23–5.

English, F. (1975) 'The three-cornered contract', *Transactional Analysis Journal*, 5 (4): 383–4.

English, F. (1976) 'Racketeering', *Transactional Analysis Journal*, 6 (1): 78–81.

English, F. (1988) 'Whither scripts?', *Transactional Analysis Journal*, 18 (4): 294–303.

English, F. (2010) 'It takes a life-time to play out a script', in R. Erskine (ed.), *Life Scripts: A Transactional Analysis of Unconscious Relational Patterns*. London: Karnac. pp. 217–38.

Erikson, E. (1950/1963) *Childhood and Society*. New York: Norton.

Erskine, R.G. and Zalcman, M. (1979) 'The racket system', *Transactional Analysis Journal*, 9 (1): 51–9.

Flowerdew, P. (2006) *Useful Ideas and Tools to Use (Based on the Theories of Transactional Analysis)*. Self-published booklet. Bristol.

Goulding, R. and Goulding, M. (1976) 'Injunctions, decisions and redecisions', *Transactional Analysis Journal*, 6 (1): 41–8.

Goulding, R. and Goulding, M. (1979) *Changing Lives Through Redecision Therapy*. New York: Brunner/Mazel.

Gregoire, J. (2004) 'Ego states as living legacies', *Transactional Analysis Journal*, 34 (1): 10–29.

Hay, J. (1992) *Transactional Analysis for Trainers*. Maidenhead: McGraw-Hill.

Holloway, W. and Holloway, M. (1973) *The Monograph Series*. Medina, OH: Midwest Institute for Human Understanding Inc.

Holmes, J. (1993) *John Bowlby and Attachment Theory*. London: Routledge.

Holtby, M. (1979) 'Interlocking racket systems', *Transactional Analysis Journal*, 9 (2): 131–5.

James, J. (1973) 'The game plan', *Transactional Analysis Journal*, 3 (4): 14–17.

James, M. (1977) *Techniques in Transactional Analysis*. Reading, MA: Addison-Wesley.

Kahler, T. and Capers, H. (1974) 'The miniscript', *Transactional Analysis Journal*, 4 (1): 26–42.

Karpman, S. (1968) 'Fairy tales and script drama analysis', *Transactional Analysis Bulletin*, 7 (26): 39–43.

Karpman, S. (1971) 'Options', *Transactional Analysis Journal*, 1 (1): 79–87.

Levin, P. (1982) 'The cycle of development', *Transactional Analysis Journal*, 12 (2): 136–7.

Lewis, C.S. (1978) *Till We Have Faces*. London: Fount Paperbacks.

Mahler, M.S., Pine, F. and Bergman, A. (1975) *The Psychological Birth of the Human Infant*. New York: International Universities.

Mazzetti, M. (2010) 'Cross-cultural transactional analysis', in C. Sills (ed.), *Eric Berne and His Legacy. The Psychotherapist* Special Issue: 46: 23–5.

McNeel, J. (1976) 'The parent interview', *Transactional Analysis Journal*, 6 (1).

Noriega, G.G. (2004) 'Codependence: a transgenerational script', *Transactional Analysis Journal*, 34: 312–22.

Noriega, G.G. (2010) 'Transgenerational scripts – an unknown knowledge', in R. Erskine (ed.), *Life Scripts: A Transactional Analysis of Unconscious Relational Patterns*. London: Karnac. pp. 269–90.

Ogden, P., Minton, K. and Pain, C. (2006) *Trauma in the Body: A Sensory Motor Approach to Psychotherapy*. New York: Norton.

Rogers, C. (1951) *Client-Centered Therapy: Its Current Practice, Implications and Theory.* London: Constable.

Schiff, J.L. with Schiff, A.W., Mellor, K., Schiff, E., Schiff, S., Richman, D., Fishman, J., Wolz, L., Fishman, C. and Momb, D. (1975) *Cathexis Reader: Transactional Analysis Treatment of Psychosis.* New York: Harper & Row.

Schore, A. (1994) *Affect Regulation and the Origin of the Self (The Neurobiology of Emotional Development).* Hillsdale, NJ: Lawrence Erlbaum.

Shivanath, S. and Hiremath, M. (2003) 'The psychodynamics of race and culture', in C. Sills and H. Hargaden (eds), *Key Concepts in Transactional Analysis – Contemporary Views: Ego States.* London: Worth Publishing. pp 169–84.

Sills, C. (2006) 'Contracts and contract making', in C. Sills (ed.), *Contracts in Counselling and Psychotherapy.* London: Sage.

Stacey, R.D. (1993/2007) *Strategic Management and Organisational Dynamics.* Harlow: Pearson Education.

Steiner, C. (1966) 'Script and counterscript', *Transactional Analysis Bulletin,* 5 (18): 133–5.

Steiner, C. (1974) *Scripts People Live.* New York: Grove Press.

Stern, D. (1985) *The Interpersonal World of the Infant.* New York: Basic Books.

Stewart, I. (2001) 'Ego states and the theory of theory', *Transactional Analysis Journal,* 31 (2): 133–47.

Stolorow, R. and Atwood, G. (1992) *Contexts of Being: The Intersubjective Foundations of Psychological Life.* Hillsdale, NJ: Analytic Press.

Stuntz, E. (1973) 'Multiple chairs technique', *Transactional Analysis Journal,* 3 (2).

Summers, G. and Tudor, K. (2000) 'Co-creative transactional analysis', *Transactional Analysis Journal,* 30 (1): 23–44.

Sunderland, M. (2008) *The Science of Parenting.* London: Dorling Kindersley.

Suriyaprakash, C. (2009) 'The transactional analysis of transformational leadership'. Doctoral research. Bharathiar University, Coimbatore, India.

Tudor, K. (2003) 'The neopsyche: the Integrating Adult ego state', in C. Sills and H. Hargaden (eds), *Ego States.* London: Worth Publishing.

Tudor, K. (2006) 'Contracts, complexity and challenge', in C. Sills (ed.), *Contracts in Counselling and Psychotherapy* (2nd edn). London: Sage. pp. 119–36.

Tudor, K. (2008) 'Take it – The Sixth Driver', *Transactional Analysis Journal,* 38 (1): 43–57.

Van Beekum, S. (1991) 'The functional model revisited'. Presentation. Maastricht TA Conference.

Voltaire, J.-M. (1759) *Candide, ou l'Optimisme.* Paris: Sirene.

Winnicott, D. (1958) 'Mind and its relation to the psyche-soma', in *Collected Papers, through Paediatrics to Psychoanalysis.* New York: Basic Books. pp. 243–54.

Index

Research Methods Books from SAGE

DISCOVERING STATISTICS USING SPSS THIRD EDITION

ANDY FIELD

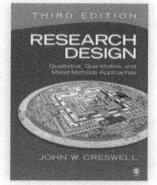

THIRD EDITION

RESEARCH DESIGN

Qualitative, Quantitative, and Mixed Methods Approaches

JOHN W. CRESWELL

Robert K. Yin

Case Study Research

Design and Methods

Fourth Edition

Second Edition

QUALITATIVE INQUIRY & RESEARCH DESIGN

Choosing Among Five Approaches

John W. Creswell

Doing a Literature Review

Chris Hart

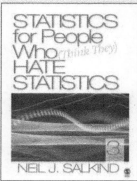

STATISTICS for People Who (Think They) HATE STATISTICS

NEIL J. SALKIND

SECOND EDITION

InterViews

Learning the Craft of Qualitative Research Interviewing

Steinar Kvale
Svend Brinkmann

THE QUALITATIVE RESEARCHER'S COMPANION

A. MICHAEL HUBERMAN
MATTHEW B. MILES

Basics of QUALITATIVE RESEARCH 3e

Juliet Corbin
Anselm Strauss

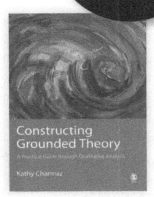
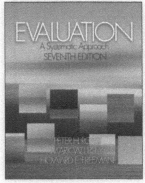
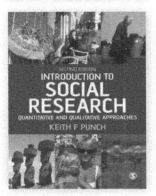